THE EMPTY BOWL

PURSUING TRUTH IN A MESSY WORLD

RIKKI WEST

She Writes Press

Published 2025
Printed in the United States of America
Print ISBN: 978-1-64742-822-8
E-ISBN: 978-1-64742-823-5
Library of Congress Control Number: 2024918958

For information, address:
She Writes Press
1569 Solano Ave #546
Berkeley, CA 94707

Interior Design by

She Writes Press is a division of SparkPoint Studio, LLC.

For Noli and all her loved ones.

CONTENTS

PART II: The Partial Fix

PART III: Getting Real

PART I

THE PROBLEM

CHAPTER 1
BELONGING

Linda and I stuffed the last morsels of Cheerios into our mouths and downed the dribbles of milk in our bowls. Scooping up our dishes, Linda skipped across the linoleum to our mother at the kitchen sink.

"Can we get out the ornaments now?" Linda asked with her gap-toothed smile. It was a brisk, snowy day, and our father was out with the work truck getting a big tree for us.

"Sure!" Mother said, smiling as she gently brushed Linda's short light-brown bangs aside.

"I want to do the little barn!" I said from my perch at the kitchen dinette. Though I was only five, I remembered a tiny family playhouse with shepherds, camels, and baby Jesus from Christmas last year.

"The crèche?" my mother asked, surprised. "Sure! Let's go find the box." She reached out to me and I jumped up to grab her hand.

Holding on tight, I hopscotched through the dining room and front hallway to the den. But when we opened the door of the dark walk-in closet, I pulled back, staring into the blackness. From a bare bulb in the ceiling hung a short chain. When Mom pulled it, the closet monsters scattered. Then I eased into the little room, my small hand clinging to her finger.

The dim glow revealed shelves strewn with our stuff. Brown boxes jumbled with rolls of colored wrapping paper. Dad's tape recorder and reels of tape lay piled near his poker chips in their special case. Mom nudged aside the chessboard with its box of pieces and Dad's new black-and-silver transistor radio. Tucked behind the electric fan, she found the special white box with the crèche pieces.

Mom brought the small carton to the living room floor in front of the coffee table near the fireplace, the warmest spot in the house. From there I could watch for Dad's truck out the big front window. Snow covered the half-acre front yard. Little bunny tracks ran down the long driveway past evergreen trees and winter-brown bushes to Dundee Road, the county highway that took our family to the shops, church, school, and train station in our little town of Northbrook, Illinois.

There was no sign of my father yet, but I already knew we couldn't count on him like we did on Mom. Some nights he didn't come home at all, but she was always there. Our clothes were clean; we ate healthy, fresh food, did our homework, said our prayers, and went to bed at bedtime because of Mom. If we got cut or fell, she had the Mercurochrome and Band-Aids. Dad was more fun but inconstant; you never knew if he would make you laugh or cry.

My eyes flicked to the driveway, searching eagerly for him.

"Here you are, little Rikki," Mom said. She opened the lid of the box, lifted out a bundle of white tissue paper, and handed it to me.

Sitting on my heels, I took the small package and unwound the crinkly paper to reveal the body of a tiny, painted character. The figure was holding a staff as tall as himself, and he was about the size of the king in my father's chess set.

"See, Mommy?" I smiled and held up the little fellow. "It's Mr. Shepherd."

"Unwrap each one gently, now," Mother said, tucking a loose strand of hair behind my ear. "Put them all out on the carpet here and then we'll set up the whole scene. I'm going to get Linda a box of ornaments."

Linda sat cross-legged on the floor against the couch. Mom handed her a collection of fragile glass ornaments to unpack that I wasn't allowed to touch. Because she was seven and I was only five, she got to do a lot of things I couldn't do yet. She could light matches, stay up until eight, and read chapter books. We were different in other ways, too. Linda liked Swiss cheese, but I hated it. She liked dolls and I liked cowboys. She pulled her hair into a ponytail, while I wore my messy blond hair short, like Peter Pan. Mom said Linda looked like an angel version of our father. They both had strong clear brown eyes and high foreheads, only Linda was missing the front tooth in the center of her smile. Dad said I looked like my mother with blue eyes, and Mom looked like Audrey Hepburn.

Linda picked an ornament out of the box and gently unfolded its rumpled newsprint. She held the sparkling ball in the light of an antique stained-glass lamp from my grandmother's collection.

"That one is hand-painted by my friend at Mary Crane," Mom said. "See the little Santa?"

Mother's charitable society, the Mary Crane Center, helped orphans, who I knew were children without parents like Peter Pan. The Santa ornament made me feel a little sad, and tears grew in my eyes. I couldn't imagine losing my family. My love for them was fierce and loyal. Especially for my clever big sister.

Suddenly we heard the front door opening. "Daddy! Daddy! Daddy!" Linda and I ran to him at once. Cold air flooded the entryway.

"It's a big one," our father said with a wide, happy smile. I loved my dad when he smiled. It made everything feel so safe and warm, like when he sang, "He's Got the Whole World in His Hands" and held me in his lap. He dragged the Scotch pine through the doorway. A sharp, bright evergreen smell burst into the house.

"You're getting dirt on the carpet, Dick," Mom said.

"I see it, Rosemary," Dad said, breathing hard as he hauled the tree into the living room next to the fireplace. Our dad was a light-weight boxer and he played tennis. His lean muscles were strong but he looked strained; his normally combed-back hair was clinging to his face. He stood, holding the tree and catching his breath, while Mom set out the tree stand.

"Hold it steady," Dad said. "Okay, on three. One, two, three!" He lifted the tree and slammed it down into the stand. It had to fit within three large screws and he missed the opening. "Dammit! Can't you hold still?" he snapped at Mom. "Let's try it again. On three!"

That time, the trunk slid into the stand.

"It's in!" Mom called out cheerfully. She began to tighten the screws that held it in place.

"You hold the tree, I'll do the screws," Dad said, squatting down.

The tree tilted off to the right. Mom straightened it.

"Quit moving!" he yelled. I picked up the miniature angel and began zooming it around the crèche pieces as if it were Mighty Mouse to the rescue.

"I didn't move it," Mom barked back.

I looked over at Linda who was sitting perfectly still, staring at Mom. My toes curled up like tiny springs.

"I think I've got it. See if it's straight," Dad said.

"It looks great, Dick," Mom said with a long exhale.

I took a breath and straightened my toes.

My father got out the tangle of Christmas lights and began to unwind them. He laid the strands out on the living room floor. After lighting a cigarette, he went out to the garage and came back with a ladder.

He climbed onto the third rung. Starting at the top of the tall tree, he clipped each bulb to a branch as he unwound the cable. But reaching too far, he lost his balance and fell off the ladder.

"Goddammit!" he growled, and the air froze.

I stopped playing with the crèche and watched him. Then I looked at Mom and she was staring at him, too. Something was wrong, and to my child's heart it felt like tears trying to break through. Linda got up and went over to the record player.

"Can I put on the Christmas songs?" she asked. She pulled out the Mormon Tabernacle Choir album and set the 33 LP record on the turntable. When she carefully placed the needle on the black stripe at the outer edge, streams of blended, soothing voices swarmed into the living room.

"O holy night," we sang along, "the stars are brightly shining."

To help the crèche people see those bright stars, I placed each of them up on the coffee table outside the little barn.

"Want me to hold those?" Mom asked Dad softly as he lifted a string of lights from his new perch on the ladder. She was walking on eggshells.

"No!" When he reached to clip a light to a branch, the bundle slipped from his hands and fell to the floor. "Goddammit, get away, you're not helping!"

My eyes flicked from him to Mom.

Setting down the camel, I felt the first brush of a wheeze in my chest. I hoped it would not flare into an asthma attack. Dad stepped down and picked up the Christmas lights.

What if he starts drinking? Once that began, we'd have to get out of his way.

Linda got up quietly, left the living room, and headed toward the kitchen. When I looked at Mom, I saw one hand covering her throat. A grimace lodged on her face while she watched Dad. I decided to follow Linda.

"There they go again," Linda said to me as we padded down the hall. "I'm getting some cookies." In the kitchen, she crawled up on the counter and brought down the bag of Oreos from the cabinet.

We took our snack into the den and stood on the couch to reach the books stacked on the shelves behind it. I pulled out a book of nursery stories. On page ninety-two, my favorite bedtime tale was about a little yellow canary who lived in a cage. Each night, his gentle, caring owner safely covered his cozy coop, tucking him in. Turning to that page, I practiced reading the familiar words.

Linda read poems in *The Big Book of Fun*. We munched our cookies and waited for Dad to get the lights on the tree. In the living room, the Tabernacle Choir record came to an end, but Mom did not turn it over.

We heard a voice in the next room. Linda tiptoed out to see if the tree was ready. When she came back, she shook her head. "No lights yet. He's drunk. Mommy's in the kitchen."

"What did Daddy say?" I asked her.

"Stupid bitch," Linda said.

Tears sprang into my eyes and spilled down my cheeks. As a first-grader I already knew those were bad words. And that Christmas decorating was over for the day. There might be yelling, or maybe Dad would pass out. Later, Mom would probably give us TV dinners in the den and we'd tiptoe up to our bedroom. I hoped Mom would come and read me a good-night story, but sometimes after fights she stayed in her room.

I turned to Linda. "Will you read me the canary story?"

Even though it was still daytime, I held out my nighttime nursery book, opened to page ninety-two.

CHAPTER 2
PRAYERS

Crawling through the dirt in our front yard on my knees, I crept under overhanging limbs into a secret evergreen chamber. Heavy branches shaded the tiny space, letting in only a dappled afternoon light. Cool air grazed my cheeks. My after-school jeans and shaggy hair were sprinkled with green needles and pollen; sticky pine goo clung to my fingers. In the surrounding bushes, I could hear the soft brushing of the wind, but the air inside my cave was still. Nothing penetrated. No one knew where I was. Alone in my private place that smelled like Christmas trees, I sat cross-legged on the earth and closed my eyes.

I had smuggled the candle out of the special hand-carved sideboard in the dining room when Mom was resting upstairs. All I had to do was reach into the cabinet, twist the waxy cylinder out of the tall crystal stand, and hide it in my jacket. The matches were easy. A smoker, my father left matchbooks all over the house. I was not allowed to play with them, but he would never notice if one packet went missing.

Because I was seven, I knew how to light candles. Mom let me do it when we had company and ate in the formal dining room. I would light each stick, one at a time, and Mother would put them in the candelabra under the crystal chandelier. Their little lights would sparkle on the polished mahogany table.

Opening my eyes, I tore a match from the small white-and-red packet. Then I closed the cardboard cover, tucking the edge behind the flinty strip. The important thing in lighting matches was not to get startled and drop the match. Holding the packet in one hand, I dragged the red head over the strip.

Zzzzip! Nothing.

I struck again and my hand jerked but I held on. The head exploded in a tiny spark, lighting up my cozy sanctuary with a whoosh. Holding the flame aloft, I picked up the candle and dipped the wick until it lit. Only then did I drop the match. Quickly I scrubbed it with the heel of my black P.F. Flyer high top, holding the candle up in one hand.

"Et cum spíritu tuo," I whispered, speaking my favorite response from the Latin Mass. *And with your spirit.*

Peering into the dark, I felt the branches envelop me. With my free hand, I reached into my pocket and pulled out the blue rosary that Grammy had given me for my birthday. Its tiny glass gems lay heavy in my palm. Closing my eyes again, I breathed, "Dear Jesus, please ask God not to send Daddy to hell."

I was in third grade at St. Norbert's Catholic School now, and I had learned enough religion to suspect my father's tantrums were sins. I wanted him to be happy and go to heaven. Not sure how to help him, I turned to the one resource I had. In 1958, at seven years old, I believed in the power of prayer.

My father didn't go to Mass on Sundays, which was considered a mortal sin. He called my mother vicious names that were swear words, which constituted a venial sin. Catholics had to confess when they sinned, big or little. But my father didn't go to confession, so Linda and I were worried about his soul. Linda said if we recited the prayers of the rosary every day during Mary's month—the month of May—it would save him. But it was September and I could not wait until May.

"Dear Jesus, please forgive Daddy," I whispered, adding, "Make him not drink tonight."

I had learned to watch his moods carefully. Most of the time when he was intoxicated, he got angry. Every few days, his accusing, hostile, drunk personality would insult and badger Mom until they were in a shouting match.

I had taken my first Communion last spring. I knew the purpose of life: to know, love, and serve God. I knew the true prayers, the one for confession, the Our Father, and the Hail Mary. But I liked to come in here and also ask for the secret thing in my innermost heart.

Jesus was supposed to listen to your prayers. But then, I was supposed to be good, obey my mother, and not fight with Linda. I wasn't sure if Jesus would really listen. Mary intervened with Jesus for people, so to make sure I was heard, I spoke the Hail Mary aloud.

"Hail Mary, full of grace, the Lord is with thee," I recited, and raced through to the end, "Pray for us sinners, now and at the hour of our death. Amen."

I blew out the candle and left it on the ground among the branches in the sacred spot. After tucking my rosary carefully back in my pocket, I scrambled out into the sunlight and ran toward the climbing tree in the orchard.

Planting one foot on its trunk, I grabbed an overhead branch and push-pulled my way onto the lowest limb. The next trick was to stand on the limb, steadying myself with other branches, then leap to the ground, flying like Superman through space. I hurled myself the four or five feet down, feeling the wind in my imaginary cape, whooping on the way. Free!

As the afternoon grayed, I ambled back to the house. "Mommy!" I yelled, letting the screen door slam in the kitchen. I ran through the house without wiping my feet and found her in the den.

"Mommy, can you help me with my numbers?" I was then the youngest student in third grade at St. Norbert's and wanted to be the first one to memorize the times tables.

"Sure, honey," Mom said. We sat in the den on the couch beneath the bookshelves and practiced different combinations of one through ten. My favorite was six times seven.

"It's the same as seven times six!" I noticed with inexplicable delight.

Mom tilted her head and frowned. "Is that the baby?" she asked, and I heard Bethy crying from her room upstairs. She was almost one year old.

"Help me take care of Elizabeth, and then let's get dinner going," Mom said.

We went up to Bethy's room together, changed her diaper, and brought her downstairs to the rocking chair in the den. I stood by the chair and leaned in over our mom's lap to stroke my sister's tiny head.

"Hello, little Bethy," I crooned. "Are you the happy little baby?" Most of the time, she was either laughing, screaming, or sleeping. I tickled her tummy and she giggled. I always made her laugh.

I tucked a bit of her hair behind her tiny ear. Already I felt protective, wanting to shield my baby sister from harm. *And Mommy needs help, too,* I remembered. Making Bethy laugh was one way I knew to take some burden off Mom.

I brought my blue-beaded rosary to school the next day to have it blessed—a second time—by Father Sullivan. We weren't supposed to get the same items blessed more than once, but I suspected he didn't keep a strict count. It wasn't the extra holiness I was after, but the magic.

Whenever Father blessed a rosary, he would make it disappear. Then he would find it in someone's pocket or sometimes he would pull it out of an ear. I couldn't see how he did it. It appeared to me that he could do real magic, the way my father did with playing cards and coins. Plus, he was tall and funny and made God seem nice. He was my favorite priest at St. Norbert's.

The school day crept slowly by. After lunch, we went out for recess. It was a fresh fall day, and the afternoon air was crisp in the bright sun. I had to wait until Father came out to supervise us kids in the playground. Avoiding my usual rowdy friends, I stayed out of trouble so I would not be sent in early from recess.

Finally, Father Sullivan emerged from church and walked onto the grass near the swing set.

At first, he seemed a little suspicious of the rosary—"Have I blessed this before?" he asked, pretending to glower—but then he blessed it anyway. He held it in one closed fist, making the sign of the cross over it and murmuring something softly in Latin. When he opened his hand, it was gone! I laughed. Then he found my rosary in the hood of my jacket. He placed it carefully in my open palm and closed my fingers around it.

"This has been blessed now," he said with a firm look, "maybe more than once."

Smiling, I looked away.

"So mind you handle it carefully." He winked at me. "No more stowing it up there in your hood."

I put the rosary reverently back in my jacket pocket. Blessings made things holy, and I was a little afraid of things that were holy. The nuns taught us that some things were so holy only boys could touch them, like the special objects used in Mass. A church was so holy that girls weren't even allowed to peek behind the altar. Only boys could do that. In 1958, it didn't occur to me or anyone around me to wonder why that was.

At school, I learned that Jesus said my soul was sacred and would go to heaven if I was good enough. But being good was very, very hard for me. You were supposed to be obedient, not a "smart aleck," and I usually felt more like a wild cowboy than an obedient child. I liked to wrestle Billy Wilkie and spin the merry-go-round faster and faster until the little kids screamed. I sassed my parents. Sometimes, if

I was clever, my father would laugh at my shenanigans. Then I secretly, sinfully, would smile and feel delighted with myself. I feared I wasn't quite holy enough for heaven.

During afternoon grammar my sinful side took over my sacred side. I tuned out the drone of Sister's voice, lost track of her words, and drifted into a reverie. I could feel myself flying like Peter Pan over our house and pool, over the neighborhood and all the houses down to Shermer Road. There was the creek where Shermer branched off Dundee and headed into town. My wings brushed the tall grasses in the meadow off Lee on the way to Church Road. Carefree, no one could harm my soaring spirit. Alone, no one could slow me down.

"Richarda! Nouns, verbs, and helping verbs."

"Yes, Sister." I jerked back into her classroom and stood. "Nouns are objects. Verbs are action words. *Has-have-had* is a helping verb." Reciting the lesson correctly, I sat relieved. Sister Mary Agnes was strict.

Even though I was in third grade, in bed at night I still feared the demons who lurked in the hallway and under the bed. Fingering my twice-blessed rosary stones, I would pray that any fiends hanging around would be content in the closet.

"Please, Mary and Jesus, keep the monsters in there." I got out of bed and propped my desk chair against the closet doorknob for good measure. Then, after my prayers for my parents and sisters, very quietly and secretly so only God could hear, I prayed earnestly that I could become a boy.

Please, God, give me a penis. Boys can roughhouse and be priests. They get to go to all the places in the world. Girls have to stay home and cook.

CHAPTER 3
MOTHER SUPERIOR

Sitting in my fourth-grade classroom in the spring of 1959, I had a funny idea.

Our desks lined up in perfect rows and columns. Seats were assigned alphabetically, so I, a *W*, sat in the back row. I decided to do a silent impersonation of my teacher, Miss Crowe (we called her Crow-face behind her back), for my fellow *T*-through-*Z* kids.

I stood in the little aisle between the wooden desks and planted my feet. Hands on hips with finger wagging, I mimicked her scolding gestures just right. I scrunched up my face to imitate her scowl. It was pretty funny, so of course the back row started laughing. Crow-face, who was facing the blackboard, whipped around and caught me in the act. I don't know if she recognized herself, but she sent me to Mother Superior.

It was not my first classroom sin. My habit of cracking jokes in class often got me black marks on the schoolroom wall chart. I was always trying to be like my dad. In my family, jokes were a respected art form, and he was the master. Besides, I couldn't respect the Catholic teachers like I once had. Hairline cracks had been forming in my faith recently. My prayers hadn't stopped my father's drinking or his bullying of my mother, nor the way he ridiculed us kids with snide comments about our intelligence or dress. Was anyone up there really listening? I couldn't help but wonder.

The foot-wide red stripe on the right side of the linoleum marked my path to doom. At first, careful to follow St. Norbert's strict rule, I walked only on the red lines. Then I started bouncing from square to square, playing hopscotch in my imagination. The antic distracted me briefly, but I quickly arrived at the office, where I knew only scolding and shame awaited me.

When I knocked on the anteroom door, my heart quivered in my throat and my shaking hands clammed up.

After I handed my slip to the secretary, I sat in one of three chairs outside Mother Superior's looming portal, my little legs swinging. When the door opened, her bulk filled the space. "Richarda Marie West! In here."

I skulked in and stood still, head bowed, in front of her desk. A tall, bulky woman, wrapped in layers of dark blue nun's habit, Mother Superior stood behind her desk with both palms flat on its surface, leaning toward me.

I got a lecture on obedience. Another on respect.

"Your duty as a Catholic student is to obey, honor, and respect your teachers," she said.

Staring at my feet, I could hear my little heart pumping hard and felt my anger building.

"Look at me when I am speaking to you!"

My eyes snapped up, but Mother Superior's gaze burned like strong sunlight, forcing me to look away again.

"Your behavior is irresponsible and sinful. I will not tolerate this in my institution."

I hated that woman. I squinted to hold back the tears threatening to form in my eight-year-old eyes. I didn't want to give her the satisfaction of making me cry.

"You have consistently misbehaved in this school and disrespected your teachers." She banged on the desk with her palm. "This time you must be taught a lesson. You are suspended immediately!"

My eyes shot to her face. Was she serious? I was a straight-A student, maybe the smartest in class!

Now I was really scared. Only really bad kids got suspended.

"We've already called your parents," she said. "Go wait in the anteroom until one of them arrives to pick you up."

I knew Mom would be furious, but I didn't know what to expect from Dad. Luckily, it was a sober father who came to get me.

"Wait here and be quiet," he said to me in the outer office. He looked plenty mad.

He went into Mother Superior's sanctum. Through the door I heard his clipped, restrained voice snapping.

"What harm did she do? Do your teachers have no respect for the children? I am taking my daughter home now, and out of this school at the end of the year."

What luck! I thought he'd be enraged, but instead my dad defended me to Mother Superior! This was a side of him I'd not seen before. Like always, just when I wanted to give up on him, my dad, Dick, pulled something so cool, or generous, or funny that I forgot all the bad times. I wanted only to be close to him.

In the car home he said I had to quit getting in trouble because it upset Mom. He didn't actually punish me. He told me to hide out in my room until it all blew over. Did my father approve of my impersonation because he loved comedy? I began to understand that he did not approve of bossy nuns because he wasn't a real Catholic. Linda told me he was secretly an atheist who did not believe in God at all.

"They peddle this nonsense about God and obedience," he complained to Mother at home—behind closed doors, but I could hear him. "I don't see why we should support that institution anymore. It's not good for the girls."

That put a few fractures in my Catholic beliefs. Shadows of doubt smudged my faith. Maybe the dogma wasn't all true. Maybe total obedience to the church wasn't required. I trusted my dad more than religion. We had almost the same name: We were Richard and Richarda. Despite all the drunkenness, he was my loyal family and I was proud to stick with him against Mother Superior and the church.

CHAPTER 4
DIGGING TO CHINA

My twenty-inch blue Schwinn Meteor sped down Dundee to Shermer Road, the muscles in my calves tightening and releasing in a pounding up-down, up-down rhythm.

Please keep him sober tonight. Please let's have a nice night.

It was a July morning, a month after my ninth birthday. Dad had woken late and discovered he was almost out of cigarettes. He'd sent me into town, just a couple of miles away, to get him a pack.

Whizzing along the asphalt on two wheels was a lot like flying. I stood up on the pedals and pushed hard, getting a good speed going. I was Superboy zooming above the treetops, doing loops in midair, faster than a speeding bullet.

When I got to the shopping center in the town plaza, I turned the bike into the parking lot and pedaled past the dry cleaners and the shoe shop, over to Hubinger's drug store.

"Daddy sent me for cigarettes," I told Mr. Hubinger. "Here," I said, fishing in my jeans pockets. "I have a note."

Mr. Hubinger took the note and set the box of Parliaments on the counter.

"I'm going to get some comics," I said, and turned to the newsstand in the far corner. I pulled my favorites off the shelf: *Archie*, *Superman*, and the new series, *Supergirl*. "Just charge it to my dad like usual," I said to Mr. Hubinger.

I went over to the five-and-dime and bought ten cents' worth of Smarties before pedaling home.

After giving Dad his cigarettes, I ran over to Peter's house.

Peter was the perfect pal. That summer we leapt from the roof of the barn onto the driveway like wild cowboys, and played baseball on the tennis courts of the Green Acres Country Club that stretched between our two houses. Daring each other, we screwed up our courage and broke into the concession stand on the golf course, where we served ourselves ice cream. In the rear part of our lot, we cleaned out a gardener's shed. It became a private fort. A tiny single room with a glass window, it was surrounded by a half-acre of scrubby woodland. Our private hideaway. There our imaginations ran wild, playing Eliot Ness and his Untouchables or the Swamp Fox. Peter even sent away for mail-order throwing knives and a revolver that shot blanks—our secret "until the end."

Today, though, we decided to dig to China—through my family's driveway.

The compressed earth and gravel of our driveway were puddled with rain from yesterday's thunderstorm. We hammered our shovels into the wet pebbles and dirt. Hard-packed ground slowly gave way. As I worked, I tried to picture coming out on the other side of the pit. *What is it like, living on the upside-down side of Earth?* We tore up good chunks of muddied soil and gravel in our enthusiasm.

When my mother looked out the window and saw us, she dropped what she was doing and ran out the kitchen door. "What in God's name are you doing?" she shouted. "That's our driveway!"

Mom was not happy with the hole to China. She sent Peter home and said I was grounded from playing with him forever. But Dad had a worse reaction. That hole was a "good enough" reason for him to get obliterated. He started with dry martinis before dinner, then he skipped dinner and switched to Scotch. We gave him the living room where he was sitting in a wing chair, nodding off. I took my homework into the den and listened for sounds from Dad while ignoring the voices on *The Ed Sullivan Show*.

"No TV until your homework is finished," Mom said in her no-nonsense voice from the doorway.

"Oh, Mom, c'mon. I can concentrate. This is easy grammar. Leave me alone."

Through the doorway, I could hear my father's voice rumble in his chest before grinding into a frightening growl. Then he was shouting, "Don't speak to your mother like that." His words were slurred and came out, "Dun spleech chur mudder like zhat." His shuffling feet approached the den; I looked into the hallway. His head sagged on his shoulders as if it were too heavy, and his eyes were red like a fire monster.

I ran up the stairs and sat on the top step. He began attacking Mom instead of me, calling her degrading names. Of course, I felt bad for her, but couldn't help feeling relieved he'd forgotten about me—because the last time something like this had happened, he'd come after me. I had locked myself in the bathroom, and when he'd started to break in with a screwdriver, I had climbed out the window onto the first-floor roof. I'd jumped down and run to my tree house.

Mother's husky, defensive whisper taunted Dad and just made things worse. He started to snarl at her incoherently. I couldn't quite understand what he was saying. I heard *fucking* and *stupid*. He stumbled back into the living room.

"You are a sick animal!" Mom screamed at him in a whisper.

Please, God, don't let him get crazy tonight. But then something was wrong, worse than usual. I heard crashing from downstairs, like a pan banging. Then he was shouting something about his mother. Glass shattered. Linda came rushing into the downstairs hall and saw me at the top of the stairs. She ran up to join me. Her bedroom was now on the first floor, and it was a bad night to be down there.

"What happened?" she whispered with a frightened look.

"I don't know. Nothing," I said. "He just went off."

Mom grabbed Bethy and hurried up the steps. "Come with me or get into your room," she hissed at us as she passed us at the top of the stairs and turned toward her bedroom. She pointed at my door. "Both of you, go!"

Linda and I retreated into my room, our faces frozen in bug-eyed fear. Our father moved from the living room to the dining room, then to the den, a fresh barrage of rage bursting in each room. It sounded as if things were falling off shelves and bashing into walls.

It went on for a long time, maybe twenty minutes. Then silence. Linda and I waited, listening at the door. We cracked it open. No noise from downstairs. We crawled to the top of the staircase and peered down.

"Holy moly!" Linda hissed, pointing to the landing below us.

Dad had passed out, face down and bleeding from both hands, in the hallway near the front door. We would have to step over his body to get to the downstairs rooms or any doors to the outside.

"Are you going down there?" I asked her, staring with alarm at my father.

"Nope," she answered. "I'm sleeping in your room."

In the morning, Linda and I peeked again. Dad was not on the floor in the hall. We crept downstairs and looked into the den where his body sprawled on the couch. Pieces of ceramic and stained glass littered the floor throughout the dining and living rooms, hallway, and den. His bloodstains splotched the front-hall carpet.

Mom came downstairs and looked around.

"Get dressed. No school today," she said in a hoarse whisper.

"Where are we going?" Linda wanted to know.

Mom got Bethy ready and bustled the three of us down the hall, out the back door, and into the car. She drove us to her friend Annie's house in nearby Deerfield and sent us off to play with Annie's kids. Instead, we spied on her in the kitchen.

Mom had coffee and a hard cry with her friend.

"I can't go on like this, Annie. He terrorized the children!" Mom's voice kept cracking, and her nose was running.

"I know, honey, Bill can get crazy sometimes, too," Annie said. She patted Mom's hand.

"This was different, he was out of control. There's debris all over the place."

"We'll send Bill over there to help clean up. It will pass. Dick isn't really like that," Annie said.

"But what if he is?" Mom said.

Hearing her words scared me; my own father had become a dangerous stranger. What else might he do?

Mom parked us at Annie's for the day and left. When she brought us home that night, the stains were covered with a rug. All the broken glass was cleaned up. Shelves throughout the downstairs rooms were stripped of the many antiques and statuettes that had belonged to Dad's mother, our grandmother Nonni.

My mother and I would never speak about that night. We would never discuss anything about the near-daily ordeal of living with Dad's demons until after he died, several decades later. I packed that violent night away in a dark corner of my mind and forgot about it for twenty-some years—until I began my own confrontation with alcohol.

CHAPTER 5
DID SOMEBODY MAKE ALL THIS?

I slipped the scapula that Grammy gave me over my neck and adjusted its little icons. It was made of two tiny religious pictures connected by ribbons so you could wear it with one image hanging in front and the other in back. The front showed Jesus's sacred heart; the back displayed Mother Mary.

Show me how to protect Mommy if it gets bad again. Help me be brave.

Despite the violence in our house, my parents claimed to believe in justice and freedom. In November of 1960, they were ecstatic because Jack Kennedy won the presidential election. They thought Black people should not have to wait in a separate line or sit in a separate part of the movie theater in Glencoe. Dad said the United States should bring the liberties of democracy to the world. He didn't "fight the war for freedom" just to see Tricky Dick Nixon take over.

But Dad was not for justice and freedom at home. At home, we had to do everything his way so he could have his Coke or his coffee or his meal or his Scotch or his martini. Everything revolved around his moods. It was time for me, now a fifth grader, to stand up to my father.

My confirmation ceremony was coming up soon. For Catholics, this was a sacrament that affirmed our faith in the teachings. During the ritual, I would kneel at the railing around the altar, and the priest would mark the sign of the cross on my forehead with a special oil. He would say a prayer, then bless me "in nomine Patris et Filii et Spiritus Sancti." The sacrament would make me an adult in the eyes of the church. Would it give me adult courage?

To prepare for the rite of passage, I copied Linda and donned the sacred scapula. I wore it under my blouse to Mass and school. It was supposed to remind me to be good, but I forgot about it except when it scraped against my skin. Then I felt a thrill of blessedness, as if I were special—so special that God would surely choose my prayers to answer.

My prayer was that the confirmation ritual would give me the grown-up bravery I needed at home. Because sometimes I knew I should knock my father out with a golf club.

"Why does God punish people for not going to Mass if they don't even know they are supposed to?" I asked from my perch on Mom's bed, using her telephone. There were phones in the kitchen and den, but Mom's bedroom gave me some privacy.

"That's a Catholic thing," Bob said. "God doesn't really care which type of Christian you are."

Picking a boyfriend had been my first act at the Crestwood Elementary Public School. My choice, Bob Kennedy, was the second-smartest kid in class. He had a curious mind, short black hair, and a sharp nose that drew his whole face into a beak. Often, we talked on the telephone after finishing our homework, and our favorite topic was religion.

"You either have to go to Mass or you don't," I said.

"You don't!" Bob retorted. "You are just supposed to follow the Ten Commandments. You don't have to follow all those other rules."

"You do if you're a Catholic. Especially if you're about to be confirmed." I paused. "Is there really a God, do you think?"

"*Somebody* made all this," Bob said.

Did somebody make all this? I wondered. Last Saturday Dad had taken me out in the front yard to look at the stars. "The stars are so far away," Dad had told me, "that it takes years and years for the light to reach us here on Earth."

I'd tried to picture a cone of light zooming down to Earth. It was backward from the way the comic-book Superman used his X-ray vision, which was like a beam he sent from his eyes. Dad had explained that in fact, light beams leave the stars, race through space for years and years, and eventually enter holes in our eyes. We'd stood beneath a wide sky, sparkling against soft blackness. Was God somewhere up there with those far-away stars? Was he listening with super X-ray hearing?

"Maybe," I conceded to Bob, "but he sure has a lot of explaining to do. You should see people fight in the parking lot after church. You would never know they had just been praying. It makes me want to cry."

"Arguing after church is something people do, not God!" Bob said.

"Well, that's my point. If somebody made all this," I said, "why did he make people so mean?"

Bob didn't answer right away. "I guess it's not God's fault if someone is mean." He took a breath. "You're supposed to follow the Ten Commandments," he said again. "People don't, though."

He was right. I coveted Linda's record album collection. I didn't honor my mother when I talked back.

"Yeah," I said. "Don't you wonder how they can go to war when it says right there, Thou Shalt Not Kill?"

"War is different," he said. "You have to follow orders."

Bob and I were going steady, which was an important fifth-grade thing to do at Crestwood. It consisted mostly of keeping each other's school pictures in our desks with our supplies and books, hanging out at recess, and talking on the telephone. This was a big change from St. Norbert's, where no one could ever have gone steady openly. And that was just one of many differences between the two schools. When I first came to Crestwood, after years at St. Norbert's, I rose from my seat to stand when called on. The other children laughed. I'd learned to stay slouched and seated while answering questions.

"If I were God," I said into the receiver, "I would not allow war. It's wrong."

"Who are you to tell God what to do?" Bob laughed at me. "Do you pray at night?"

"Yes. Sometimes."

"Me, too," he said. "I pray for my family."

Bob was a Protestant, like most of the kids at Crestwood. Protestantism was a different religion with different rules. Each religion said the other one was wrong, but they didn't fight over it. Of course, I had no understanding of the historical conflict between them. But I was curious about the differences—so, a few weeks prior to this conversation with Bob, on a cold fall Sunday, I'd decided to investigate for myself. No one noticed when I snuck out of the Sunday school line and took off through the parking lot. I dashed across the street, heading to the Presbyterian church that most of my friends attended. I'd been running down the broad hilly lawn in front of the heretical church, when the next thing I knew, I was waking up.

I found myself on a couch indoors, woozy and thirsty in a small dim room with my mother and the Presbyterian pastor, who were coaching me back to consciousness. My mother told me I'd slipped on an icy patch and knocked the back of my head, where a nice goose-bump arose. I never got inside that mysterious Protestant church. Had God blocked my way?

"What do you pray for?" Bob asked me, bringing me back to the present.

Last May, I'd said the rosary twenty-eight of thirty-one days for my father and hoped that Linda had the bases better covered. I regretted my weakness. Each time I'd missed a rosary, I'd doubled up the next day, hoping to make up for my failure. Mary was supposed to be merciful. Still, I'd feared I was not helping my dad very much. And I had long since lost the blessed blue-stone rosary.

"Sometimes I just repeat the prayers," I answered. "But does it help anything? People are still starving in India." *Daddy still gets drunk and hurts everyone.*

"Maybe God has other plans," Bob offered.

"I hope so," I said.

CHAPTER 6
HOMETOWN

My hometown was a small, mostly Christian village among many that expanded as white people moved out of Chicago in the 1950s and ’60s. Our township built a second high school in 1962 to accommodate all the new students. Northbrook had one Catholic and one Presbyterian church, and no other places of worship. It never occurred to me to notice that we had no synagogue, mosque, or Quaker meeting place. In 1963, I was not aware that such places existed.

For better or worse, my young friends and I were insulated from the real world as we grew into adolescence. We rode our bikes around town without ever locking them. Shopkeepers knew us by name. In our daily lives, we didn’t encounter crime (many of us didn’t lock our house doors), racial conflict, or poverty. Almost nothing of Black Americans’ terrible struggle for basic justice penetrated our white adolescent enclave. When news of the civil rights movement eventually trickled into our awareness, we heard adults around us refer to it as “the Negro question.” So, while Martin Luther King was protesting in Birmingham, I was sprawled on bedroom floors at my friends’ houses listening to folk rock while other girls chattered about how to grow into women.

On one typical rainy Saturday in April 1963, four of us gathered, as we often did, at Sally’s house. Sally sat cross-legged on her bed reading the current *Seventeen Magazine.* Each month you could read beauty and makeup tips, advice for dating, how to tell if you are in love, and if he is the right one. Or how to jitterbug and do the mashed potato.

"Listen to this," Sally began. "This article tells you ways to meet boys. 'Go to exhibits at the library, local stores, the museum, the town hall, places that offer things a boy might be interested in,'" she read. "They list boats, cars, fishing, photographs of the town's fire or police department, and softball games."

"They're building a new fire station out on Dundee near Skokie," I put in. "We could go scouting down there." Riding our bikes over to the station sounded like fun.

Sally laughed and turned the page. "Here's a way to set your hair to get a pageboy," she said.

"Let me try that on you," Marty said, looking up. "We can use your sister's curlers."

Marty and Sally gathered up Marcia's rollers and went into the bathroom while I went into the kitchen to get a glass of water. Mrs. Stonebraker stood at the counter, chopping potatoes and celery.

"Hello, young lady," she greeted me with her bright half-smile that made it look a little as if she were teasing. "How's the A-team doing today?" Her left eyebrow went up. She glanced down and sliced a potato lengthwise.

My throat constricted and I felt myself withdraw. Sally's mother was always kind to me, often asking about my life with real interest. But I worried that she knew, maybe through town gossip, that my father got drunk and violent. He had a case of Scotch delivered every week by the Otis & Lee liquor store on Waukegan. What if employees talked and my family had a reputation? What if Mrs. S. was trying to show me what a normal home could be like because she knew my family secrets?

"Good afternoon, Mrs. Stonebraker!" I said, covering my shame with exaggerated energy like Eddie Haskell on *Leave It to Beaver*. I hoped my smile didn't look too phony. "How are you today?"

Mrs. Stonebraker put down her knife. She rested her elbows on the counter, put her chin in her hands, and leaned toward me. "So, what's the latest in Rikki's life?" She gave me that crooked, quizzical smile again.

I wanted to let the words come pouring out and tell her how crazy things were. That last weekend my parents had somehow crashed the Cadillac and left it on the train tracks near our house, and that a train had smashed it up. That I felt on the edge of panic half the time.

But I couldn't bear to expose myself, my family, or our secrets. Instead, I picked at my fingernail and chewed on my bottom lip. "I'm fine." I nodded a few times. "We're reading that Joseph Conrad book *Lord Jim*. I'm working on a book report."

"I remember that one, I think. The sailor who abandons ship? Well, you keep up the good work. Do you girls need a snack?" Mrs. S. always asked. "Take this," she said, handing me a bowl of Ruffles.

Part of me just wanted to hang out with her in the kitchen. I wasn't sure I was ready for the move toward dating and womanhood that was going on in Sally's room. In seventh grade at the junior high, some of my friends were already thirteen, but I wouldn't even be twelve until June. I still liked to play football with Peter. I liked to read The Hardy Boys mysteries and ride my Schwinn at the speed of the wind.

But I dutifully took the chips and padded back down the hallway toward Sally's room.

In the bathroom, Sally sat in front of a mirror with half her hair bound up in brush curlers.

"Who's going to the sock hop?" Marty asked as she wound a fresh strand.

"Me." Sally held up a hand.

"Me, too!" chirped Nancy.

"When is it?" I asked.

"What planet are you on? I've been waiting weeks for this!" Nancy said.

"Saturday night," said Sally. "I think Marcia can drive us."

My stomach clenched. I dreaded dancing, moving my body in front of all the kids at school. And it could kick off asthmatic wheezing. I carried one of those new bronchodilators with me by then, so the risk was small. But just talking about dancing made me want to go home and hide. And I tried to stay away from home as much as I could.

"What are you guys wearing?" I asked, feeling heat rise in my neck and ears. A nagging voice whispered at the edge of my mind. *I never seem to wear the right thing.* Skirts were required at school, but on weekends most girls wore tight jeans and stretchy sweaters. I chose oversized shirts with button-down collars. It would be years before I needed a bra.

Marty sighed. "Probably a plaid skirt and sweater like always."

I marveled at Marty. She was a straightforward, honest girl who seemed to have no secrets. *Whereas I always feel like I'm hiding something.*

"No jeans?" I asked, my hopes fading.

"Not for girls!" Marty said.

"The boys have to wear a tie," Nancy put in.

I hate skirts. I look so stupid in them. I tried to picture myself doing the foxtrot with Rick Suez or Tommy Weckler, and my body froze inside. *How will I ever endure a sock hop?*

Yet that Saturday night, I did shuffle my way through our band's versions of "Venus in Blue Jeans" and "Sealed with a Kiss." I wore a plaid skirt and a baby-blue cardigan that I buttoned to my throat. I performed a stumbling foxtrot with Rick Suez and goofy versions of the jitterbug with two boys I didn't know. Between dances, I stood awkwardly near the bleachers or doors and looked for girls to talk to. Sometime around nine thirty my torment ended when Sally's sister Marcia gave us a ride home.

Home . . . with my parents Dick and Rosemary, who, I knew, would be hung over tomorrow, as they were every dreary Sunday morning. It seemed there was nothing I could do to break the cycle. Dad would go on a bender and disappear for a few days, leaving Mom a confused mess. Little Bethy would try to comfort her. Or Dad would insult and attack Mom until she was in tears and then he would pass out. Sometimes he would hit her. Then he would do something to make up for it, such as buy her a new car or promise not to drink for a week.

I didn't even have Linda to commiserate with anymore. For high school, she'd chosen Marywood, a Catholic boarding school for girls an hour away in Evanston, and she had been gone all year.

I just wanted out. I wanted out of my family, but I didn't know where I could go.

As it turned out, Mom slept through the Mass schedule that Sunday—so, to my relief, we did not have to attend.

I'd grown weary of Catholic rituals since I'd been going to public school. We rarely went to church as a family, and I hadn't been to confession for months. In fact, I didn't even talk to God anymore. Junior high kids were into the Top Ten hits; they wanted to dance, hang out, and TP the houses of popular kids on Halloween. No one was talking about God. No one but me worried about sins. My heart wanted to stay right with God, but my mind wasn't sure he was real.

Five months later, I was rushing down the corridor from lunch to English class on a chilly fall day, thinking about Tom Sawyer, when an urgent voice rang out on the public announcement system. "All students report to the gymnasium for a school meeting. This is not a drill. All classes are canceled. All students are to report to the gymnasium immediately."

I obediently turned around and headed back down the linoleum toward the gym.

Eighth graders were the kings of the mountain at my school. We were on our way up and out into the world. Yet privately, I felt like a winner only when compared to seventh and sixth graders. Among my peers, I was ashamed to dance, scared to talk to boys, and too anxious to speak in front of class. I knew how to get an A on a test but not how to flirt. And I had very quiet, disturbing rushes of warmth around some of the other girls. Kimmy Gibson, maybe. I just wanted her to like me. My mind would go blank and my cheeks would heat up whenever I tried to talk to her. And I knew this was a secret thing I could never talk about.

But when I ran into Kimmy on the way to the gym, I was almost too curious to blush as I blurted out, "What's going on?"

"No idea. Must be serious, though," she said.

"Someone's been shot," said Ben Haskell. "I heard my shop teacher talking about it."

Six hundred students crowded into the bleachers on both sides of the gym floor. Mr. Courdray called everyone to order in solemn tones. "Please take your seats. I have a very difficult announcement to make," he said into the loudspeaker. "There has been a shooting in Dallas." He waited for the shuffling to settle. "President Kennedy has been shot."

Silence thudded like wet clay. "He has been taken to the hospital. We are waiting for news." The static of whispering broke out across the benches of confused students. Courdray raised his voice. "Classes are canceled for the rest of the day. Students will wait in here until your parents pick you up. You can go to your lockers and get your things."

"What happened?"

"Where were they?"

"Who did it?"

"Did they catch the guy?"

Questions rang out as students tried to absorb the shocking and unbelievable facts.

"He was shot while riding in a motorcade in Dallas. We do not know his current condition," Mr. Courdray said.

How could this have happened, in this, the safest country in the world? Presidents don't get shot. Tears welled up in my eyes. He was Dad's hero. He got us through the nuclear missile crisis with Cuba, when we school kids had to scrunch our necks under flimsy wooden school desks. Now President Kennedy could die! How could life be so unpredictable?

"There is no information about the shooter," Mr. Courdray added.

Mom's eyes were red and swollen when she picked me up from school. Bethy was already in the back seat; her first-grade class let out at 1:00 p.m.

"Is there any news?" I asked as I opened the front door of the new Oldsmobile Cutlass convertible.

"He's dead," Mom said, a tear gently sliding down her cheek.

We drove in silence for a few blocks, then I switched on the radio. The police were searching for the gunman who had shot a policeman while escaping.

We drove home. I did homework in my bedroom at the desk under the window. Then I went next door looking for Peter, to see if he wanted to play pool or something. Anything normal.

Life was going on, but something had changed. I felt like a little kid who just learned there was no Santa Claus. The facts of the world had finally crashed into my life. What I learned was something I already knew from my family but had kept hidden from myself. Now I spoke it aloud: "You can't count on anything. Don't ever trust anyone (except Linda)."

That night, I lay in bed in the semi-dark with my night-light glowing, my toes curled tight, and my hands pressed into fists. I wished Linda were home. Eventually, I talked to God about the killing.

“Why do you let these things happen?” I demanded. “Why can’t you be on our side? I hate you!”

God made no sense to me; what was he for? He was no use in the fight against evil. He couldn’t even help me stop sinning. I wrapped the blankets tightly around myself to ward off the threatening intrusion of the world.

Snuggled in bed, I peered into the dark, feeling edgy and frazzled, as if someone might be sneaking up on me. My jaw ached. Then I got up and did something I hadn’t done for years. I dragged my desk chair over to the closet and wedged it under the handle of the door so the monsters couldn’t get out.

Back in bed, I bumped my lonely way down into a jumpy sleep. But I knew it was too late; the monsters were already out.

CHAPTER 7
CHICAGO HIGH

Sally lifted a Spartans football jersey out of the cardboard box she'd dragged into the cafeteria during the second month of high school. She held it up with a happy grin.

"We had fifteen made, so everybody gets one," Sally explained as she handed green and gold shirts to Peggy, Nancy, Mindy, and me.

"Why do they say *Nablies* on the back?" Nancy asked. But the other girls just giggled.

As new freshmen (it was very important to say *freshmen* rather than *ninth graders*), our gang of friends from junior high created a Glenbrook North Spartans girls' fan club called the Nablies. It took me a few weeks to realize that the name was an anagram of *lesbian*, but when I figured it out, I was secretly delighted. The whole notion was titillating. I never did learn who came up with that, but we wore our provocative shirts playfully to the games, and despite my vague worries that broadcasting any hint of sexual deviance was dangerous, no one ever asked us about it or teased us. My little football pullover became a teen treasure.

Although I was a year or more younger than my Nablies friends, high school was easy and fun for me. Our English teacher decided that a more contemporary version of Shakespeare's *Romeo and Juliet* might offer a refreshing introduction to its themes. Instead of forcing us to slog through the original work—an education in itself—we read the screenplay of *West Side Story*, which had been out for several years. The course was useless; we already knew the words to all the songs, which told the whole story.

Algebra was a breeze. When my math teacher saw how quickly I understood the concepts and mechanics, she let me help coach other students during class. Ms. Rosen also directed the fall melodrama, *He Ain't Done Right by Nell*, in which I played Nell.

I was having fun, feeling comfortable in my own skin and with my peer group. While succeeding socially and academically, I was too busy to worry about a boyfriend. What could possibly go wrong?

"This will be easier for Daddy," Mom explained as my freshman year drew to an end. "He'll be close to work. He won't have to drive in all that traffic."

Mom and Dad wanted to move to Lakeshore Drive in Chicago, near Daddy's advertising office. I knew Mom hoped that if things were easier, Dad might not drink so much. I had my doubts, but I also knew my dad needed something. Maybe, as he used to say, this was the ticket.

The summer after my freshman year, in 1965, we left our little town and moved an hour away to the fortieth floor of the DeWitt building on Chestnut Street in Chicago, overlooking Lake Michigan. We didn't sell the Northbrook house right away. Instead, we locked it up with much of our old furniture inside.

The new apartment was spectacular, with ten-foot-high windows for exterior walls, looking out over the city and the lake. Mom said she could see all the way to her relatives in South Bend, Indiana. There was one big central room including the kitchen, plus three small bedrooms. The floors were made of intricately patterned hardwood squares that gleamed when the morning sun flowed in. It was a huge improvement over the big old drafty house on Dundee.

The whole family was ready for a fresh start. Linda had been boarding at Marywood, but she came to live with us in Chicago. She took the "L" to school each day, while Elizabeth and I walked to our new local schools. I missed my bosom buddies Sally, Mindy, Katie, Nancy, and Marilyn, but I went back to visit Northbrook at least twice a month and spent nights at one of their houses. As long as we had these regular visits, I loved living in Chicago.

Dad had a contract to create radio ads for Baby Ruth candy bars, and he hired me to be the voice of a happy gobbler. He got me a Social Security number and a bank account. One weekday in August, we walked together a few blocks to his recording studio near LaSalle.

This part of Chicago piqued my interest. Flashy entertainment clubs dotted the infamous Rush Street nearby. Dad and I stopped outside one.

"Here's where your Uncle Bill started out," he said, referring to a close friend who'd done standup until he found a role on a TV sitcom. "Look in here."

I pressed my face against the darkened window of the small bar, straining to see the little stage and microphone beyond the cocktail tables and chairs.

"Have you ever done stand-up, Daddy?" I asked, staring at him with admiration.

"I've done open-mic here and down the street a few times," he said. "But I'm pretty busy with the radio commercials."

We stopped at the famous Mister Kelly's jazz hangout on the corner of Rush and Chestnut, where Dad first saw Barbra Streisand. Just down the street, I spied a bar displaying poster-size photographs of song-and-dance performers in glamorous costumes. They looked like heavyset, beautifully made-up women.

"Actually, honey," my dad said slowly, "they are not really women."

My face skewed into bewilderment. *What?*

"They're men, dressed as women."

Holy cow! I could hardly believe it! I'd had no idea men dressed as women. What other secrets did Chicago hold?

I got my answer one night a few weeks later when the whole family went to have dinner in the Old Town District. My Uncle Bernie did the bartending at Chances R, a 1940s retro tavern. The floor was covered in empty peanut shells. Mom ordered me a Shirley Temple cocktail and a burger, but I gorged on the peanuts. I loved throwing the crushed husks under the table.

After we ate, the five of us strolled among the novelty and tourist shops in Old Town. Down the street, I saw odd-looking people walking around in men's suits or wife-beater tank tops. They seemed out of place to me.

I tugged on my dad's jacket sleeve.

"Are those regular men, or . . . ?"

"No, honey, those are women. They like to wear men's clothes and act like men."

Actual living lesbians! I had no idea women dressed as men! It bewildered me even more than men dressing as women. *Is it even legal?* I wondered.

"How do you know God exists?" I insisted during religion class in my second month at my new school. "He doesn't perform miracles anymore."

Two or three of the other kids looked up from their reading to see how Father Ricci would handle me.

I attended Holy Name Cathedral High School now, where the kids were a mix of white, Mexican, Puerto Rican, and Black. Here, knife fights after school and guns hidden in jackets were real things. It was thrilling and scary. I was suddenly in the big, unprotected world, not the sheltered burrow of the suburbs watching a musical. But one aspect of this school was familiar: It was a Catholic school, which brought the dogma and rituals back into my life.

The religion class at Holy Name was taught not by a nun but by a visiting Jesuit priest. I knew the Jesuits had a reputation within the Catholic church as intellectual mavericks, which was just up my alley. I liked to ask challenging questions.

Father Ricci was a short man with brown hair in a crew cut. He wore the white priestly collar under his dark blue wool sweater, but his clear, intelligent eyes and sturdy build made him look more like a coach than a priest. He was ready for me.

"God wants you to ask these tough questions," he answered with a hint of a tease. "Here's how I look at it: people discover that God exists by listening to their hearts."

I cringed silently. In my heart, I coveted a junior from my old high school, Mark Stanchion, who hung a broken cross on a well-worn leather thong around his neck. It seemed like several intoxicating sins at once: the broken cross itself, the pride of wearing it, the arrogance of rebellion. He reminded me of Sal Mineo in *Rebel Without a Cause*. I yearned to be cool enough to talk to him. Never, ever, ever in a million years would he notice me. Still, I was quietly relieved to be attracted to a boy—an older, sexy, mysterious, forbidden sort of boy—rather than a girl like Kimmy Gibson. Or like the lesbians in Old Town.

"What do people hear?" I asked Father Ricci.

"The right thing to do. The truth." He watched me take this in.

I knew in my heart that the right thing to do was certainly to avoid being alone with boys. But it was okay to like them. I had always liked boys. They were no mystery to me when we were kids. We played cowboys, football, and kick-the-can. We fought sometimes and got yelled at. But this was different. Older boys lived in a special world of their own with special powers. They were dangerous, which was exciting. They joined varsity sports clubs and knew about sex firsthand. Girls knew about sex from gossip.

"I don't believe God is watching each person to catch you in a sin," I told Father Ricci. Now half the class was listening.

"Maybe he's more like a coach," Father offered. "He urges you toward righteousness. But you still have the freedom to ignore him."

That was the hard part. I had the urge to kiss boys on the weekends, and the urge to be righteous during the week. I resolved not to talk back to Mom, yet when she asked me to put my coat away, I sassed her. Was I ignoring the urging of God? Did he actually care?

"Mary, help me stay chaste," I whispered in prayer when I was alone. "Give me the willpower to resist."

And then, I made plans to go to Northbrook for the weekend. I was hoping to see Mark at the varsity game.

CHAPTER 8
LAST CONFESSIONS

Everything started to go to hell when Peggy McAllister discovered the six-branched candelabra among a collection of silver and crystal that an Indian raj had given to my great-grandfather. Then she unearthed my mother's long wooden matches from the sideboard.

I found out about it when I heard her scream.

"What the hell is going on?" I screeched as I ran into the front hall and found Peggy stomping on flames. "What are you doing?"

"Sorry," Peggy slurred, and emptied a can of Old Milwaukee on her feet.

"Oh my god." I peered at the floor. "The whole carpet was on fire! It's black!" I stared at Peggy in astonishment.

A few people came over to observe the wreckage before backing away and disappearing into the crowd.

"Okay, people!" I shouted. "That's it! Time to go!" I clapped my hands and shouted, but I could barely hear my own voice over the mayhem of the party.

I was only fourteen and the house was packed with older teens I didn't know. Once I'd decided to have the party, my girlfriends had spread the word to the upperclassmen, who could drive people and bring alcohol. Friends had called friends and told them everyone was coming to Rikki's house at 846 Dundee Road, the one with the pool, the next Friday night. And we'd been lucky! Piles of teenagers had arrived in souped-up Pontiacs and Chevys and pickup trucks that stacked up in our long, circular driveway. They'd brought their own alcohol: cases of beer and bottles of vodka.

Now people swarmed through the house, upstairs and down. I'd kept them out of my parents' bedroom, but couples were making out in every other room. They played stacks of 45 rpm records in the living room, twisting to Herman's Hermits and singing "Wooly Bully" aloud as they reveled in its sexual suggestion. Splashes of spilled drinks stained the living room couch and den carpet. And now this fire in the front hall!

After checking the carpet for sparks, I moved down the hall toward the big living room and den, calling out, "Time to go!" and tapping kids on the shoulder.

"Party's over, friend. Time to go," I shouted six or seven times.

But they wouldn't go. They looked at me as if I'd fallen off a tomato truck. This crowd of drunken sex-crazed teenagers wasn't going anywhere until it had exhausted itself with the magic of booze and rock 'n' roll. The party didn't peter out until midnight, when the oldest boys finally left, clearing the driveway.

I locked up and got a ride with someone to Nancy's house.

Nancy, Peggy, and I spent all day Saturday cleaning the house. But the burn mark was still there, and my parents' alcohol cabinet had been reduced to half a bottle of gin. I knew I was in serious trouble. Mom and Dad were coming to the house Sunday, and I was supposed to meet them and ride back with them to Chicago. In desperation, I ran away to Mindy Mueller's house.

I hid in Mindy's bedroom and told her not to tell her parents. Then I called home to talk to Linda and explained where I was, extracting a promise of silence. But Linda broke under questioning Sunday afternoon, and soon some very angry parents picked up a remorseful teenager.

"What were you thinking?" my father shouted at me. Thank God he was still sober that day. It was "good Daddy" that I was dealing with. Still, he looked as if he would slap me if I ticked him off another notch.

"It was just a party," I whined, grimacing. I stared at my ragged fingernails, wishing to hell I'd gotten away with it.

"This is not a party house! This is our home. How dare you insult your mother like this." He shook his finger at me. I hated it when he accused me of hurting Mom. What about his bullying?

"It wasn't just a party," Mom cried out. She was holding herself together with her arms wrapped around her chest. "This place is a mess. You've torn up the carpets and gotten stains on the furniture." Mom was yelling like she hated me. "You look at me when I'm talking to you, young lady!" Her eyes were cold and unblinking, shutting me out completely.

"I'm sorry, I didn't—"

"Don't start your 'sorries' with me," Mom said with a steely look that shut me up.

"You are grounded," my father said abruptly.

"Oh no, how long?" I started to complain. My whole life centered around my friends. How could they cut me off?

"Forever," Mom said. "Now be quiet."

Alone with my miserable self, I contemplated my sins. I had a lot to clear up. I worked on a list of transgressions, afraid to come clean yet scared to be dishonest with God. In case I died, I didn't want to go to hell. On Monday afternoon, when my religion class went to confession, I got it off my chest. I recited each violation to the priest on the other side of the little sliding door in the privacy of the confessional.

"Bless me, Father, for I have sinned," I intoned. "I accuse myself of the following sins." I knelt on the little cushion in the dark, whispering at the screen that separated me from the priest on the other side.

It smelled like wood or leather polish in there. The priest cleared his throat as if he were the one about to speak. Then I began. It came out in a rush.

"I had a party at my house and lied to my parents. I ran away from home. I let Tom copy my homework. I told Mom to go to hell. I hit Linda." Thank God I did not know the priests at the cathedral. Whoever it was didn't make a sound. Was he still awake? "I humbly beg and penance and absolution of you, Father."

"You've been giving your parents a lot of trouble, I think," said a soft, throaty whisper. "Are you sorry for your sins?"

"Yes, Father," I said.

"Your penance is thirty Hail Marys, ten Our Fathers, and one Apostles' Creed," he told me, and I was free to go. I went out into the church, knelt in a pew, recited the prayers—and that cleared my soul. I was safe again, for the moment.

"Want a beer?" a strawberry-blond boy, probably a junior, asked me with a smile.

We were at a party in Northbrook a few weeks after I'd been grounded. My parents had finally relented and let me visit my friends on the weekend.

"Sure," I said hesitantly. I had never had a beer. Just sips from my father and uncles. It seemed very grown up.

"I'm Jackie," he said, handing me a Pabst Blue Ribbon can. He had punched two triangular holes in the top. "Jackie Peterson."

It was a Friday night in December. My friends and I had gotten a ride from Nancy's older sister, who'd dropped us off at a two-story four-bedroom house that was already crowded. There was slushy snow on the ground, but the night was clear and not too cold, so a few people were standing out in the driveway. There were lots of upperclassmen whom I didn't recognize. Most of the guys wore jeans with V-neck sweaters, while we girls were in plaid pleated skirts and blouses. I wore jeans and a white button-down blouse with a wool vest.

I'd lost track of my friends early on and was sitting on a couch in the breakfast nook of a vast kitchen. A long countertop separated the sitting area from the cook's space. From another room, I could hear Manfred Mann and Roy Orbison on a record player, and people were dancing the twist and the jerk right in the kitchen.

"Are you a freshman?"

I blushed, looked away, and sipped the Pabst. "Sophomore," I said, "can't you tell?" I was a year younger than my peers, having started school at five instead of six. On top of that, I looked young.

It was cute the way Jackie laughed. He had short, wavy hair that he parted on the left side and combed back from his forehead. His smile made his whole round face look like a baby's.

"Cigarette?" he said, pulling out his pack of Tareytons.

"No, thanks." I shook my head and took another sip of the bitter-tasting brew.

"Who are you here with?" he asked as he held his lighter to his smoke.

"Marilyn, Nancy, and Sally." Where were they? I glanced down the hallway to the living room.

"Sophomores? Don't know them. I'm a junior. Are you girls at Glenbrook North?"

I was running out of interesting things to say. What was his name again?

"I used to be. We moved to Chicago."

"Want to dance?"

I froze. *Yes, I want to dance! No, I would be utterly mortified to dance! Yes, I want to chug this beer and twist the night away! No, I cannot get up off this couch.*

"Not yet," I said, squeezing the beer can in one hand and chewing a fingernail on the other.

"Okay, you finish your beer and I'll see you later." He got up and moved toward the music.

I was suddenly aware of being alone in a bubble of intense, personal silence. People moved around me in small clumps, telling jokes, arguing, and sipping drinks. Cigarette smoke hung in the air like a barrier between me and them. I looked at the beer in my hand and saw relief. Tilting it back into my mouth, I chugged and swallowed. Bottoms up! Then I stood, ready to go find another. It was party time.

My mind swam back into consciousness in an upstairs bedroom with three other people. A window looked out on a streetlamp shining on a short icy driveway. We were polishing off a bottle of tequila. The boy named Bill had access to his parents' liquor cabinet and said he could get more if we wanted. My friend Marilyn sat at the head of the bed next to him and I was lying at the foot of the bed next to Lou, whom I had apparently met at the party.

My head was spinning but I felt terrific. Lou was a junior on the varsity wrestling team. He had short blond curly hair that circled his cherub face with its unexpectedly gentle blue eyes. At sixteen, he was too old for me—I was fourteen—which pleased me no end. We were talking about getting in Lou's car and going to get Bill's bottle. "I have to get back to Nancy's house by eleven o'clock," I said, worrying a little now. Where exactly were we? What time was it? Where was my coat?

It turned out not to be ten yet. We piled in Lou's car and drove maybe ten minutes to Bill's for the extra bottle. Then we sat out in the car in the December chill with the heater on and drank, listening to the car radio and making out quietly. Lou got me home by eleven.

What to say in confession on Monday afternoon?

I was pretty sure I was in love, according to everything I had read. Although I had been blackout-level intoxicated, I knew I loved kissing him. How was I going to deal with this strange and exciting new wonder in my life? A boyfriend! A really cute strong nice boyfriend with a car!

"Bless me, Father, for I have sinned. I kissed a boy. I lied to Mom. I stole $20 from Daddy."

The priest doled out my penance. I said the prayers. Did I get the account cleared? Was I set for another week? I did not want to fall into sin, but I wanted to see that boy again even more.

"Does confession really work, Father?" I asked Father Ricci that week in religion class.

This one got several glances from the girls.

"It's a sacrament, a special work of God. It always works if you are sincere," he answered.

I felt sincere when I was praying. But I felt longing for Lou even more. Maybe I wasn't as earnest as I hoped. I brooded over it for weeks.

This was the best I could do: I worked out an agreement with God where I could make out with Lou on weekends, but then I would show up on Monday for confession. I would do my best to avoid venial sins and to earn straight A's in school. How much harm could there be in having a cool boyfriend?

"I'll come pick you up in Chicago," Lou said on the phone on December 31, 1965. "There's a party at Bill's house."

"I could take the train . . ." I ventured without enthusiasm.

"I'll come in the morning, before traffic, and you can hang out at my house."

Lou lived outside of Northbrook in a sprawling, slightly dilapidated fifteen-room home that housed all of his family. He had twelve sisters and brothers, all younger. They had two big refrigerators and an elk-sized freezer in the garage.

Lou had become my official boyfriend. I felt safer with him than anywhere else. I could hold his sturdy wrestler's arm and count on his calm, friendly voice. I could ride through town in his '64 Chevy Impala 425 with dual overhead cams and oversized tires instead of in a godforsaken sedan with my parents. When he drank, Lou got funny or happy, never angry or violent. I felt a calm with Lou that I never felt alone, or at home.

The new year looked full of happiness, love, and friendship.

One night at dinner in spring, Dad started to talk about writing comedy in California.

"My advertising agency has been so successful, winning awards in multiple categories. I talked to a Disney executive, and they need writers like me."

Linda and I glanced at each other. I was shaken and rolled my eyes. Linda didn't react because she was leaving Chicago anyway, headed for college next fall. Only Beth's life and mine would be ruined!

But Dad wanted to write comedy for television.

"I think you should take the job, Dick. It's what you've always wanted," Mom said. I knew she hoped the change would help him stop drinking.

I hated the idea. I had everything I needed right there in Illinois. It seemed like my father drank anyway, no matter what the family did for him. Why did I have to suffer?

Beth was too young to care, Linda was going off to Creighton University in Nebraska, and no one listened to me. Arrangements were made, despite my vehement objections.

I had barely finished sophomore year when we packed up the apartment, put both our homes up for sale, and trekked off to Los Angeles.

CHAPTER 9
FIRST GLIMPSE

On a warm September afternoon in 1966, a day bright with the fragrance of blue gum eucalyptus, I began exploring the secrets of my mind.

My parents, sisters, and I had arrived in Southern California's San Fernando Valley a few months earlier. With a new friend Kim from my California high school, I had scored a $10 one-ounce bag of clumped green-brown leaves. Kim and I took the stash up to my bedroom and put Dylan's "Rainy Day Women #12 & 35" on the record player. Singing along, we shouted out our favorite lyric inviting everyone to get stoned while rolling our first-ever marijuana cigarettes.

Back in Illinois, my biggest thrill had been to slam Old Style beers with the boys during beach parties at Lake Michigan. In LA, there was something much bigger going on. A fantastic new vision—of expanded consciousness, of social equity, of peace among nations—filled the minds and music of young people here. It pulled us all into a vortex of rebellion against the old regime. I quickly embraced the nascent peace-and-love culture that seemed to radiate from the hippies on Sunset Strip and spread into the surrounding mountains' wild, winding canyons, which my pals and I would hitchhike carelessly to the Pacific Ocean.

Up in my room, Kim and I scraped out the stems and seeds from the bag of weed, then broke up the lumps. I rolled a few little cigarette papers around a pencil to get them started. Kim took one of those curled tissues in her fingertips and sprinkled shredded leaves in the trough. After a few tries, she produced two fat, wondrous, life-changing joints, with the papers twisted tightly on both ends. We smoked both of them, burning incense and cigarettes to fool my mom, and ended up giggling so hard we could barely navigate the stairs to the kitchen when we got the munchies.

With this act, we joined the tribe of California young people who were exploring altered consciousness. We became part of a fast-growing transformational movement. Anyone who flashed the peace sign and took a hit could be part of it.

At school, girls were required to wear below-the-knee skirts, but my out-of-school dress quickly changed from Midwestern jeans and shirts to West Coast hip-hugging corduroy bell-bottoms with a three-inch wide belt, peasant blouses, and jackets with fringe. My hip friends and I trusted all "dopers" but were suspicious of "surfers and narcs." We hated law and order, rudely calling officials "the man" and "the fuzz."

On weekends, we painted symbols of love, peace, and psychedelic visions on our bodies with glowing body paint that we bought at a head shop in West Hollywood. Our generation had an attitude against the whole cultural and economic establishment. In protest, we put our nonviolent values right up in the face of anyone over thirty.

Occasionally my mother could not resist the temptation to tease my hippie persona. One afternoon, we were driving down Ventura Boulevard when I spotted a police car.

"Watch out for the fuzz!" I alerted Mom.

She burst out laughing.

"What?" I asked, bewildered.

"Fuzz?" she blurted. "It's fizz, not fuzz! I can't believe you said fuzz!"

She had me. I blanched; my mind raced. I flashed through multiple scenes of me saying *fuzz* in front of my friends instead of the correct *fizz*. My face burst into flames of embarrassment for my many stupid faux pas.

Then my mother completely broke down in laughter. I started to giggle along with her, tentatively, not sure I got the joke. Then it started to become clear. She was just messing with me; I'd had it right all along.

That was my family; anything for a laugh. And to this day, my sister Beth and I use the verb *to fizz* when someone pulls off this kind of jest.

But that day in the car, I laughed to cover my more nuanced feelings—like feeling pretty unhappy about being ridiculed.

"Now children," I said to my AP science class in my deepest growly voice, "I *respectfully* request that you open your *lab books* to page sixty-two." I began fake-coughing, patted my imaginary coat pockets for a hanky, and cleared my throat. Half the class was laughing.

"Today, we shall *experiment* with an experiment." I expected that well-used phrase to get a laugh, but the class had gone silent.

Uh-oh. They were staring over my right shoulder.

"Impressive, Miss West," Mr. Levi said.

My science teacher had been late to class, so I'd stood up in front of the room and impersonated him—my father was a successful Hollywood comedy writer, after all. But now Mr. Levi was standing behind me. He'd been in the anteroom getting slides and heard the whole thing. I peeked over my shoulder at him.

"And now you're headed to the principal." He sent me to the office on suspicion of drugs.

I was easily landing straight A's in my classes, except in home economics, where I had inadvertently sewn a sleeve into the neck of a blouse I was making. But I wasn't interested in school. Who wanted to be indoctrinated by the military-industrial complex that Eisenhower warned us about? They would try to teach me that war and oppression were unavoidable and acceptable. In revolt, I'd been skipping school and acting up in classes.

The previous week, my friend Kathy and I ditched music to spend extra time in the darkroom developing photographs. When the chorus director sat down at the piano, we just climbed out a window in the rear of the classroom and took off running. I'd served detention for that excursion.

Today, I handed the pink reporting slip to the secretary, who gave me a strange look.

"You should see the nurse," she said.

The nurse shined a flashlight in my eyes and took my pulse. "Stick out your tongue," she said, and peered inside my mouth. Then she sat back and looked at me. "What are you doing here?"

"I was goofing around in science class. I'm not on drugs," I said with defiance. I was scared, and a little angry, and inclined to resist her authority.

"I can see you aren't on drugs," she said, "but I wonder what you were up to." The nurse was part of the establishment, and I was an anti-establishmentarian. I wasn't open to a dialogue.

"I told a joke," I said stiffly.

The nurse sent me back to class with a clean report, but the school called my parents.

Mom worried I was becoming a juvenile delinquent. They sent me to a psychiatrist.

"So, your parents set up this appointment," Dr. Bergman began, "but why don't you tell me why you think you're here."

Dr. Bergman had longish salt-and-pepper hair growing down the back of his neck that stuck out at the sides. Wearing a full, neatly trimmed beard and perfectly doctor-ish round glasses, he looked steadily at me from behind his desk while I sat cross-legged on the small leather couch facing him.

I had a lump in my throat and my palms were sweaty. Who was this guy? In a gray cardigan sweater over a white shirt and tie, he looked every bit the authority I loathed.

"I did a great impersonation of my science teacher and they freaked out?" I tried.

"You are a comedian?" He surprised me with a smile.

"My father is," I said.

"Tell me about cutting music class," he said, squinting at me.

I had to come up with something to keep him off my case. "I just wanted to escape. There was a big scene at our house the night before. I wanted to hang out with my friend. Music class is no big deal."

"Say more about the scene that night."

This was the hard part. I wanted to seem reluctant to blame my parents. "Well, my dad got drunk and yelled at my mom."

"That sounds upsetting." He waited with his hands neatly folded on the desk, looking at me. I sat on my hands to keep from fidgeting.

"Yeah, kinda," I said slowly. "You get used to it."

"What do you get used to?"

"The drinking. Fighting. Moving was supposed to help, but . . ." I stopped. I was saying too much.

Dr. Bergman let the silence hang while I started again on my fingernails. It was so claustrophobic in there I could hardly breathe. How much longer did I have to go on?

"Tell me more about why you moved," he said.

I looked away. "I don't know. It's okay. He's just not that happy right now." I had revealed more than I wanted already. Our family was none of his business, really.

"How is that for you?" he asked.

"Fine." I was done. I had nothing more to say for the rest of the hour.

That night, the psychiatrist called my father. When I heard Dad talking on the phone, I was sure I was in big trouble. But when he hung up, he seemed more sad than angry. All he said was, "That was Dr. Bergman. You don't have to see him again."

One morning, unshaven in his shorts and T-shirt, Dad came out to the kitchen while I was eating cornflakes and just asked me straight out: "Can you get Nembutal at school?"

It was spring break, and Dad had gotten overwhelmed by some dark feeling or other earlier that week. He'd stayed locked in the den for days without eating. We'd all been walking around the house on eggshells, waiting for him to sober up and come out of hiding.

I knew what he wanted Nembutal for; it was the drug that killed Marilyn Monroe. But why did he want to die? After a year in LA, Dad had started writing for famous comedians like Dean Martin. He wrote spots for *Rowan and Martin's Laugh-In* and *The Smothers Brothers Comedy Hour.* You couldn't do better than that. But my father made me feel like happiness was impossible. I thought he should be able to end his life if he wanted to.

I got on the phone with my friends, hunting down some barbiturates.

Linda was home for the week, and she overheard one of those conversations.

"What in God's name are you doing?" she demanded, standing in the kitchen doorway. She startled me. Linda was never intrusive like that. She jerked the receiver out of my hand and slammed it down on its cradle.

"Daddy asked me . . ." I stammered, suddenly seeing the terrible truth.

"Oh, good Lord. Just stop. He can't do that; he can't ask you that." She spoke with authority like a judge on *Perry Mason*. Case closed.

I gave up the calls, and with my heart burning, I left Dad to figure it out for himself. He never asked me again, and he didn't try suicide for several more years.

As a good Catholic schoolgirl, I used to pray for my mom and dad all the time. But the old God of my youth did not fit in my new world. I no longer knew to whom I should pray. The psychedelic scene said to look inward, rather than outward, for some kind of universal consciousness. It promised an alteration in my self-concept and an awakening to my "cosmic nature." Maybe I could be part of that if I turned on, tuned in, and dropped out.

Exploring these ideas seemed very grown up, but in this new spiritual world I still felt wobbly. There was no one to lean on. I was on my own, naked and solitary, seeking something I could not quite name.

I hoped that smoking pot would help me see more deeply into unknown cosmic secrets.

CHAPTER 10
FREEWHEELIN'

The police siren behind us set my heart slamming in my chest.

"Shit," Linda said.

We were both high on pot, heading toward home on Santa Monica Boulevard. The cop probably snagged us for curfew, but my mind panicked. Images of handcuffs, tiny cells, and cruel interrogation overpopulated my thoughts.

"Don't say a fucking word," Linda hissed. "Just be quiet."

I held by breath and kept my eyes down while she talked her way out of it. By the time she was driving again, I was so freaked out that I swore off pot for life.

It was the summer of 1967. After months of smoking dope, rather than having celestial insights, I'd begun to have fearful thoughts. The first few times it happened, a jittery sensation hit my belly and my thoughts got dark and repetitive. I became convinced that my friends and I were going to be arrested. And then that my friends hated me. Over time, more fearful fantasies—that I would have an accident or be assaulted—started to pierce even my ordinary states of mind.

But after the terrifying cop stop, I knew couldn't handle the heavy, paranoid thoughts anymore. Just after Timothy Leary, Richard Alpert, and Jerry Garcia launched the Human Be-In in San Francisco, and just as "turning on" became the rallying cry for the counterculture movement that engulfed me, I quit.

Instead, I thought about taking lysergic acid diethylamide-25. I read everything I could find about it. LSD, or acid, was available in dots, tabs, and sugar cubes. A lot of people took LSD to have sex, even group sex, but that wasn't my interest. To me, the allure of acid was not merely to have a "groovy high." I wanted a radiant, colorful, amusing mystical vision, from which I would emerge a changed person—more loving, patient, peaceful, and wise. I wanted the real thing: a mind-blowing, consciousness-expanding, ego-altering trip.

The only risk I discovered in my reading was that I might have a psychotic breakdown instead. Still, I kept looking for a good opportunity to try it.

Up until Timothy Leary's call to "drop out" threatened Johnson's war effort, LSD had been produced legally. In October 1965, those labs had gone into hiding. Now LSD got to my hippie pals in San Fernando Valley through chains of friends. It could take weeks or months to find some, but I knew some would show up eventually.

Rick pulled a baggie holding torn bits of blotter paper out of his backpack and smiled ear to ear. "The real stuff," he said, dangling the bag in front of our faces.

It was a Saturday morning in the fall of '67, and I was hanging out with my good friends Sam and Rick in Rick's parents' converted garage, listening to the Doors.

I trusted both Sam and Rick. Sam looked straitlaced, with a short haircut in a time of defiant long hair, but he was a freewheeling artist at heart. He drew portraits with earth-toned pencils on wide sheets of sketch paper and had a gift for capturing a nuanced look or expressive moment. My mom loved his drawings. And Rick was a blue-eyed dreamer, a soft-featured long-haired good person, draped in beads and buckskin, who got along with everybody and raised a smile wherever he could.

The stuff Rick wagged in our faces was genuine "blotter acid," not some capsules laced with amphetamines. I decided to take the plunge.

I told my mom I'd be over at a friend's house and would get a ride home late. Sam, Rick, and I piled into Sam's camper and drove up into the Santa Monica Mountains for our trip. We found a good picnic site and swallowed the laced blotter slips.

As we came onto the drug, my mood grew warm and gentle, as if I were playing with a puppy. The comfort of friendship bloomed into affection. All three of us kept smiling and saying, "Oh, no, you talk," feeling only kindness. Both of the guys seemed wondrously beautiful and precious to me, for no special reason.

Over the next few hours, we began to communicate without speaking. We imagined a glowing globe that we passed among ourselves like a balloon. Whoever had the "mystic orb" could speak to the others telepathically. In those silent transmissions, we spent the evening discussing the fragile beauty of all creation.

As the trip unfolded, the experience of unity and love only deepened. These guys were my intimate brothers. No loneliness or any sense of isolation or fear ever arose, as they often did in my normal state of mind. Rather, feelings of belonging, harmony, and beauty wove through my trip like flowing water.

We spent the afternoon and evening at the campsite in a state of radiant, inexplicable union. Hours slipped by. Near midnight, the intensity faded but the goodwill remained. Relaxed and happy, as if everything were normal, we drove back to the valley and stopped at the all-night restaurant on Ventura for eggs and bacon before Sam dropped me at home.

I got there sometime after 2:00 a.m.

I went to my bedroom to sleep, but my mind was too active. Somehow all the rules of physics had been broken yesterday while mental boundaries dissolved. I had felt oneness, bonding, and intimacy with those two big-hearted souls. But now I was by myself, crashing. The sense of trust faded. Was the experience up in the mountains even real? Did that communication happen? My mind clouded with doubt.

Lying alone in bed I felt dislocated. Could other people hear my thoughts now? Slowly I began to fear that people *could* hear my thoughts; then, that everybody was part of some secret plot to trick me. It wasn't clear what the trick was, but I was sure it involved everyone in my surroundings, even my house and family. Then it began to seem that the physical world—like the house and bedroom—was a facade in the plot.

Unnerved, I took a blanket downstairs to the living room and snuggled up on the sofa, unable to sleep.

Linda was home from college for the summer. When daylight rose, she came into the living room and found me awake, still in my clothes from the previous morning.

Clearly, I looked exhausted and distraught because she asked gently, "How are you doing, Rikki?"

"Don't talk to me," I whispered. "I know you are part of it. You are all part of it."

I'd had many adventures with my beloved big sister. Linda was cool. One time during spring break, Linda and I had dropped those little amphetamine pills called "white crosses" and painted everything in our room—including walls, stereo, sculpture, and telephone—a pale sage green. On summer nights, we hung out on the Sunset Strip with the movie stars and hippies. One night we'd picked up the actor Warren Beatty and followed him to a party at movie director Roman Polanski's house in the Hollywood Hills. The following summer that house would be the scene of the grizzly Manson murders, but when we were there, we enjoyed a pork chop dinner with Warren, John and Michelle from the Mamas and Papas, Mia Farrow, and Roman. I was too young for anyone to take seriously. It was Linda who'd caught Warren's attention. He'd asked her out a few times, but Linda had decided he wasn't her type.

"Did you do acid last night?" she asked softly, knowing I'd been thinking about it.

"I'm not talking to you." I bit off my words. The paranoia was so deep I didn't even trust my most trusted friend in the world.

"Okay, that makes sense," Linda said. "If you think we are all part of it, don't talk to me. It makes sense. Just try to get some sleep."

Her unexpected words made me feel I was thoroughly understood and cared for. Still reeling from the acid, a feeling of warmth and love bloomed within like a ringing bell.

Linda tucked in the blanket and patted me on the shoulder, leaving me alone with my fantasies. But my fears had melted away. I slept.

When I woke later in the day, I remembered the sacred, invisible orb that enabled us to hear each other without speaking. Was I losing my mind?

That couldn't have happened! I thought. People were made of atoms, cells, and brains, not metaphysical (I looked the term up) stuff like consciousness.

Then I read in a magazine—perhaps it was *Time* or *Look*—that Aldous Huxley, whose *Brave New World* we'd read in school, took mescaline, a drug like LSD that's extracted from cactus rather than fungus. The article cited his published account, *The Doors of Perception*. In it, he claimed his stoned eyes were opened to the "naked existence" of all things. Simple objects like a chair, trousers, or flowers, he said, radiated with a light that illumined their sacredness.

In my *heart* I felt that's what we touched on during our trip, but I couldn't understand it in my *mind*. The whole love festival might have been a mere hallucination, a chemically induced brain spasm.

But maybe . . . maybe there is something to it, I thought. The words to the Beatles' "I Am the Walrus" ran through my mind, about me being you and you being him as we are one together. Maybe "Lucy in the Sky with Diamonds" took us somewhere real.

Which was it, reality or fantasy? I did not know. With these dim flashes of intuition, I began exploring the inner world of my mind. What was this higher consciousness that everyone was talking about, and could it explain my trip with Rick and Sam?

CHAPTER 11
EIN-EH-MAH

"Kenny's picking me up on his motorcycle," I told my sister Bethy a few months after that first acid trip, on a Saturday morning in March. I'd been dating Kenny, a sculpture artist I'd met through my friend Laurie, for a few weeks.

"We're going to the beach. Don't tell Mom about the bike." I charged Beth with my secret.

I was a high school senior now, class of '68, turning seventeen in a couple of months. Kenny was eighteen, lived on his own, and made colorful mechanical art with gears, cranks, and engine parts that were lying around his yard. Four of us—Laurie, her boyfriend, Kenny, and I—would hang out at Kenny's amid all his brightly painted leftover bits and debris and make fat corned beef sandwiches to eat with cold beer. Sometimes we'd smoke a joint.

But last week when we were over there, the three of them had slipped into the bedroom with a spoon and a lighter. Kenny took a rubber tube to wrap around his upper arm.

"Just stay out here; you don't want to watch this," Laurie had said. A few minutes later they'd emerged, relaxed and smiling, not dopey but pretty blissful.

LSD was one thing; shooting heroin was something else altogether. I wanted nothing to do with it. It scared the hell out of me.

Kenny rumbled up on his Triumph, then sent me back inside for a heavier jacket. “It’ll be cold from the wind,” he said, “despite the sun.” So, bundled in a parka, I slung one leg over the bike and scrunched behind Kenny in the saddle. I put my feet on the passenger pegs and wrapped both arms tightly around him. There was no “sissy bar.”

With his strong upper body and sturdy legs, Kenny steered the bike east on Ventura, then south on Sepulveda. His dirty-blond ponytail streamed down his back and flew in my face as sunbaked pavement wafted warm waves at our legs. The bike eased through the wide but persistent curves of the Sepulveda Canyon onto the plateau of Los Angeles. Cool wind blew in our hair and whisked our voices away. The motorcycle thrummed beneath us, and the words to “Ruby Tuesday” drifted through my mind. I hugged Kenny, rolling with the easy motion of the bike.

We rounded a tight curve when suddenly he braked and slid into a pullout on the left. We neared a stretch of pavement where a car lay on its side, the front frame crushed against a guardrail. The horn blared. Kenny stopped the motorcycle and told me to hop off and stay there. He kicked the stand down and ran to the car. I walked after him.

Trapped in the driver’s seat, a person with long dark hair screamed. I stopped, staring at her hair, and wrapped my arms around my suddenly shivering body. Kenny was talking to another man who had parked around the curve. Then he walked over to me and pulled my arm.

“Hey, let’s go.” The terrible noise tearing the air and the mangled mess of the driver and car had seized my attention. I could hardly pull my eyes from the scene.

“Can’t we help her?” I asked.

Kenny steered me back to the bike. “They already called the police. There’s nothing we can do.” He threw his leg over the saddle and motioned for me to hop up. Then we zoomed back onto the pass toward the ocean.

Dear God, please take care of her, please get the ambulance there fast. The prayers screamed in my mind, unexpected and surprising. I began reciting the Hail Mary without thinking. I hadn't prayed at all since we left Illinois, but the longing to seek help, comfort, or solace in the great beyond exploded in my heart. *If not God, then let universal consciousness care for her. Something. Some good somewhere, may it spring forth and protect this woman.*

For weeks, the accident haunted me. The trapped driver's screaming or the image of her dark hair would burst into my mind unbidden.

It made me yearn for there to be a power who could help us when terrible things happen. I missed talking to God. When I looked within, I could sense a source of courage and comfort. But I didn't know how to call it up. And when I looked at the world outside, I found no evidence of any guiding heart. I seemed to be alone.

My mother read in the *Los Angeles Times* that the Beatles' guru, Maharishi Mahesh Yogi, was sponsoring seminars at UCLA. She knew I was interested in consciousness stuff. The article explained the yogi's Transcendental Meditation, jauntily abbreviated to TM. The practice was simple: Silently repeat a special sound, called a mantra. This would slow the chattering mind so that in quiet gaps between thoughts it might discover a silent awareness hiding. I had little idea what this meant. But in my heart, I hoped, in a groping, inarticulate way, that TM was tapping into the loving power I longed for.

I asked my friend Joanne to come with me to a seminar.

"It's supposed to make you happier," I whispered to her one day in her kitchen. "The Beatles are doing it." Joanne lived around the corner from me. Her father had cancer and was dying at home. We always had to be very quiet at their house.

"How does repeating a sound make you happy?" Joanne murmured.

"I don't know. Maybe it's like the *Magical Mystery Tour*. An invitation for us to make a reservation!"

Joanne laughed. "All out for the Mystery Tour," she cried. "Okay groovy. I'll go along.

"Hush in there!" called Joanne's mom softly from the next room.

"Don't fight the darkness. Bring the light, and darkness will disappear," the speaker said, his face animated and smiling brightly. The way to bring the light, he asserted, was via the quieting effects of silent chanting. Joanne and I learned that the benefits of this simple technique included calmness, creativity, and well-being.

"You will also take yourself less seriously and laugh more." He chuckled lightly and told us that life finds its true fulfillment in ever-growing happiness.

It was late March of 1968, and Joanne and I had driven over the hill to the UCLA Westwood campus to hear a talk on TM. The presentation was given by student followers of Maharishi Mahesh Yogi to a crowd of several hundred in a lecture hall.

Each new meditator, we learned, would receive a private mantra, specially tuned to their mental quirks. The student yogis were authorized to give them out during private, one-on-one sessions. To receive mine, I scheduled an appointment the following Tuesday afternoon.

"Aren't you going to get one?" I asked Joanne.

"No," she said, and reached up to finger the tiny silver cross she wore. I had never noticed it. "I guess I'd rather look to Jesus for happiness." She shrugged and smiled. "We already have a relationship."

I could respect that, but I had left Jesus in Illinois with my Catholic school days. Dark memories of his suffering, painstakingly mapped out in the stations of the cross, studded my childhood like bruises. I'd gladly let them fade.

"Reality is a transcendent field," one of the speakers that night had told the crowd. When I got home, I looked up *transcendent* in *Merriam-Webster's Collegiate Dictionary*: "extending or lying beyond the limits of knowledge and material existence." Then I looked up *reality*. Definition 2b seemed relevant: "something that is neither derivative nor dependent but exists necessarily."

I tried to puzzle this out. They claimed that what existed was not stuff made of atoms and space but was a field of being beyond understanding. I shook my head in confusion. Trying to picture something like a magnetic field beyond the universe made me wonder: How did they know about it if it lay beyond their grasp?

Again, I drove to Westwood. I met in a small room with a young man who wore a flowing white cotton blouse and long hair nearly to his shoulders, which made him look like familiar pictures of Jesus.

"Tell me what you hope chanting might do for you," the flowy man asked me with a gentle smile.

I hadn't expected to be quizzed.

"Peace of mind, I guess." I thought for a moment. "Less worry, more confidence." I hoped that was good enough.

"Those are excellent expectations!" he told me. Then he gave me the mantra "EIN-EH-MAH," chosen especially for my mind. He said I must keep it a secret. Of course, that made me wonder how special it was. To this day I don't know if anyone else was assigned my sound.

But I gave him my mother's check for $35 and listened to the instructions. I was supposed to sit quietly and recite EIN-EH-MAH in my mind, silently, plowing right through any thoughts that came up. The rest was magic, up to the transcendental field.

A secret key to happiness had been transmitted to me. In some arcane way, I might open a locked passageway to cosmic truths, in just two twenty-minute sessions a day. "The *Magical Mystery Tour* might be coming to take me away!" I quipped.

I was excited to start.

A few days later, when my mother shouted for me to come downstairs, at first I didn't move. Sitting in a cross-legged position on the floor, I was noiselessly reciting my mantra. Then I heard, "Rikki! Come down here and see this!" That sounded urgent but not angry.

I ran down the stairs to the living room. Walter Cronkite was saying that a bullet had exploded in someone's face, that he had been assassinated in broad daylight. I soon learned he was talking about Martin Luther King Jr.

The TV news reported that people in Harlem were out en masse, enraged, confused, and grief-stricken. Over the next few days, Los Angeles detonated; people streamed into the streets, and some got violent. A lot of people I knew went out to protest. But to me, real progress in social justice seemed impossible while there were people who were holding so much hatred. I thought we had to transform both cruelty and bitterness before we could live in peace.

I turned with more intensity to Transcendental Meditation. It gave me hope for this conflicted, unjust, angry world. I wanted there to be something pure, something more powerful than brutality and hate.

But could I keep it up on my own? None of my friends were mantra-repeaters. Everyone was an antiwar activist by then, or a civil rights activist, or a hippie dropout. No one was praying for peace. They were demonstrating for it, arguing for it, and resisting the war for it. "Johnson just increased the draft," my friends bemoaned. "How is meditation going to help?"

I had to admit, so far nothing much happened when I repeated the mantra, besides me getting bored. My mind would calm down a little but did not seem to expand. No transcendent happiness, lots of mental activity. I tried to bring more light and laughter, but I was at a loss.

Unfortunately, there wasn't much helpful literature in those days.

I found a copy of Aldous Huxley's book about mescaline, but it was over my head. Swami Yogananda's *Autobiography of a Yogi* had been around for decades, but it would not cross my path for many years. So I listened to Jefferson Airplane, repeated EIN-EH-MAH once or twice a day, and waited to graduate high school, wondering if I should try acid again.

CHAPTER 12
THE ANTI-MASSACRE MOVEMENT

But before I could graduate, somebody plowed a bullet into Bobby Kennedy's head.

For weeks, my friends and I had been out at peace rallies, inspired by the hope that Bobby, a US senator running for president on a peace and justice campaign, would win the California primary. On June 6, my mom and I were watching Kennedy's acceptance speech on TV, broadcast live from the Ambassador Hotel right over the hill in Los Angeles. He went off-screen while his handlers bustled him through a hand-shaking crowd in the kitchen. Suddenly the news camera was pointing down at his bleeding head. Someone in the crowd had shot three times, and Bobby had simply dropped.

Along with all my hopes for peace and justice.

A balloon deflated in my chest. All around me, people under thirty had believed the time for a real social revolution had finally arrived. Bobby was our symbol, our leader. The mood on the street had been buoyant. It had seemed my generation was winning the culture war. But no, the bad guys won every time.

Any vision I had for wide-scale awakening disintegrated. Human beings were just too violent to reform themselves through meditation. Alone in the green bedroom Linda and I had painted, I lay face down on my bed and wept with helplessness and rage. Without Bobby, we would be stuck with Nixon and the endless machine of the Vietnam

War. In the last month alone more than two thousand Americans had died there, and who knows how many Vietnamese soldiers and citizens had been killed or injured.

I gave up the useless mantra. Who could wait for everyone to learn to meditate? Things were falling apart right now.

A week after Bobby died, I skipped my graduation ceremony. I knew my always distracted, often intoxicated parents wouldn't even ask about it. *Who cares,* I pretended. *Who wants to wear one of those stupid gowns, anyway.*

Later, I told Mom that I had graduated with honors, which she expected anyway. And which was true if you didn't count my being on probation from the detentions that had piled up.

God willing, in two months, I would leave home to join Linda at the University of California at Santa Barbara, to which she had transferred the previous year.

Later that summer, on a hot August afternoon, Mom sent Linda and me shopping with her credit card for school clothes at a Bullock's department store. We tried on jeans and long-sleeved fall tops and bought one outfit each. When we were walking out through the women's section, I spied a beautiful short-sleeved cashmere sweater that was just my mom's style. I loved giving things to her. Though we argued, I wanted to lift her out of the doldrums that came over her when Dad disappeared for days or raged through the house—to rescue her from the cycle of bullying, the role of scrunched-up victim, and the despair of hiding the secret abuses she endured. Besides, I would miss her September birthday this year since I'd be away at school.

The only money I had was a small allowance from my parents—not nearly enough to buy that sweater. But I knew it would make Mom happy and would look beautiful. So, even though I'd never done anything like this before, I didn't hesitate. After looking around for observant store clerks, I walked right over to that sweater, yanked it off the hanger and stuffed it in the bag of items we'd already purchased.

Linda saw me but didn't react.

"Let's get out of here," I said to her under my breath, and we headed to the exit.

We quick-stepped to our car, the little gray Hillman Minx Dad had given us on my sixteenth birthday last year. We'd named it Mammon, Linda's idea after studying Milton, in mockery of society's money worship.

After unloading the bag containing both legal and contraband clothes, I thoughtlessly tossed a joint in the glove compartment. We locked Mammon and returned to the shops to finish our shopping.

On our way back to the store, two officers blocked our path. I turned to run but a third was standing behind me. She grabbed my arm and pushed me in front of her. I struggled, and she shoved me to my knees.

"Don't make me add resisting arrest to the shoplifting," she said, pressing me toward the cement.

Shit. They were following us the whole time!

"You are under arrest," I heard one of the other cops say to Linda. I twisted my head to see her from my crunched position, face inches from the ground. I could see her handcuffed wrists behind her back.

Oh my God, what have I done?

"Possession of a Schedule I illegal drug. Nice," he said, and pushed her toward a patrol car.

They broke into my car and found the joint! Now they were pinning it on Linda. She was over eighteen; not a juvenile like I was. I was horrified! My sister was heading for jail, and it was all my fault. And I had this jerk cop holding me down. My head spun; my mind filled with noisy static.

The policewoman prodded me toward her vehicle and opened the back door.

"In you go, sweetie," she ordered me. "You can wait here while we contact your parents."

The patrol car with Linda in it drove away.

"Get in the goddam car and don't say a word," my mother snarled at me when she arrived outside Bullock's.

After a brief exchange, the police released me into her custody with a summons to appear in court. During the twenty-minute ride home, the air in the car was frozen with rage. There was nothing I could say, and my mind was a mash of hatred and shame.

"I don't want you in my home," Mom spat at me when we got inside the house. "Get the hell away from me!" She pointed to the street. She was crying so hard you'd have thought I'd murdered someone.

"I'm leaving!" I shouted back. "I can't get out of here soon enough."

"You are so much trouble. Why can't you act like a normal person?" She went into her bedroom and slammed the door.

"I'm sorry," I said stupidly to the door, not sure if I was.

I stood in the hall feeling angry and forsaken, my limbs and head sagging. I just didn't care about the rules the way you were supposed to. All I wanted, at bottom, was for my little family to be happy together. Yet I'd thoughtlessly lifted that sweater, sabotaging my own goals. *Why do I make things worse?*

My parents didn't speak to me over the weekend. I was in a panic over Linda, stuck in jail. I didn't find out until she came home Monday morning that Dad had hired a top-notch lawyer who got them to drop the charges and release her. But still, we couldn't leave for Santa Barbara until I appeared in juvenile court later that week.

Mom hid in her bedroom until the day of the hearing. She was already in the front seat when I slid into the back of my parents' car, rigid with fear. We drove to the county courthouse in silence. *What if they send me to juvenile hall?* I knew only one guy in the whole town who'd been sent away. Kids in my social group did not get arrested for shoplifting.

This was turning into the worst thing that had ever happened to me. But despite feeling frightened and mortified, I reeked defiance and disrespect. Slumping in the back seat with arms crossed, I sent angry vibes to Mom and Dad. They were part of the unjust system that Bobby Kennedy was supposed to reform.

"Shoplifting is a very serious charge. So is resisting arrest," said the stern, robed man behind the bench. My parents and I sat facing him in three metal folding chairs behind a railing.

I started to protest. "But I—"

"You don't speak without my permission in this courtroom, do you understand me?" the white-haired judge snapped.

I nodded, fixing my wide eyes on the bench.

"If convicted, you will go to juvenile detention, do you understand that?"

Blood drained from my face and my jaw throbbed. I was genuinely terrified of being locked in a facility for who knows how long with actual delinquents. And the judge could see it.

"Yes, sir," I stammered, unable to meet his eyes.

He kept talking; the hammering in my head blurred his words. Then, suddenly he was saying something about the charges. I looked up and paid attention.

"I never want to see you in this court again. I expect you to go to college as planned without breaking any more laws, and to grow up into a decent citizen like your parents." He stood and left the chamber.

Holy smokes! He's letting me go!

A clerk handed my father some papers. I stared without breathing, fearing I was mistaken.

Dad signed the papers.

"Let's go," he said.

Like that, we were done.

As we had on the way to court, we drove toward home in stone cold quiet. I looked out the window at the flow of traffic. Slowly the shock of arrest and horror of detention subsided, and my mutinous attitude started to creep back. *I've had a brush with the law,* I thought, *just like Arlo Guthrie.* The folk singer had stood up to local cops using music and humor. I began to think of a verse from his epic antiwar song, "Alice's Restaurant," where he called our war protest the anti-massacre movement.

Instead of feeling remorse for the theft, I now began to regret that I had not stood up to the judge. I wished I'd told him that the joint the cops found was mine. I wished I'd had the courage to start singing the famous chorus from Arlo Guthrie's ballad. I wished I had told the judge I was part of the Alice's Restaurant anti-massacre movement, instead of cowering behind my parents.

When we got home, Dad told me to leave for school immediately.

"Your mother has endured enough. Get yourself packed for college and go. We've told Linda we want you both out by tomorrow."

Fuck you rushed through my mind, but I kept it to myself.

Mom went to her bedroom, Dad to his office. Linda was out. Bethy had gone to her friend Dana's.

I slumped off by myself to smoke a joint, feeling nothing. We went our own ways as always, with our separate pain and confusion. None of us knew how to help the others.

The next day I packed up the little Minx with my college life supplies. Clothes, my guitar, a sculpture of a sailing ship Lou—my childhood boyfriend from Northbrook—had given me years ago. I'd get cool school gear when I arrived on the UCSB campus.

"Drive safely," my mother said stiffly at the front door.

"Study hard," said Dad.

"See you at Thanksgiving," Bethy said, hugging us with tears running down her face.

With Linda in the passenger seat, I drove away.

"Free at last," I joked as I took a last look in the rear-view mirror. We rocked with the FM radio, greatest hits of 1968. But beneath my cockiness burned a deep sense of loss. These were the people I loved most in the world, and we could not manage to take care of each other. Everything we did created another wound. I hated them for not stopping me even as I fled.

Where do I belong now? I looked at Linda—my older sister, the one who had taught me to read from *The Magical Land of Noom* when I was four. The one who had shared a stuffed animal family with me under the massive homework desk in our Northbrook bedroom. The one whom I had put in jail for the weekend.

"I'm so sorry," I began.

"Let's not talk about it. It was an experience I'm glad I had."

Her short, clipped words meant *Shut up about it forever* in sister-language. And in all the years that followed, she never did share with me even a glimmer of what she'd been through.

I could still rely on Linda like nobody else in the world, and I'd be fine in Santa Barbara with her close by. But decades later, I would wonder if this was one of the moments that weakened both her trust of me and our bond. I was, perhaps, not an easy person to love.

CHAPTER 13
HIGHER EDUCATION

"Hit?" offered the long-haired young man wearing a multicolored Indian blouse. We sat on Linda's front landing in the late afternoon sun, long yellow streaks piercing the sea fog. Josh gripped the joint between thumb and forefinger as he held it out to me.

"No, thanks," I said. "I mostly gave it up. I'd take a hit of acid, though, if you know anyone." I lit a cigarette.

Josh took a toke, then exhaled. Soft breezes from the ocean brushed our skin and blew our smoke away.

Linda shared this upstairs apartment on Del Playa, across from the beach, with two other students. They were letting me sleep on the couch for a few weeks until my dorm opened in September. So far, the student town of Isla Vista seemed like paradise.

Young people with wild hair, wearing beads and army surplus shirts, hung out everywhere and adult supervision was nowhere. All along the main drag, head shops mixed in with bookstores, cafes, and clothing outlets. Acid and pot were ubiquitous among the thousands of students who cycled or walked down the middle of the street ignoring car traffic.

Josh did know someone, as it turned out. He went out for a while and came back with a single tab. It cost $5.

I held the little pill in my palm and looked at it.

Do I want to trip alone or with people?

Alone. I swallowed the tablet.

"I'm going down to the beach for this," I called out to Linda. "See you later!"

I don't know what possessed me to trust the acid or the night. Both were risky. The pill could have been anything at all, and a beach at night is always unsafe for a lone woman. Yet I trusted both and plodded along the path down the cliffside.

When my feet reached the sand, I took off my shoes and made my way to the water. Tar stains from a recent offshore oil spill blotched the beach and left the scent of something burning in the air. I walked in the surf for a while, listening to the rhythm of the waves.

I found a good spot to plop myself down. After clearing a space of tar globs, I sat near a pile of dry seaweed with my back against the bluff. The night was very dark, and there was no moon. Slowly the drug permeated my brain and brought on a feeling of quiet happiness. I felt at home in the dark.

My body began smiling. The tide was going out; I could hear gentle waves unfurl, one after another in wide arcs, hissing when they drew back across the beach. Their white edges glided eerily over the dark expanse. As I lay watching the stars gleam in the black night over the sea, something in me softened and spread out, like the waves running over the sand. The inner sensation of this made me laugh.

The solidity of my body kept melting as my eyes looked into the ebony night, with the Milky Way standing out like a real splash in the black, light-studded heavens. I belonged here, on this beach, against this cliff, among these stars, in this darkness.

I lay alert in the quiet night, smelling the salty fish and oily tar, while time eased by and the experience deepened. I no longer felt like me, a person, in a little body pressed against a sandy cliff. There was streaming starlight embracing our little patch of planet, and I was part of it. Something about me—call it my soul—spread out among those stars. Each point of light seemed a lovely part of my being.

I'd lost myself but felt entirely safe. Waves rolled closer, inching toward me as the tide came in. When the whispering water reached my toes, I got up and separated myself from the unity of water, stars, and me. The acid was wearing off. When I moved my hands, I could still see those telltale visual trails, the iconic hallucination of LSD, but my mind slowly returned to my body.

I put my shoes on, walked back to Linda's apartment, and found her hanging out with friends.

The acid trip stayed with me as a warm sense of belonging. I had scribbled a note sometime during the night in my journal. When I opened it, I found "God Is" scrawled across a page. Apparently, I thought this sentiment adequately expressed the unity I'd felt on the beach. For days afterward, I wrote about the peace of feeling one with the stars, about sensing God everywhere, about the happiness of coming *home*.

As a freshman, I didn't have a lot of freedom in choosing my classes, but I had room for one elective in winter quarter. The Religious Studies Department had a course in the Buddha's teachings "from the Indian tradition." Maybe I could learn something from the ancient yogis about the source of this simple feeling of participation and love.

"Nice to meet you. Now c'mon, you're with me." My new roommate, Tina, pulled on my arm.

I looked at the dormitory welcome pamphlets in my hand.

"But I haven't even unpacked," I muttered, eyeing my suitcases. "Or even met you."

"Okay, one more time, hi. I'm Tina from Newport Beach, and I'm a lit major. Now let's go, they're waiting for us," she said.

I grabbed a sweatshirt and followed her out of the dorm to meet a friend who had a car. She drove us to a political rally in downtown Santa Barbara, outside the courthouse. A Black man had been arrested for something—it might have been possession of pot. About a hundred people, Black and white, gathered in the street outside the courthouse where he was being held.

We joined a small crowd of young folks who were linked arm and arm beneath the windows of the building. Fear constricted my belly and amped my heartbeat. There was a lot of noise. Someone was shouting an incomprehensible chant into a bullhorn. One group of five near us was shouting, "Power to the people!" Between us and the building loomed a wall of police.

About twenty city cops stood behind a makeshift barrier across the entrance to the courthouse. Blue and black uniforms and unbreakable white helmets blocked our access. For me it was a line of malevolence; the cops stood for government authority and the military machine.

It was my first face-to-face resistance action with the police. Sweat bloomed on my face, and my breathing sped up. I watched everything going on with wild eyes, terrified we would confront menacing billy clubs and get cracked in the head.

Just when it seemed we might storm the building, a protestor with a megaphone began bellowing for attention. He told us to stand in doorways. The organizers wanted us to inhibit access to local businesses and to be a public nuisance.

Within seconds a guy with a long beard positioned me in a doorway of a local building, yelling at me to "Block this door no matter what!"

I stood erect and determined in the building's doorway for a few minutes before an angry, helmeted city cop strode up with his baton raised.

"Get the hell out of there!" he shouted.

I wasn't interested in finding out what would happen if I refused; I scurried quickly away and ran down the street into the throng. I found my friends and we scuttled to a parking lot where we watched a few people in the front of the crowd jostle with the police.

A cadre of Black students stood with military bearing around an information table in a corner of the parking lot. I asked what they were promoting.

"A rally tomorrow with Brother Bobby Seale," replied a young man wearing a black beret. "At the football stadium."

"Brother Seale will talk on behalf of the Black Panthers," another said, his voice strong and his afro wild. He raised his fist in front of him in a brief salute. I thought he was cool.

"We'll be there," Tina said.

There were hundreds of students in the bleachers at the football stadium the next day. When Bobby Seale took the microphone, we all got quiet. In a sincere and urgent voice, he explained the need for Black people to understand their political situation and to demand solutions to their social needs, like jobs, decent housing, and an end to police brutality. He demanded that people stand up to the rigged system.

He didn't sound like a menace to me. He sounded righteous.

"I can't believe what Black people have to cope with," Tina said. "The cops even harass the Panthers for giving out food."

A tall skinny guy with shaggy hair under a blue bandana grabbed my arm. "Come join the Students for a Democratic Society," he said, and corralled us to their information table. In 1967, SDS was a mostly white resistance movement that supported the Black Panthers. Tina told me that SDS, which would devolve into the Weather Underground terrorist group over the next few years, was already under government surveillance. We both signed up on the spot, not caring about "the man."

Bobby's speech smashed through my illusions that Black people enjoyed the same civil liberties and protections as I did. I began to understand why they had to fight for things I took for granted.

Later that day, I heard some upsetting news. I caught up with Linda at the student union to tell her about it.

"The fuzz are arresting Panthers in Oakland for running a health clinic!" I told her.

She was as appalled as I was. "What happened to democracy in this country?" she demanded.

We were still learning.

"I'm afraid it was ever thus, Linda," I said. "I'm losing hope for political struggles."

"Still," she said, "people have to fight back against oppression."

"It's the human heart that has to change," I insisted. "Meditation and drugs are the only ways I know to precipitate experiences that have a real impact."

"You're not going to get too far with the human heart," she said bitterly, shaking her head.

But it may be our only hope, I thought. I wasn't ready to give up on us.

"Sitting tall and relaxed, let the breath flowing in and out be the focus of your attention," my professor said in a soft, slow voice. We were practicing a method of meditation from northern India.

The instructions were simple: Observe the constant activity of the mind and consider what it is that remains unchanged throughout it all. One consistent thing was the steady flow of breath.

"Note the breath brushing the nostrils, the rising of the chest, the tickle of air on the way out," he went on.

Instead of inwardly reciting the EIN-EH-MAH mantra, I began to sit on my cot in the dorm and observe the passage of my breath.

"Why do you bother?" Tina asked.

"Buddhists teach that when the activity of the mind subsides, the 'true nature' of mind will be revealed," I answered her.

"What does that even mean?"

"I have no idea," I admitted. "My activity of mind never subsides."

Tina looked at me with something like pity.

"It helps me stay calm," I mumbled, feeling a bit defensive. "If everyone would mediate, we might end this stupid war in Vietnam."

"Well," she said with a shrug, "I'm headed out to see what's happening on campus. Want to come?"

At UCSB I enjoyed a year of protests, coursework, Buddhist studies, and parties. My life of freedom and exploration had begun. But now that I had escaped home, I yearned to go further north, to San Francisco.

"It's all happening in San Francisco," I urged Linda. "We should go."

The center of hippie and spiritual culture was the magical Fog City, perched between the Pacific Ocean and the enormous San Francisco Bay. During the Summer of Love two years earlier, an invasion of hippies had taken over the neighborhood at Haight and Ashbury, near Golden Gate Park. People could still get Owsley acid on the street—the pure kind on blotters like my friend Rick had years ago. Beat poets, including Allen Ginsberg with his sacred chanting, still hung out at local bookstores, and the Zen people had a meditation hall right in the city.

Meanwhile, across the bay to the east of San Francisco, the UC campus at Berkeley was roiling with antiwar and civil rights activity. Berkeley students led demonstrations in Sproul Plaza all the time. In Santa Barbara, we looked to Cal Berkeley as the center of our movement. We called our UCSB campus "Little Berkeley."

"Maybe," Linda said. "I'll be done with school in May."

It was only February. But I applied for a transfer and was accepted into Cal Berkeley for the winter quarter of 1970, just a year away.

With any luck, I'd be living in San Francisco in June.

CHAPTER 14
FOG CITY

"I don't want you to worry, but I have to go home for a few days," Linda said in her no-nonsense, big sister voice. I felt the familiar rock that lodged in my stomach whenever the phone rang unexpectedly. *Mom or Dad?* It was early, not yet eight o'clock.

"Why, what's wrong?"

"Everything is okay, but Daddy broke his leg or something. Mom needs help. I'll be back Tuesday."

At least he didn't slit his wrists or overdose.

I didn't give it any more thought until Linda returned to school and told me what happened.

"Daddy went on a binge," she started. "No surprise. I think Mom kicked him out. Anyway, he ended up staying at the Sportsman's Lodge."

Things like this had happened before, so I wasn't disturbed. But while at the Lodge, he had fallen down a flight of stairs in a stupor. He had shattered some foot and ankle bones and torn some ligaments. Confined to a wheelchair, he had to go home.

"I helped Mom set him up in the downstairs den," Linda explained. "She'll have to take him to rehab and doctors by herself."

After Linda told me all this, I tried to put it out of my mind. Thinking about my father always opened a dark chasm in my chest. If I let myself feel what I imagined was his pain, I would fall endlessly into that empty pit. I was grateful to forget stories like this one. His needs and feelings took up all the space, even when he was sober. Being around his depression was like having an asthma attack. There was never room for me to breathe. I couldn't get far enough away. Santa Barbara was too close for comfort.

"Let's get the hell away from Los Angeles, Linda."

"Okay. Yes. Let's do it."

We made a plan to move to the home of our poets and our rock 'n' roll heroes like the Airplane, the Dead, and Big Brother. We saved some money, and after classes ended on June 1, were ready to take off. With our friend Jalice, we hopped on a Greyhound bus at five in the morning and rode the three hundred miles north to California's City by the Bay.

We stepped off the bus and out onto San Francisco's Mission Street in high spirits. It had been almost two years since the "flower children" staged the notorious Summer of Love in the Haight-Ashbury District. According to gossip I heard at UCSB, hippies still overflowed those streets near Golden Gate Park, freely sharing music, food, health care, housing, and drugs. The lyrics to Scott McKenzie's "San Francisco" hummed in my head, calling on me to wear flowers in my hair when I joined the gentle people here.

My system was clean; I hadn't used anything since the LSD trip on the beach eight months before. I wasn't looking for drugs so much as fellowship and camaraderie. Along with my small suitcase I carried a Yamaha acoustic, on which I could fake-strum my way through the basic chords of most Dylan songs up to *Highway 61 Revisited*. Dressed in corduroy hip-huggers and a work shirt with crocheted decorations under a jean jacket, I was a living emblem of the Love Generation. "Peace and love, baby!" was my greeting to strangers.

Now that we were here, we had to find a place to stay—hopefully, an apartment we could rent. We didn't have a specific plan, but as long as I was with Linda, I felt safe and ready for anything. Free of the shackles of childhood, we were together on a new escapade, searching for our tribe in the cultural Mecca of our times.

The three of us found seats in a cafe. We grabbed a couple of local papers and spread them out next to a city map, some coffee, and sandwiches. After studying the map, we began to search the papers for flats near the corner of Haight and Ashbury.

"This one on Masonic sounds good," Jalice said. "Let me see the map." She ran her finger along the panhandle of San Francisco's Golden Gate Park. Anything off Fell or Oak was in the right neighborhood.

I peered over her shoulder. "That's a good location," I said. I tapped the map with my pen. "How much is it?"

Jalice went to the pay phone with a handful of dimes and called the landlord.

She came back shaking her head. "We're too late," she said. "The apartment is already rented."

"Let's try this one on Hayes," Linda said, circling the ad.

She went to the pay phone and called; no luck on that one either.

I wasn't worried yet. Young people on the West Coast trusted each other. We were a movement of rebels and hippies who stuck together. I was sure something would turn up.

After a few more failed tries, though, I got frustrated.

"Let's just go down there and look around," I said to Linda, opening my arms to possibility. *Why not?* I shrugged.

"Shouldn't we know where we're going first?" Jalice asked, appealing to our common sense. She tucked her chin-length hair behind her ears and looked at both of us in turn.

Linda put down the *Renter's Realty* she held and gestured at the papers scattered across the table. "Calling about these ads isn't working very well," she said with a frown.

"Maybe we'll see signs for rentals. Let's just try," I pleaded.

Linda nodded. I grabbed my suitcase and guitar, and we headed for a bus stop.

Standing on Market Street, we were working out our bus route when a clean-shaven young man with short black hair approached us. He was wearing a pale blue button-down dress shirt tucked into khakis with a well-pressed pleat. He looked nothing like the love children I was hunting for—but he did have a sweet smile.

"Hello, I'm Ken, and I want to ask you, are you interested in happiness?" He stuck out his hand.

I shook it readily. "Peace, friend."

"Hi, Ken," Linda said. "Of course, I'm interested in happiness!" She returned his smile with her own bright laugh. "But right now, happiness is a place to stay." She waved a hand at our suitcases.

"You don't have a place to stay?" Ken asked. He glanced at each of us. "Where are you from?" Another disarming smile blossomed on his face.

"Santa Barbara," Linda and I answered.

Jalice hadn't said anything. She was staring closely at Ken.

"Come to a meeting with me," Ken offered, "and you can stay at my mom's tonight. Tomorrow you can figure out what to do."

"What kind of meeting?" Jalice asked, squinting.

I lit a cigarette and began to wonder if this was the friendly break we'd been hoping for.

"Buddhist," Ken said. "A Nichiren Buddhist meeting. We use our practice to overcome obstacles in our lives. The power we get from chanting helps us plow through challenges. Come to a meeting with me and find out for yourself."

His laugh was warm and reassuring. I was interested but skeptical. *Is he for real?*

While we waited at the bus stop, Ken told us that the sect was founded centuries ago by a Japanese monk named Nichiren. The modern group was on a global mission to enroll new members and revolutionize humanity in pursuit of peace. That resonated with me. I had kind of given up on meditation as I slogged through classes the past semester. Maybe this was a wake-up call from my spirit self.

Going with him seemed both practical and interesting. We were aware of the risks of trusting strangers, but we were in sacred San Francisco, and there were three of us. We could always leave and find a hotel.

Linda ran her fingers through her brown, gently curling hair, pulling it up and away from her face. She studied Ken, then said, "Why not? You seem like a good guy." And flashed her own charming smile.

I nodded vigorously.

"All right, then," Jalice sighed.

"Most of us are in a mental condition like hell half the time," a man named Ko explained, "but we also have a state of peace and wisdom within us. By chanting, we come into harmony with this higher state," he went on. "Then good things begin to appear."

Ken had driven us a couple of miles to a flat-roofed Victorian with white-washed front steps on a crowded street in what we would come to know as the Mission District. There, we'd found a group of eight or ten people kneeling on their heels, Japanese-style, in a small, carpeted front room. We'd listened while they repeated their mantra, "Nam-Myoho-Renge-Kyo."

"The writing on the scroll represents ordinary states from misery to joy. But at the center is a symbol for 'Buddha nature,'" Ko continued.

They'd been reciting their chant in unison while facing a little scroll covered with Japanese lettering, which hung in a small wooden cabinet set on a table.

Ko's words reminded me of the Beatles' Maharishi and his Transcendental Meditation. "Buddha" nature seemed akin to the Yogi's "higher consciousness." I sat still and paid attention.

The man pointed to himself. "When I started chanting, I had

nothing, couldn't get into school, was completely lost. Now I am a high school history teacher." His face beamed.

My legs were starting to ache from sitting on the floor, which seemed like a hell state. I slid off my knees and into a cross-legged posture: Ahh, happy state. I smiled, echoing Ko's enthusiasm.

Other people shared their stories about the influence of chanting.

"I was in a terrible fight with my mother," said a young woman with long brown hair and a yellow flower painted on her cheek. "So, I chanted about it. And my mother literally came into my room to apologize! That's never happened before. We really connected." The woman was genuinely moved.

A thirtysomething Black man with a scraggly afro raised his hand. "Chanting helped me find my job at Caterpillar," he asserted—eyes bright, lips curved into what I would soon come to think of as the chanter's smile. "I was in line at the supermarket talking with a brother, and he knew about it. He recommended me. It was like a stroke of luck, but exactly what I chanted for."

That was intriguing.

Could you create good luck?

After the meeting, Ken drove us to his mother's house where we met Nancy, who like her son, had recently joined the Buddhist movement.

Nancy greeted us in a confident, strong voice and gave each of us a friendly hug.

"Hi, it's wonderful to meet you." She was in her early forties, and her soft brown hair framed a small, animated face. She welcomed us to her flat in the Richmond District.

"We can't thank you enough," Jalice said.

"You're too kind to strangers," Linda added.

Displaying more friendliness and generosity than I had hoped to find, Nancy said we could crash in her spare room and on her couch. Once we settled into Nancy's cozy home, she encouraged us to use the magic invocation to find jobs and an apartment. "We chant to achieve our goals and overcome obstacles. Just follow along with me, keeping your mind focused on what you want. You'll see. Things will start to happen."

Not only did Nancy provide a place of rest, she let us use her phone, newspaper, and kitchen. Out of respect and appreciation, we joined her in the daily chanting ritual. Jalice started to enjoy it, and Linda looked as if she were being polite. But I was curious. I had traveled hundreds of miles to discover new things, and already I had encountered a fascinating, modern Buddhist sect. Fog City was living up to my daydreams.

"I found a job," I told Linda a few days later.

I'd landed an entry position as a communications monitor for the Santa Fe-Pomeroy Construction firm, working the switchboard, telex, and mail distribution. Linda and Jalice had also found good-paying work in the Financial District.

"Oh, terrific," she said. "Now we can nail that flat at Twenty-fourth and Fair Oaks in the Mission."

Maybe it was the chanting, but within a week, we three had moved into a large fifth-floor one-bedroom Linda had found in the paper. We worked out our new commute routes, using the public transit system to get around.

Shortly after we moved into our San Francisco apartment, I turned eighteen. I figured my life was nearly perfect. I lived and worked in San Francisco, the hippest place on the planet. I rode the city's streetcars, walked its infamous hills, and bought food in its corner groceries.

My own life, away from family chaos, was falling into place.

"Peace and love, Jajo!" I called out to the clerk at the laundromat a few blocks from my apartment. "Can I get a roll of dimes from you?"

Jajo was a poet. His black hair hung straight a few inches below his shoulders, and he curled the back into a topknot. We'd met at that infamous home of beat poets—the City Lights bookstore in North Beach. While I waited for my clothes to dry, he read to me in his deep resonant voice from *A Coney Island of the Mind*.

"That one for sure is about sex," I said after listening to a Ferlinghetti poem about spilled seed.

"They're all about sex!" he laughed. "Or social justice. Hey, have you seen the Black Panthers' exhibit yet?"

"Where?"

"The de Young. You need to go. It's images from the movement. They're amazing."

"Okay, maybe we can go this weekend. My sister and her boyfriend love Golden Gate Park. And the museum."

When Linda had left Santa Barbara, her boyfriend, Rick, followed her up to San Francisco. Rick was staying with us in the Mission apartment while he wrote his doctoral dissertation on a psychological theory of perception. None of us understood a word of his paper, but because I adored him, I always listened attentively. I loved that my sister had found someone so cool. He drove a tan Mustang convertible, played a mean guitar, and because he was older than me, he knew much more about everything. An added bonus: He looked like Ricky Nelson and sang like Dylan.

The dryer buzzer sounded. I gathered my clothes into a bag and headed for the door.

On my way out, I flashed Jajo a peace sign.

Thus implanted in America's '60s counter-culture, I gave little thought to my parents and their troubles. But Linda and I did keep in touch with our younger sister, Bethy, through long-distance phone calls. Things weren't going well at home.

Twelve-year-old Bethy was stuck in the house with my parents.

"Mom is ignoring Dad. If he doesn't come out to eat, she just lets it sit there. I have to take it in to him after she goes to watch TV," she told us.

"How's his leg injury?" asked Linda.

Since the accident, the soft tissue in his leg was healing slowly and demanded daily deep-tissue work. With Mom checked out, Beth got roped into the adult role, becoming our father's caretaker and unwitting enabler. She massaged his torn ligaments, got him food, and cleaned up his booze bottles. She tried to coax him away from destructive thoughts.

"It doesn't seem to get better. It still hurts him like crazy," Bethy said.

There wasn't much I could do for Beth at such a distance. In truth, I was relieved to be four hundred miles away. As soon as we hung up, I put the home scene out of my mind.

Fifty years later, Beth would tell me that the reason Mom made Dad stay at the Lodge in the first place was that he kicked our dog, Alphie, to death—a story that would shock me, even though I knew well my father's drunken cruelty. Could Beth be wrong? Picturing it made me nauseous. I had always believed Alphie had been hit by a car.

Was it really that bad? I would ask myself for the zillionth time, but I knew Daddy's demons overwhelmed us all. It took Mom a few more years, but she would finally divorce him and replace him with a sober, though still narcissistic, companion. Dad never recovered from his sense of being helplessly abandoned.

"I suspect the secret to consciousness has something to do with DNA," I confided to Rick one Saturday. We lay on towels spread out at the Pescadero nude beach south of the city.

Linda and Rick were my absolute favorite people in the world. Many evenings, the three of us and Jalice would polish off a gallon of Gallo Brothers' red—often drinking out of the basket-wrapped bottle—while playing guitars and singing bad harmonies on protest songs. We read poetry aloud, and on weekends we joined antiwar marches in San Francisco. On warm Sundays like this one, we drove to beaches like Pescadero to sunbathe and walk along the breathtaking Pacific Coast.

It was a gorgeous, sunny day. Rick, Linda, and I had dropped some acid. A deep, wide stretch of golden sand, sparsely populated, welcomed us so we had plenty of privacy. I was too shy to go naked but lounged in my bathing suit, watching the waves billow and crash. I'd been taking a genetics class at City College, and as I came onto the drug, all I could think about was cellular biology, DNA, and cosmic archetypes.

Rick, who lay face down on a towel, unabashedly naked, turned to look at me.

"You've been reading Jung?" he asked. "Don't let his erudition fool you. It's nonsense; there is no universal mind and no archetypes."

"No, it's this class I'm taking at City. This amazing DNA molecule," I said.

At the local college, I was learning about the DNA double helix, which had just been discovered in the 1950s. The fascinating genetic mechanism infiltrated my hallucinogenic trip, filling my head with the notion that consciousness and DNA were intimately related.

"Well, don't let your imagination get carried away." He closed his eyes. "Figure out how to design experiments to test your ideas."

After that acid trip, I wanted to know everything I could about this twisted molecular ladder that hid in our cells, and how it dictated the emergent details of the body and mind. There seemed to be a great secret hiding there. And I knew just the place to go to learn all about it—right across the bay.

In December, our little band of merry pranksters parted ways. Linda and Rick returned to Santa Barbara while Jalice took an apartment of her own. I, meanwhile, was set to begin my formal study of deoxyribonucleic acid at UC Berkeley's world-class molecular biology department, in which I had enrolled for the winter quarter of 1970.

"Where are you going to live?" Linda asked as we said our goodbyes.

"I found a place on Dwight, just a few blocks from campus."

The past seven months had been the most idyllic and magical I'd ever known, filled with spirituality, music, and camaraderie. Yet as I hugged my sister goodbye, my eyes looked east to the UC Berkeley Campanile rising against the hillsides of the university campus. There was so much at Cal to learn.

My gaze returned to my sister's face, and a question occurred to me: "Are you guys going to get married?"

Linda laughed. "*So* bourgeois. But yes, probably."

"Wow, groovy. I'd love to have Rick as a brother-in-law. And you two will make beautiful kids."

"We'll soon find out," Linda smiled, and I grinned back.

Had chanting helped me establish this fabulous life? The more I used the mantra to uplift myself, the more I seemed to succeed. I was about to study genetics at perhaps the highest-ranked scientific institution in the country, which was also a center of student protest and anti-war activity. And through the work-study program, I'd landed a job in a biology lab, prepping Petri dishes. My life was taking off, well-equipped with some saved money, a Buddhist practice, and ambitious curiosity.

My parents were hundreds of miles away, and I imagined I was free.

CHAPTER 15
MODERN PSYCHOLOGY

"Are you sure you're not a baby dyke?" Peg arched an eyebrow at me. She was the cook at the Brick Hut Cafe, a great corner bacon-and-eggs grill across the street from the Ashby Flea Market that also happened to be a lesbian collective.

I certainly looked like one: My hair was cropped short to keep it out of my face, and my wardrobe was jeans with work shirts. But I wasn't gay; I simply enjoyed the ambiance at the Hut.

"You might not be ready yet, but give it time," she smirked.

"See, now that's what people worry about, Peg," I said with a mischievous grin.

"What's that?" She squinted at me from behind the three-person breakfast bar.

"Recruiting!" I told her, laughing.

Peg made the scrambled eggs with the onions perfectly caramelized and, at thirty-one years old, regaled me with stories about her life as "an SOL—slightly older lesbian." I'd sit at the counter doing the math for my lab work on a slide rule, talking to her. The cursed ten-inch Pickett used logarithms to do multiplication and division, so I had to write down what I was doing to get a valid result. It was messy, but I could do it if I went slowly. There were often food stains on the calculations page in my lab notebook.

"Well, thanks for breakfast," I said, stuffing my work into my book bag. "Have a great day, Peg."

"Take care of yourself, pretty baby." Peg waved.

I unlocked my bike and rode a couple of miles to Latimer Hall for my first lecture.

"Rikki, right?" A short stout young man with shaggy brown hair and a trimmed beard appeared at my table, where I sat in a padded folding chair.

As usual, I'd ridden over to Telegraph Avenue after that day's classes and ordered a coffee on the outdoor patio of a cafe across from Moe's Books, where, it was rumored, secret planning went on for all the antiwar actions in Berkeley.

The man smiled. "I'm Richard," he said, touching his chest. The April afternoon was warm and sunlit.

"Hi, Richard," I said. I slipped a bookmark between the pages of my text. On a small round table next to me, a white ceramic mug filled with coffee and cream served as my lunch. "Psych 101, right? How's your paper coming?"

"Yeah, Psych 101. It's going pretty good. Want to compare notes?" He unzipped his backpack and pulled up a chair.

"Sure." I dug around in my book bag for a notepad. Then I looked at him. "Have you noticed anything strange about Attwood?"

"Ha!" Richard guffawed. "That guy comes in drunk every day!"

Professor Attwood, who was probably in his late fifties, seemed angry that he had to teach undergraduate classes. Often arriving late, he would stumble to the lectern and slur his way through talks so boring even he fell asleep. He espoused behaviorism and tried to convince us to explain humans solely through measurable actions, without reference to inner thoughts, feelings, or motivations. He would drone on about how people were bundles of tissue that sought out pleasure and avoided pain. The human personality, with its passions and weaknesses, the one I struggled with, was nowhere to be found in Psych 101.

"I hate that class," I said, lighting a cigarette.

"Me, too," said Richard, "but you can understand his point. Have you read *The Naked Ape*?"

"Not yet," I admitted, flushing. I picked at a torn cuticle on my thumb. "What does it say?"

"My paper is about it." He waved a handful of typed pages at me. It looked as if he was already done. "Morris says that human features and behaviors evolved from apes. The point is, our behavior is not coming from some mysterious soul with free will. It's driven by our biology. Just like any other animal."

The waiter ambled over to our table and Richard ordered a coffee. I sipped mine, grimacing at its cold bitterness.

"What's your paper on?" he asked me.

My paper was unorthodox and difficult to articulate. I wanted to critique the scientific view of the human psyche. "Sciences like evolution, psychology, and cell biology explain why we behave the way we do. Right?"

Richard nodded. I took a puff of my Marlboro and blew the smoke over his head.

"They present a human being as a collection of cells"—I shaped the air with my hands—"that are organized into organs and tissues, wired together with the nervous system and a brain. Which supposedly produces our experience through electrical signals."

Richard nodded again. "Yep. And all those cells are packed with molecules that obey the rules of molecular biology. And those molecules are made of atoms that obey the laws of chemistry and physics."

That was exactly my point! Science reduced a human to a machine. I tapped my cigarette on the ashtray.

"So, behaviorism portrays a human personality as a little machine that can be trained through rewards to do anything," I said.

"You disagree?" Richard asked. "What's your critique?"

"That there's no place for human experience or an actual human person in the picture!" I exclaimed, warming to my topic. "Psychology doesn't even mention morals or consciousness. How can you say that it 'explains' a human? It's all about measurable behavior." *What about self-hatred? What about my father?*

Richard pointed his finger at me. "You think there is something special about humans," he said. "But there isn't." He pointed out that even our genes were nearly identical to genes in chimpanzees. "We aren't made in the image of God. And we don't need God anymore to explain our existence," he concluded.

"Okay, forget God for a minute. Still, what about our own minds? And our sense of right and wrong? Something is missing if you leave those out," I said.

"Attwood's not going to like it. You should pick another topic." Richard shook his head.

I loved science. I loved the explanations, the way details snapped into place, the way you could predict the behavior of things with calculations. In my family, Linda was the expert in literature; I wanted to claim the realm of science as mine. Maybe even go to medical school.

In physics classes, I calculated the relativity effects of imaginary speeding rocket ships, and in chemistry I measured molar concentrations and triggered reactions. In our molecular biology lab, I learned to spin down samples of mutated *Drosophila melanogaster*—fruit flies—and isolate the DNA, tightly packed into neat little chromosomes. Then, under a microscope, I examined layouts of chromosomes to look for structural changes that mapped to mutations in the fly's anatomy. Yet, I knew something was missing from materialistic analyses of humans.

I also knew that if I wanted to pass courses, I would have to play by the rules. Buddha, God, and plain old awareness just didn't fit in the interpretations available in the modern materialist worldview.

"I suppose you're right," I conceded. "Maybe I'll just write about the monkey experiment he lectured on."

We both laughed.

"A much wiser choice!" Richard said.

And thus, I slid down the slippery slope, pretending to be satisfied with materialistic descriptions of ourselves and our world. Knowing that my intuitions about inner spirit wouldn't be well received, I decided to go with the prevalent scientific understanding at Cal. I pushed my own understanding away, behind rational and abstract thinking.

But not quite out of my heart.

CHAPTER 16
PEACE AND WAR

The news sparked a wave of anger in our class.

"This is a war crime. Kissinger can't just drop bombs on people in another country!" cried Christine.

"I agree, Christine, on the face of it, invading Cambodia looks pretty illegal," our poly-sci professor said. It was the end of April 1970. The morning newspapers had announced that the US Air Force had attacked the Viet Cong in Cambodia, illegally invading a sovereign nation.

"I'm going down to Sproul," said several students at once.

The antiwar movement was, at this point, serious business. The draft sucked up over fifteen thousand men a month. It wasn't just immoral; it was lethal to thousands of them. There had been massive nationwide demonstrations against the Vietnam War in recent months, but President Nixon and his secretary of state kept escalating. The conflict had become impossible to ignore.

Now this invasion. How long had it really been going on? My colleagues argued that the only righteous thing to do was demonstrate. Several people in class, including me, left to join the protest action that would likely develop in Sproul Plaza.

On the way, walking near Sather Tower, we saw dozens of people running from the direction of the plaza.

"What's going on?" I called out to a woman who was speed-walking toward us.

"The cops are out in force!" she said, panting. "They teargassed Sproul."

We stopped in our tracks. I watched a dozen people pass me, while I pondered what to do. One man shouted, "They're shooting rubber bullets this time!"

I wanted to turn and run. I looked to my classmates—what would they do?

"I'm going back to class," said Everett.

"Not me, I'm going to see what's happening," said Christine.

I opted for safety. Taking the back route, I hightailed it to my apartment. And felt ashamed for hiding out. *Maybe I should have gone to the action. How was the war going to end if people like me are scared to get arrested? Next time,* I promised myself, *I'm heading into the thick of it.* This time, I stayed off the streets all day.

Until a few weeks later.

"Four students at Kent State University in Kent, Ohio, are dead and more are wounded," I heard a television announcer say in a shaky, urgent voice. The newscaster's words pierced the usual cacophony of the Student Union.

"What the hell happened?" I asked the woman next to me, who stared at the Union's downstairs TV.

"They shot at student protestors," she answered, not looking at me. Around us students milled and chatted as if it were an ordinary day on campus.

"Who did?" I demanded, my eyes focused on the screen, too.

"Cops in Ohio," she said, turning to me now.

"Did they kill people? Really?" I met her wide-eyed gaze.

She nodded.

I was stunned, flabbergasted. This could have happened to us, to me. Just like students at Berkeley, the Kent State kids were protesting expansion of the war. What had become of our First Amendment rights and the free country we thought we lived in? Another naïve childhood bubble burst. The reality of cops killing white students shocked me into understanding that dangerous authoritarian forces were always at work in our democracy. And that Black citizens encountered these forces continually.

I suddenly wondered how I ever imagined that widespread spiritual transformation would bring peace. We needed real democratic change. Now. Thousands of Berkeley students and residents launched a raucous protest action in Sproul Plaza. This time I went.

I had never seen so many outraged people. I couldn't hear a word coming from the speaker at the podium. A yelling, angry crowd that grew larger and more unruly dragged me with it into the roadway. People were shouting at cops, jostling each other as we clamored down Telegraph Avenue with no particular destination. My breaths came in gasps as the mass of warm bodies squeezed out the air. Men near me started throwing bottles and debris at shop windows, and I got scared.

Ahead at a corner, I could see cops in helmets and bulletproof vests pour onto Telegraph swinging Billy clubs. On my right, a man threw something heavy at a shop window and it shattered. I stopped moving but the bodies behind pushed me forward in stumbling lurches. Then, pops like gunshots exploded nearby. My eyes looked toward the sound but suddenly burned like hot fire and teared up. When I squeezed them shut, I smelled something sharp like vinegar.

Peeking out, I saw a canister spewing smoke into the road. I turned left, pushing through the crowd until I reached a side street. I headed back toward the plaza, steering around another canister that blew streams of tear gas down Bancroft Way. In the plaza, cops with long machine guns were herding people toward Sather Gate. I darted across the plaza and through the gate, toward Moffitt Library. There the air was clear and only a few students stood talking on the lawn.

My knees buckled into the grass and a coughing spasm engulfed me. I tried to gather my wits. My heart slammed into my ribs. I couldn't stop the shaking in my hands, and my breath came in shreds. Lying on my back, I stretched out my limbs and rested with my tearing eyes closed, trembling.

"Are you okay?" My roommate Carla met me at the head of the stairs when I finally got home. "I heard they are teargassing everyone."

"Yeah, I'm fine. I came back on Shattuck to steer clear. Do you think I should have gone?"

"No, we're not supposed to be in riots." Carla was a Buddhist, too. "We're supposed to keep our vision of peace and chant for that. No matter what," she said, almost mechanically.

"I guess so. To tell you the truth, I was scared."

"You should have been! I bet a lot of people got arrested," Carla said.

I didn't dare to be one of them, which made me feel ashamed and conflicted. I wanted to avoid the violence yet remain aligned with the resistance.

Seeking clarity, I chanted for hours while contemplating the best course of action for myself. Finally, I decided to support thousands of students in boycotting university lectures. Though I might flunk every class, courses that cost me real time and money, it was a small price to pay for opposing war.

One by one, over the following week, my professors announced they would discontinue classes. Grades would be based on coursework completed so far, they said. Finals and papers were canceled. It seemed as if the entire university were standing up against this war. *Maybe even God will get involved.* I couldn't help but hope.

But sadly, the war didn't end that spring or the next, nor for several more. It wasn't until 1973 that the United States worked out a peace agreement with the Viet Cong and combat troops started coming home, which took years. I couldn't say protesting helped end this almost twenty-year war. Nor did chanting seem to have much impact, if I were honest.

In 1973, with a year of physics and two years of math, biology, and chemistry as the foundation for my degree, I still had upper-division biology classes to complete. And I needed elective courses, including anthropology, German romantic lit, art history, Western philosophy, ancient mythology, and modern poetry, to round out my education.

I retreated from protesting to focus on my studies.

CHAPTER 17
LAST ROUND

I signaled the bartender for another Scotch, rocks, and he reached beneath the bar for the bottle. He scooped clear, round chunks of ice into a glass and poured a honey-colored shot. I watched it trickle through the cubes to the bottom. The glossy wooden bar curved away under glass shelves that held glistening bottles of amber, red, and clear liquor. Blinking reflections of streetlights in the mirror behind the bottles made me feel a bit woozy.

My Buddhist colleague, Tom, and I sat on stools at the end of bar where it rounded into a dark corner. Tom was a vice chair of the student movement in San Francisco, and I was flattered he would hang out with a struggling undergrad like me.

Despite my growing intellectual atheism and insistent doubts about the usefulness of spirituality in the changing world, I still chanted twice a day. The ritual boosted my sense of worth and confidence. Chanting gave me hope that I could overcome obstacles and create a successful life. Besides, the organization's leaders said you had to chant every day, or negative things would start to happen.

As a member of the Buddhist student group, I helped encourage new chanters. But the sect had a strong Japanese style, which was almost military in its strictness. If you didn't chant for sixty minutes, or bring in x number of new members, or study the teachings for so many hours, you were going to be a loser in life. And you had to say

"Hai!" to any leader's statements or requests. "Hai!" meant yes, but it also meant something like, "You are right!"

There were several Buddhist students at Cal. We wanted the organization to modernize and adapt to the university culture. We had been talking about changing our meeting formats and doing study groups. And that's how I found myself in a rare situation, out late, having a drink with a Nichiren Buddhist leader from San Francisco at a Berkeley bar.

After an evening spent discussing strategies for Buddhists at UC Berkeley, the two of us were taking a break. We'd skipped dinner, but at least we had a plan. Tom was throwing shots with beer backs down his wide throat, jutting the hard line of his black-stubbled chin toward the ceiling. Drinking like this was a luxury that I could not afford, but Tom was on a PhD student stipend. He was buying. Still, I couldn't keep up; I was just 108 pounds to his six-foot, 180. I would be under the bar while he was still drinking. I threw my hands up.

"I've done my best, but I've hit my max," I slurred. "This is it." I tipped my freshly filled glass at him. "We're almost on last call anyway." I took a sip. "Give me a lift to Mary's?"

I was house-sitting only a few blocks away on Ninth Street at my friend's. The bar where we sat was on University near Sixth. I could walk to Mary's in fifteen minutes if I could even stand upright, and if Berkeley were safe for walking single women.

"Sure," Tom said, finishing his beer. "Let's go."

I swallowed my drink and squashed my cigarette. Pulling my sweater over my denim shirt, I pushed my wallet into my rear jeans pocket. I never carried a purse. You didn't carry a purse walking around Berkeley at night. Maybe a backpack, with books, firmly strapped to your back. But a purse was just asking to be mugged.

I tottered toward the rear door to the parking lot when Tom reminded me that the exit was locked. We steered toward the front, spilling out onto University Avenue. We made it to his car, drove the few blocks, and arrived at Mary's. I stumbled up the half-flight of steps to the front door. Pulling the keys out of my front pocket, I jabbed the house key at the face of the lock. Tom took the keyring from my hand and slipped the thick, brass key into the slot. The lock turned. He opened the door and dropped the keys into my hand.

"Okay. Good night, thanks," I said.

"Aren't you going to ask me in?" he asked, smiling.

Is Tom flirting with me?

"At this hour?" I grimaced. "No."

Tom pushed past me through the tiny hallway into the room. He stared at me, then grabbed my shoulders and pulled my body against his. He grabbed my buttocks. I pushed back hard, with both hands, on his chest.

"No, man, we're not that kind of—"

He smashed his mouth against my face. I pushed away again. Confused, I wanted to be cool, a good friend, an open-minded modern woman. It was 1975. Why was I so uptight about sex? Couldn't I just enjoy a quickie after a long day?

"No, get off! I'm not up for this. Let's just call it a night." I twisted away from him, and with one hand on his chest I shoved him toward the door. "See you later." He finally turned and went out.

I shut the door and spun the deadbolt and walked across the hall to the small bathroom. I pulled down my jeans and sat. Suddenly there came a loud banging on the front door. I jumped up, fumbling with my pants.

"Who is it?" I called, guessing Tom had left his keys, but I wanted to hear for sure before I opened the door. All year, the infamous Berkeley rapist tagged "Stinky" had been attacking women alone in their homes late at night. It might have been Stinky.

"Me." Tom's voice, friendly. I cracked the door and peeked out.

"What happened, did you—"

Tom slammed his hand against the door, banging it open. It hit me in the head. He pressed through the entryway into the front room, picked me up, and put me down on the faded green fabric couch that Mary had collected from Goodwill.

"What are you doing?" I cried out, completely off balance. Tom was engaged to marry a friend in our circle. We were colleagues with no sexual history. Suddenly, his weight was on top of me and one hand was tugging at my already-unbuttoned jeans.

I was drunk, I couldn't get him off me, and I felt more confusion than rage. "Get off, Tom!" I grunted and pushed him as hard as I could with two hands. "Go home! Ugh." I twisted uselessly underneath him. He pressed harder, trapping my arms. And then—I don't know why—I gave up.

I was pinned. He wanted to fuck, so fuck it. What the fuck, who gives a fuck.

He held me down with his left arm, pulling my pants and underwear down with his right. He was smiling and saying something, aroused by my surrender. Suddenly he jammed into me. The scent of his hair oil instantly assaulted me; my stomach turned. His head kept bumping into my face; it seemed too large and full of harsh angles that cut into my vision.

Out the front window, a translucent curtain covered the lamplit darkness on the street. A neighborhood dog began to bark. Sinking into myself, I waited. He finished and dropped out. Did we say anything to each other? I cannot recall any words. He zipped his pants and left.

Collapsing on the couch in disbelief, I shivered in the cool night. Did that just happen? Disgusted, I threw my clothes into a pile in the bathroom and turned on the water in the shower. Steaming spray embraced me. I leaned my forehead against the tile, water streaming down my back. Tilting my head back I bashed it forward. Bang. A flash of light. Bang. Heavy and sharp at the same time, in a circle around the crown of my head, bang.

I dried off and pulled on flannel jammies, trying to get warm, relieved to be alone. I snuggled into myself in bed and wrapped my arms around my chest, letting the world fall away.

When early gray light suffused the little bedroom, I woke in a dim funk and untwisted myself from the sheets. "Ahhhhh," I sighed, empty-heartedly reaching for a cigarette. Shaking one out of the pack, I went looking for a match. The cardboard packet announcing *Berkeley Bar and Grill* in black cursive lettering over green plaid lay on the counter like a garish souvenir. I didn't even like Scotch. My father drank it, over ice, and I thought it was sophisticated. But what was sophisticated about last night?

A sickening shame shuddered through my chest, and I squeezed my eyes shut for a moment. Then I tore a match from the packet and scraped it over the emery until it burst into flame. I watched it burn down to my fingers before I dropped it in the kitchen sink. Tearing off another, I held it in front of my face and put my left palm over the flame.

"One, two, three," I counted aloud slowly, then dropped the match. The pain stuttered through my body. My thoughts stopped churning as endorphins hit my brain. I lit another, this time holding the little flame up to a Marlboro and taking the first hit of the day.

"Shit," I exhaled, a little swirl of lightheadedness passing over me. I felt as if I had eaten stones. To Tom this was normal sexual behavior—aggressive, dominant, masculine. What was it to me?

I took a drag off my smoke, then pressed the hot coal into the soft white skin of my forearm and exhaled as the rush lifted me and spun me around. Better.

I must have invited it. Because I think he's hot. He knew. Sitting on that complicit couch, I let my forehead sink into my palms while I slid into a hidden place within, a disappointed, lonely place.

"It was just sex," I said aloud, "so who cares." I refused to let this turn me into a victim.

I filled the Mr. Coffee carafe and scooped grounds into the filter. The dark, bitter scent sparked my habitual coffee craving. I lit another cigarette while I waited.

Blowing smoke rings, I thought it through. *It was just a friendly fuck, Rikki, don't worry about it.* I coached myself while the stones in my belly rumbled. *I guess you're pretty hot. Tom was totally into you.*

I held the cigarette out in front of me, then pressed the coal down on my arm again. "One, two, three." I shut my eyes as my body shuddered and let the pain soothe me.

It's not rape if they don't beat you up, really, I reminded myself. I knew from *The Daily Californian* that a New York court recently said it's not sexual assault unless you oppose the man to the utmost limit of your power. The resistance must be genuine and active. If you freak out and shut down, you fail the resistance criteria. It amounts to consent; men had the right to penetrate you if you were not sufficiently combative. It was my fault he thought he could get away with it.

I stood up and began pacing the tiny kitchen. Two hot red rounds marred my forearm; they would scab up later. A small knot had swollen on my forehead where the door hit me last night. Or maybe it was the shower tile.

I drank the black coffee while packing my book bag and dressing for class. I had to get up to LeConte by eight forty-five for microbiology and then to Life Sciences by ten for a biochemistry lab, so I had to bring my lab book and slide rule. Glancing at my small Buddhist altar, I decided to skip my chanting practice today. Maybe forever. Something about it made me feel heavy and discouraged.

My bike was padlocked to the stairs outside. I skittered through the numbers until the lock clicked in my hand. Ahead of me rose a busy day full of diverse projects to complete.

Pushing the last scrap of remorse out of my mind, I filed the whole night under *Drunken Sexual Adventure*. It would be more than forty years before I remembered the scene with horror and a dawning realization that it was rape. That it had wreaked terrible repercussions in my life. But that morning, I strapped on my backpack, mounted the bike, and began pumping my way uphill, east toward UC Berkeley's Sather Gate. I didn't have time to wallow. I had things to do.

CHAPTER 18
CATHOLIC GUILT

Alone at my shared flat above the dry cleaners on Ashby, creepy memories roiled around my mind and disturbed my concentration. I desperately wanted to convince myself that I was a strong and free individual—sexually liberated and in control. I could not bear to be a nothing, dominated and trashed by Tom.

The whistle of the dented teakettle on our ancient black six-burner industrial stove shattered my blue reverie. I yanked the kettle off the flame and splashed boiling water over the noodles in my Styrofoam cup. Tearing open the flavorings packet, I dumped the seasonings in and stirred slowly. Little green onion bits swirled in my noodle soup with snippets of carrot. Lunch and dinner in a single serving.

A few months had passed since the violent tryst with Tom. Just the thought of admitting I'd been assaulted and degraded against my will repelled me.

I took a hot mouthful of soup and burned my lips. Bile rose and burned the back of my throat. It felt as if all my organs cringed to escape shame.

I padded back to my bedroom, got out my notes, and scattered them over the card table where I worked. My paper on the ethical implications of human genetic engineering was due Friday.

Genetic counseling for chromosome-related diseases was just beginning, but we imagined a time when Western medicine might manipulate individual genes. There were many open questions. My Olivetti portable electric, a gift from my father, sat waiting next to a stack of blank sheets.

I was having a dark day. A hangover was banging on my head, creating wavy nausea. A nasty version of myself ragged on me: *You're way behind on your reading and you'll never get these papers written!* I felt stupid and ill-informed; depression settled in like dank fog. My forehead fell into my palms while I tried to think about the ethics of research on human DNA. But who was I to think about these things?

These were problems for responsible adults. My ethics seemed pretty low. *Promiscuous. Slutty.* What other words did society have for me? I'd been drinking too much. How about the simple *Drunk*?

Stop it, I admonished myself, *that's patriarchy talking. That's Catholic guilt haunting me. I'm above that.* I sucked on my cigarette, then stabbed it out in the ashtray. I refused to be controlled by social tyranny or religion. My mouth slurped a few mouthfuls of hot noodles while I flipped through my notes.

What kind of damage could we do by messing around with our genome? Did we even understand how genes interact within a cell? Which would do the least harm: research that leads to medical miracles, or a moratorium that protects us from our darker impulses and careless mistakes?

I pushed all my anxious feelings and the urge to smash something underground: my usual response, as betrayed by my frayed nails and chain-smoking. I took a puff and started typing.

> *Who would own the new genes—the research firm that did the genetic editing, or the person in whom the DNA originated? In the Western ethical system, we respect the individual, but we respect the corporation even more. A person's genes could end up being owned by some pharmaceutical firm.*
>
> *And what would we do if someone figured out how to boost*

intelligence or enhance sporting ability through DNA manipulation? Would the wealthy and well-connected have access to enhancements that others could not afford? How would that square with democracy?

I methodically typed out my thoughts, but when I read them, my words seemed like crap. I felt like an imposter, posing as an intellectual. Last quarter, I had barely scraped through with a 3.85 GPA and 3.25 in the sciences. Hardly competitive. My thoughts seemed childish to me, unsophisticated. I wanted to hurl my soup against the wall. Instead, I ripped the paper out of the typewriter and crumpled it, flipping it over my shoulder to the floor.

I thought about going down to the Hut in the morning for eggs and bacon with hash browns and toast, saying hi to Peg while she worked the grill, eating comfort food in a safe place. If I got up on time, I could get down there before my first class. But when I dumped out my backpack and fingered through the debris for breakfast money, I found only three quarters, four dimes, two nickels, three pennies, and a packet of Marlboros. I tapped one out.

Back in the kitchen, I grabbed the red and blue cardboard box of stove matches and used one to light my cigarette. The intoxicating smoke soothed my mind for a moment, and I blew it out in rings. I needed to apologize to someone for existing. To make a good Catholic confession. My teeth ripped at a scraggy cuticle.

I stared at my cigarette for so long it burned down to the last puff. Then I pinched off the coal and held the little butt of tobacco shreds, once part of a huge green leaf that was dried and cured and rolled into this little tube of paper. There was DNA in each cell in each shred. Now the DNA and the cells and the shreds were burnt, gone, vaporized. They once existed, and I had watched them disappear, like dying flowers.

Maybe just being alive itself is sacred, I thought. *Worthy of respect because body and soul have gone to all the trouble of existing, putting organic life together, growing, and maturing.* But I didn't know how to put ideas like that into an essay.

Shake it off, Rikki. You are a sexually liberated modern woman of twenty-three. I needed some aspirin, coffee, and a pencil sharpener. I was good to go.

I reheated the water and used it to dissolve an overflowing spoonful of Maxwell House instant. Back at my desk, my head dropped down to the table. I felt like shit and my ideas were idealistic and my coffee was bad. I didn't have enough change for breakfast at the Hut. Disgusted with my life, I worried I was a crummy scientist and would never get into medical school.

Who was I kidding? Pretending to be a student at Cal, I was just faking it.

After a moment, I sat up, took a deep breath, and rolled a fresh sheet into the Olivetti. *Tap, tap, tap.* Then nothing. My brain stalled. I couldn't think of anything to say.

I pulled out the sheet and placed it on top of my notepad on the table. Then I closed up the typewriter, took out my lab books, buried my face in my hands, and wept.

CHAPTER 19
A FREE INDIVIDUAL

In early 1975, after finishing all the coursework for my bachelor's in genetics, I finally admitted my Buddhist practice was a farce.

Doubts had grown over the past year. I'd lost respect for the organization, and I disliked the constant demand to recruit. Besides, what kind of teaching said you could "create good fortune" by repeating magic sounds? And where was that pure Buddha nature we were supposedly bringing forth? I should have felt peace, compassion, and wisdom by now. Instead, I was acting out, harming myself and others.

After seven years of chanting—I'd first met Ken in 1968—I doubted that I had become a better human being. To me, the whole idea of an inner Buddha was tarnished. *Maybe there is a Buddha nature*, I thought, *but this can't be the way to find it*. I decided to quit the practice. I packed up the little altar and put it away.

Still, in the back of my mind, I worried: What if the chanting Buddhists were right? What if the sect had found the streamlined path to awakening? Had I just endangered my inner Buddha—which bore a striking resemblance to my Catholic soul? I wasn't sure I could trust my judgment. I seemed to have more faith in the dogma of organized religion than in my own inner voice. It had been a decade since I engaged in Catholic rituals, but fears of hell still rose in my belly.

How long is it going to take you to escape this cult? I badgered myself.

My Buddhist colleagues noticed that I had stopped showing up to meetings. One of the older ladies in my local group called to warn me I had made the wrong choice.

"All your negative karma will rise up and ruin you. You cannot find true happiness without chanting," she cautioned me.

"I'm not sure that's true, Mrs. Kawata," I replied. I recalled the Catholic claim that missing mass blackened your soul with sin.

"You won't be able to create any good fortune," she nagged, sounding very much like the "God will punish you" threat from my childhood.

"I'll just have to face my fate as it comes," I told her with growing confidence.

I wrenched myself free, but I had to cut off contact with the fanatic Buddhists. For better or worse, I needed to listen to my intuition. Deep within, I knew the Nichiren folks weren't helping me awaken to my higher consciousness. None of our behavior showed the least sign of any enlightenment worth its salt.

After graduating in June of 1975, my final overall GPA record came in. I made an appointment with the career counselor at school. We met in a small cramped office in the basement of Sproul Hall behind a frosted glass door that read School Counselor.

"We have your final grades here, and I wonder what your next goals are?" the balding, jowly man in a lumpy brown suit told me. Stacks of paper and folders littered his messy desk. He held my record at eye level and peered at me over his reading glasses.

"Well, I'm pre-med," I explained.

"Ah. Well. Looking here," he waved my file, "I'm not seeing competitive numbers."

My heart fell forty floors from my chest to the pit of my stomach. That was the end of it. My grades were not going to get me into a medical school. All along I'd secretly hoped that chanting would create a miracle for me, a pathway to become a doctor.

"Candidates have 4.2's, 4.5's with extra, graduate-level classes. And volunteer hours on medical wards," he said.

Neither of these was possible for me. Carrying an advanced science load at Cal, I also worked twenty hours a week supporting myself, and I sweated getting A's in my classes as it was. I chewed a loose cuticle.

"You might look into Guadalajara," he said, tapping my records with the eraser on his automatic pencil. "But frankly, I don't recommend a woman studying alone in Mexico."

I stopped listening. He rambled on about the four-year foreign program being too rigorous and exhausting for women, blah blah blah. Then I heard him say I might do better as a genetic counselor. That caught my ear. I looked up.

"What's genetic counseling?" I asked, trying to find a path forward.

I learned that genetic counselors work with doctors to advise parents about genetic risks. My degree could get me into graduate study in that field. But I wanted to be the doctor, not the counselor. My chest muscles tightened, and I knew I was going to cry. My secret dreams were shattered. Was it because I quit chanting?

I left that counseling office a woman without a plan, feeling as blue and empty as I ever had been.

What am I going to do now?

There was a little bar on Shattuck, near my workplace. As soon as the clock struck five that day, I trotted over there for happy hour.

The owner-bartender, Jan, poured me a shot of Dewar's White Label and a Heineken back. They went down perfectly. As the warmth of the booze ran through my system, my blue mood fell away and my buoyant side rose to the surface.

"I am feeling mighty fine, Jan!" I quipped from my barstool. On my right sat a man drinking shots of tequila. "And who am I meeting here?" I said to him with a quizzical look. "My name is Rikki."

"Groovy, sweetheart." He looked me over, taking in my faded jeans, Doc Martens, and tousled hair. "Let me buy you a drink."

Another Dewar's appeared in front of me.

CHAPTER 20
THE WASTELAND

"Howdy-do, Jan," I said, plopping onto that same barstool a few weeks later. "The usual, please."

A shot of Scotch and a beer appeared in front of me. But I had meant to order white wine! That very morning, while nursing a hangover with coffee and scrambled eggs, I'd resolved to ease up. No hard booze. Because lately I'd found myself at late-night joints where I could drink until I blacked out. Entire nights had disappeared from memory.

Then again, it was just past four on a warm June weekday, and I had nothing better to do, having finished my part-time work. I slammed the shot.

Oops.

"Hey, Rikki," a voice called from behind me. "Come join us!"

Pam and Adrienne, work friends, waved from a small table near the back. I gulped the rest of my beer and walked over.

"What're you drinking?" Pam said.

I glanced at the table. Two wineglasses.

"White wine," I said with a smile, wondering if I'd end up in bed with one of them tonight. When intoxicated, I slept with friends—both men and women—who should have remained friends, and with strangers I should not have met at all.

After I got my glass of wine, our small talk quickly turned to gossip about the law professors at work. Did we know that Barbara was speaking at such-and-such a fundraiser? Anyone see Singer's new book yet?

All the while, I gauged my wine-sipping to match the rate of my friends.

Around five, Pam and Adrienne said their goodbye-see-you-to-morrows. The red swallow Pam left in her glass caught my eye. Most people did not drink with my zeal; I never left anything in the bottom of a glass.

On the way home, I stopped at Wild Times for a bottle of Pinot Noir. As soon as I walked through my front door, I beelined to the kitchen, took out a jelly jar, poured to the top, and gulped the red warmth down.

That steadied me. I refilled the glass halfway and took it to the kitchen table while I pondered my predicament.

For no reason, my heart ached. The truth was my attitude over the past several months had turned sour and combative. *Fuck* this and *fuck* that. I had even started to drink during the day to block out nagging angst about what to do with my tiny, meaningless life.

I'm turning into my father! Flashed through my mind, leaving a tingle of fear and pain. Sitting forward, I shook my head to disengage that terrifying thought. I was only twenty-four; I should be carefree, enjoying my life. *How did I get here?*

My fist slammed the tabletop over and over. *I refuse to be like him!*

My mind needed something constructive to do, something worthwhile to get me on a more productive track. I took out a fresh legal pad and a pen.

Law school? I wrote, as I brainstormed. Even if I couldn't get into medical school, I could continue my education.

Write my novel? That would involve research, and I needed intellectual challenges.

Biochemist?

Teach English overseas?

What about graduate study in philosophy or literature? I had many philosophical questions that didn't seem to bother other people. *What is consciousness, where do our minds come from, why is there suffering?* Was there any way I could investigate things like this? Maybe there were insights or secrets in the Western intellectual tradition that could help me find my place in the universe. Pursuing that could occupy my mind for years.

"For your graduate work, you'll have to pick a theme and ensure your studies prepare you both to write a dissertation and to pass oral exams," my mentor in the Philosophy Department had explained. She was a visiting professor from France who spoke English as if she were reading from the college handbook. "Prep work will include medieval studies, art appreciation, appropriate philosophy and literature courses, and seminars in the humanities."

But the crème de la crème of my program at San Francisco State University was the dissertation. For that, I planned to research three artistic pieces that represented the period between the two world wars: T. S. Eliot's poem *The Waste Land*, the choreography of Martha Graham, and Picasso's painting *Guernica*. I would be looking for themes from the zeitgeist of the times.

"This is so exciting," I told Linda, who was in town for a visit.

We sat in the living room of the bungalow I shared with my friend Phil in Berkeley, drinking hot tea with honey. Gray fog drifted up the hills from the bay, creating a gloomy fall day. I was explaining my ideas with almost manic energy to Linda, because she was the only person I knew who would listen.

"Each of these masterpieces breaks from traditional rules to express fresh, raw human truths. Look." I shoved a picture of *Guernica* under her face.

Linda sipped from her mug of Good Earth black tea, examining the image. "My God. Of course, I see the turmoil and disruption."

"It's definitely not beautiful, but it's *true*," I said. In the blue, black, and white oil painting, Picasso had expressed a deeply disturbing image of social mayhem. "I asked my art professor about it."

"What did he say?" Linda asked.

"She." I reached for the teapot and topped off our mugs. "She asked me to describe what I saw when I looked at it. What do *you* see?"

"I see horror." Linda grimaced. "Bodies dismembered. Broken warriors. Dead children."

"Exactly! Me too. Then my prof asked me why Picasso would paint that."

I waited to hear Linda's answer.

After a moment, her face opened in surprise. "It's a warning," she said. Her eyes flicked up at me. "A very dire warning."

"Wow, yes, I see that," I said. "And it's the kind of warning that couldn't have been expressed using nineteenth-century rules of artistic beauty." I lit a cigarette and got up to find an ashtray.

"Is that your thesis then? That old forms or structures in art broke down between the two world wars?"

"Not just art, but government. Physics, everything. Politics. Women got the right to vote in 1920."

"Fascinating. Okay, I'm already familiar with Eliot's poem." Linda had been an English lit major. "But what about this Graham dance?"

"I'll show you! We have tickets to a Graham-inspired performance on campus by my dancer friend's class tomorrow night."

As anticipated, my friend's class performance ignored all the sacred notions of beauty in classical ballet. Instead of arcs and uplifts that pointed to godlike perfection, Martha Graham's style used down-to-earth, breathing, organic body shapes to display raw human emotion.

"Your friend is a great dancer. But I see what you mean," Linda said as we walked home with other Berkeleyans through the grassy hills of campus, bundled up against the chill. "The focus was on human experience, instead of transcendent values. And the shapes were angular, like we are."

"Yes, exactly!" I cried. "And this dovetails with the existentialists I've been reading. Meaning, or worth does not come from above but from the human experience alone."

"I thought grad school was supposed to be hard work," Linda said, "but it sounds like you're just having fun!"

I laughed. Nobody in the world understood me like my big sister.

"Who founded the school of scholasticism?" my colleague Diane asked me.

Diane and I were taking medieval philosophy and French existentialism in the spring semester of '77. We studied together on Wednesday afternoons at her place—a huge Victorian she shared with a number of roommates—in the Sunset District.

My gaze turned toward the window as I searched for the answer. Tiny motes of dust, defying gravity, swirled in the shafts of lights that streamed onto the faded floral carpet. Diane got up to pour snifters of brandy.

"Anselm of Canterbury," I said. We lounged on her bed, our books and notes spread out around us, quizzing each other.

Diane set her glass down on a side table. She inched closer to me, and to my surprise, began stroking my shoulder. Then she brushed the bangs out of my eyes.

"My boyfriend, Daniel, and I are in a committed relationship," Diane began, "but . . ."

I didn't catch on right away to her cryptic hint. I assumed she wanted to try sex with women on the side.

"Okay . . ." I said uncertainly, waiting to hear more. The scent of her patchouli oil hit my nostrils, and I turned my head to avoid it. Musk or amber, yes, but patchouli I did not like.

"I mean, if you're into it, Daniel would like to be involved. Participate."

Oh! That. A threesome. No, thank you.

"Want to see a picture?" Diane walked over to her desk and came back with a framed photo. I took it.

Daniel was a good-looking guy, and I felt some heat with Diane. *What the heck*, I thought. I had no valid objections. I mean, people had three-ways all the time.

And therein lay my problem—the curse of being a narcissist's child. Just because somebody wanted something from me, did I have to give it?

Immersed in graduate work on philosophy and art, I was studying the leading lights of the brilliant and creative early twentieth century. Diane and I delved into the medieval Saint Augustine, and I'd read the ancient Plotinus for another course. What had I learned from all this thinking?

My answer was disturbing. Picasso depicted the darkness of something fragmented, distorted, and violent. The infamous Nietzsche trashed notions of truth, goodness, and beauty. He left a hole in the pit of my stomach; even rock 'n' roll expressed truth, goodness, and beauty. Jean-Paul Sartre convinced me that meaning and value had to be conjured up by each individual. So, navigating this frightening and crazy world was completely up to me. There was no authority or guide besides myself.

And yet I could not derive an iota of clarity about how to conduct my life. How to respond to Diane, for example. Where was the attunement that might help me hear my own voice about Daniel—the one saying, *No, thank you*?

Instead, I heard the zeitgeist of my times crying *sexual liberation!*

Diane and Daniel asking for a *cool threesome.* People telling me that religion and morality were the *opiate of the masses!*

I handed back the photo with what I did not then recognize as a sigh of resignation, or perhaps sadness, for abandoning myself.

"Simone de Beauvoir did it," I said with a half- smile. "I guess we could try and see what happens."

"Great!" Her face lit up. "I'll let him know he can come over."

CHAPTER 21
GAY AS SPRINGTIME

Daniel came over. The three of us carried on the affair for a few months, but eventually I squirmed out of it. Daniel just wasn't my *thing*.

Because I finally had to admit, I was as gay as springtime. The time had come to own it.

It was 1978, the year anti-queer sentiment in California led to a voter initiative to prevent gay people from teaching in public schools. One of our lesbian icons, singer and songwriter Holly Near, asked the hidden "women's community"—a euphemism for lesbians—to "come out of the closet" to our family and friends. We needed voters to realize that they already loved and respected a gay person. To discover they already trusted us around their kids. We were teachers, friends, grocery clerks, and family members.

I gathered my courage and slowly talked to people: coworkers, friends, and family.

"There something I need to say," I started, "about the Briggs Initiative."

My boss and I were sitting at a local café, eating salads. She chewed and nodded.

I took a breath. "You probably know it will make it illegal for any gay person to teach in public school." I held my breath and hoped to hear a murmur of affirmation.

"Uh-huh, I'm familiar with it," Amy told me. "Don't worry, I'm voting against it."

Don't worry? That stunned me. *Does she already know?*

I pressed on. "Lots of good people are gay. They aren't perverts." I should have said *we*. But this was all new to me.

"Of course not. You know, I have lots of gay friends." Amy greased the skids for me.

"In fact, well . . . I'm gay too." I stopped, depleted from the effort.

"Really?" Amy's eyebrows lifted in a humorous tease.

I laughed. "You probably knew before I did," I said, relieved and appreciative all at once.

Emboldened after my smooth conversation with Amy, I told a few coworkers. One responded, "Big secret. I already knew." Nobody seemed shocked.

I called my family, too. Mom said, "I just want you to be happy. Do you have friends?" She didn't even hesitate. Maybe she'd guessed.

Elizabeth joked, "You finally noticed!"

And Linda said, "Well, Rikki, I am not surprised. I'm glad you came to terms with it."

My ear against the phone receiver burned crimson. I'd been holding my breath and squinting to protect myself from feared judgment and derision.

"In fact, this is a secret, too, but my boss is gay," she said in a conspiratorial whisper. "Let's just not tell the kids yet." Linda's children were still in grade school. It made sense that we should shield them from . . . well, from perversions. And in 1978, being queer still felt depraved to me.

"Okay," I agreed, with a slight flush of humiliation.

But the next day, she called me back.

"Why should I hide it from the kids?" she asked. "I don't know what I was thinking. There's nothing to be ashamed of."

“Thank you!” Finally, I’d made it out of the closet!

But was she right? Was there really nothing shameful about these forbidden desires? I wondered if maybe we *should* hide it from the kids.

CHAPTER 22
THE REAL WORLD

"Let's sit here." My friend John gestured to two red leather stools at the dark end of the bar.

We were having drinks at the White Horse, a gay men's bar on Telegraph Avenue in Oakland. From his chosen perch, John could view the whole throng of men talking and flirting at the club.

"Looking for anything in particular?" I teased, and glanced around the smoky room.

John laughed. "I'll wait for him to find me," he said, and raised his glass to me in a toast to that possibility.

I downed the rest of my drink after his toast, and when the bartender swung by, I asked for a glass of Pinot Noir.

"Life just is the way it is," John said. He drained his drink and slammed the glass down, jingling the ice. "It doesn't give a shit about us." He looked me in the eyes and said, "You have to get what you want for yourself."

John had endured a loveless childhood and an adolescent life on the street. He was a former chanter like myself. Being an avid reader of Kurt Vonnegut, he loved cynical humor and bitterly joked that life was just chaos happening in time.

Since earning my master's degree a few years earlier, I'd been hanging around Berkeley doing nothing much, supporting myself with a data entry job at a legal firm. I had become a rather arrogant existentialist. I thought of myself and other humans as completely free agents, unbound by any external rules, living as isolated bits of self-consciousness in vulnerable bodies on a rock hurtling around a star.

Bringing my wineglass to my lips, I tasted a complex stream of grape, alcohol, and wood scent while I pondered John's pessimism. *Is that all there is? Just achieve and acquire?*

I lit a cigarette and blew the smoke out in a stream. "I'm afraid there's no 'higher plan' for humans overseen by a transcendent entity of any kind," I said with a sigh. I had come to appreciate Jean-Paul Sartre's humanist insights and to admire Friedrich Nietzsche's bold critiques of social morays. I looked down on those who used religion as a crutch. "Not what I'd hoped."

I swallowed my drink as John went to the bar for refills. Around the room, men were slow-dancing in each other's arms or making out in the leatherette booths. I felt my toes curl when I glanced at them kissing, before my eyes slid away.

Wow, what is that? I was surprised at my discomfort. *The hetero-normal standard is really embedded in you.* Did I feel the same distaste about my own behavior? I put it out of my mind as John approached with the drinks.

"What is it you really want?" I asked my friend when he sat down, distracting myself from that tinge of homophobia.

"A relationship," he said. "Love. A decent job. Why are those things so hard to get?"

"It's not much to ask. But you get tired of trying," I reflected darkly.

"You have your smarts, your looks, your education!" John guffawed in my face. "What are you complaining about?"

He couldn't see beneath my exterior, into my inner life where emotions continually troubled me. Without any spiritual connection, I fell prey to anxieties and depression, wasted my time in bars, feared going far from home, and drank too much. Self-pity ground ruts in my psyche. Like my father's.

"I have got to get something going in my life," I said. Why was I still entering data twenty hours a week when I had a master's degree under my belt? It was time to move on. "But what am I going to do with one undergrad science and one graduate humanities degree?"

"You should try publishing," John suggested. "You could read for a living. Since you read all the time anyway."

"That's a hot idea, John. Maybe I could read science books!" How fun it would be to combine my two great loves: reading and science. I lit up at the thought. "I could have a life of discovery and learning!"

Within a week, I'd reached out to a managing editor at one of the big book publishers.

"I hate to disillusion you, but to be an editor, you needed to get a literature degree," said Clive Raymond. We were in a high-rise in San Francisco, enjoying lunch on his expense account.

After speaking with me briefly on the phone the previous week, he had agreed to meet to discuss the career path of an editor. Our chat proved to be about as encouraging as that interview about medical school with the counselor a few years earlier.

Clive, a middle-aged man with chin-length graying hair, brushed a lock away from his eyes. "Also, the hours are endless, the pay is poor, the field is crowded, and success is unlikely." He smiled and placed his hands flat on the table. It was the best he could say.

I thanked him and decided to look for another profession.

Not long after my lunch with Clive, a friend's mother told me about her work as a technical writer for a new software company.

"It takes a mix of technical understanding and skillful writing," Carol said. "You would be great at it." The pay was in a whole different category from my hourly wages in data entry. "I get a monthly salary, vacation hours, and stock awards," she went on.

My eyebrows shot up. "That's for me. How did you find the job?" I asked.

"An ad in the *Mercury News*," Carol answered.

So, that weekend, I scoured the Sunday paper for technical writing positions. There was an open house the following Saturday at a computer manufacturing company in Cupertino, about fifty miles south of Berkeley. I spent the week preparing my resume. On Saturday morning, I drove down.

Astonishingly, the company was looking for someone with a science background *and* writing ability to join the new manufacturing documentation and training group. My degrees proved I had both skill sets. I was offered a job on the spot at $25,000 a year, a huge salary in June of 1981.

I'd managed to graduate from anguished student to professional writer. Having money and a little social status healed a lot of woes. I got a new apartment and quickly earned praise from my new boss. These accomplishments gave me a fresh confidence and sense of pride.

Drinking was part of the company culture, which meant I fit right in. With my new riches I bought finer wine and better Scotch and drank them so frequently that I, ashamed for anyone to see all those bottles in my bins, hid most of the empties in other people's garbage cans.

Perhaps John had been right: It wasn't that complicated. You just had to take what you wanted to make this life your own.

At home, I raised a glass in imaginary salute to Kurt Vonnegut and swallowed all the golden liquid.

CHAPTER 23

TWENTY QUESTIONS

Late one Saturday night in June of 1982, I sat at the wooden kitchen table in my quaint rental cottage off Telegraph Avenue in Berkeley. Looking through bay windows onto a small, shared courtyard, I smoked my Tareyton down to the filter. Then I walked over to each window in the kitchen and front room and turned its crank, closing them all tightly.

In the corner of the big kitchen stood an old-fashioned gas stove, with an exhaust pipe snaking out the back wall. I sat down next to it on the yellowing linoleum floor and traced my finger along the red striping on the once-white tiles. Leaning against the stove, I guzzled from my fifth of J&B whisky.

From the cloud of confusion that was my drunken mind, a darkness of self-pity and shame rained down on me. Maybe it was years of booze-fog clogging my thought pores. Maybe I felt guilt about my drunken exploits. I knew my problem wasn't my job, where my responsibilities and rewards had grown. I had friends and money and health. But in some frightening way, I hated myself; I wanted to stop being. I just couldn't bear myself anymore.

This was the first time that depression slammed me into the floor. Over the next thirty-five years, I would work with it, learn from it, even grow from it. That day, my sense of solidity shattered; I felt scattered and lost. Dread weighted my thoughts and gave me feelings of desperation. It was like falling off the Empire State Building in my imagination, scrambling for purchase on something I could count on. Nothing was there.

Instead of walking through it, I blew out the pilot in the old stove. I turned on the gas, stuck my head in the oven, and inhaled deeply. Then I pulled my head out, exhaled, and took a swig. I went on like this, perhaps half an hour or so, until everything went blank.

When I woke around two thirty in the morning, moonlight streamed through the kitchen window and gas still streamed into the room. The air smelled of garlic. I was curled in a fetal coil on the floor. I got up, turned off the flow and stumbled miserably into bed.

You couldn't even do suicide right, I chastised myself. *At least you're smart enough not to light a cigarette.* I slept until dawn's smudged light seeped into my bedroom.

When I woke, I knew I needed to call Linda. She was living in Minneapolis, where she had moved with Rick and their two children after he landed a teaching job at Augsburg University. I could call at 7:00 a.m. my time since it would be two hours later in her time zone.

"You need to get sober, Rikki." Linda's voice on the phone was harsh and impatient. "Starting today." The gray morning had grown brighter, and yellow streams beamed into my kitchen. I opened the bay windows.

"It's not drinking, it's my life," I sniveled. "There's something wrong with me." I stretched the snaky loops of the beige Princess phone cord across the room to the sink.

"There's nothing wrong with you except alcohol," Linda said. Holding the phone away from my face, I vomited into the kitchen basin. When I came back, she was saying, " . . . promise me you will get some help."

Linda had gotten sober herself about six months before. She didn't sound sanctimonious as much as serious.

"Go to the county and ask for a counselor," she told me in her no-nonsense big-sister tone.

I knew she was right. I still had a shot at controlling my drinking before I turned into my dad—who was chronically depressed, full of self-pity, and dangerously self-destructive. At thirty-one, I was well down the alcoholic path. After drinking heavily for years, it was time to get control.

On Monday, I took a long lunch break to check out what the county offered. The offices were just a ten-minute drive down Stevens Creek Boulevard. I told no one else what I was doing.

At the county building, I slipped across the lobby with my head down, pulled a ticket to get in the queue, and sat in one of the flimsy plastic waiting chairs. Locking my eyes on the tiled floor beneath me, I tried to disappear.

"Next!" A clerk at the counter called my number. Standing at the open rectangular window, I stared at my twisting hands instead of her face. "Can I help you?" she asked.

My eyes searched a sign on the wall that listed various county services. I straightened my hunched shoulders and cleared my throat.

"Can you tell me do you have any counseling available?" I tried to meet her eyes.

"Depends," she said crisply, "on what you want. Marriage, addiction, adoption? Here's a list." She handed me a poorly xeroxed sheet of county support services.

"Oh." I studied it a moment, as if choosing an ice cream at Baskin-Robbins. "Addiction?" I asked.

She gave me an appointment at 2:00 p.m. three days later. But when I arrived that Thursday to meet with the counselor, I was convinced I had been too melodramatic when I signed up.

"I don't think I need to be here," I began, clearing my throat and using my assertive managerial voice.

"Maybe not," said a prim, middle-aged woman in a green plaid skirt and beige blouse that tied at the throat. "Before you decide, try taking this quiz," and she handed me a brochure.

I took the triple-folded, glossy handout with the title, "Twenty Questions." Unfolding it, I saw a list of irritating inquiries like these: Have you ever tried to quit drinking? Do you sometimes drink more than you planned? Do you get the urge for a drink? Is alcohol affecting your relationships or work performance?

I looked up at the woman I remember as Mrs. Brown. "I think I flunked," I said, a little bewildered.

"I flunked, too, dear," Mrs. Brown said gently. "No need for us to feel ashamed. It's a disease. And there is treatment." She explained the disease model of alcoholism: Basically, that some of us had severe physical and psychological reactions that we could cure by swearing off entirely. She gave me leaflets about AA meetings and asked me to promise I would go, then come back and report to her.

"Here," she said, handing me another photocopied sheet, "is a list of meetings around the South Bay." And circling one entry with her blue pen, she said, "This one is a gay meeting at the Unitarian Church. You might be more comfortable starting there."

My eyes froze; then I looked away. How did she know?

Four years after coming out, I still imagined strangers couldn't tell. Maybe it was my dress style: khakis or jeans with polo shirts like the men. But I kept my private life to myself, and I thought I passed for straight. Mrs. Brown took me by surprise.

Flushed but grateful, I gathered my papers.

"Thank you, Mrs. Brown. I'll get to that meeting. I promise."

PART II
THE PARTIAL FIX

CHAPTER 24
TRITE SLOGANS

I balked.

The heavy double doors that lead into the gay Monday night AA gathering at the Unitarian Church in San Jose were my last barrier. I'd been fretting about this moment since last week. That night, I left work at five thirty to get a bite to eat, swallowing my meatball sandwich as if it were my last meal. I arrived here at six forty-five, unsure of where to park. Finally, I stood on the sidewalk outside. If I could get through that doorway, maybe something in my life would change.

Taking a deep breath, I pulled open the portal. Inside, fluorescent lighting revealed an ordinary room with twenty or so people milling about. Folding chairs were set out in rows. No one noticed me. The air, warmed by California's June sun, exhaled heat while a breeze rippled through the open windows. A clutch of people in jeans and polo shirts crowded around the coffee station.

On the wall, a huge poster listed things you had to do to quit drinking. I looked at the first two or three instructions—they were about being powerless, about needing God—and felt my heart sink. *Shit. I didn't come here to learn that I'm powerless,* I thought. *I came here to learn how to control my drinking.* I slunk over to the coffee bar, wishing I were anywhere else.

My eyes scanned the crowd for the most attractive women as potential dating material. Peering discretely over a Styrofoam cup, I hoped I was invisible. An athletic-looking woman, maybe a tennis player, with short black hair and bright blue eyes was telling a funny story. She did not look like a drunken loser, and I wondered if she was single. That was what I was thinking about, rather than recovery. I imagined loneliness was the reason I drank so much, fantasizing that finding a partner would fix many woes.

A handsome young man—he said his name was Alan—stood behind a table in the front of the room and called out to the group.

"Okay, everyone. Let's get started. If you'll take your seats, I've asked Heather to read the Twelve Steps."

I sat near the back. They began reading their materials while I looked around. Brief slogans on laminated posterboard were taped up on two walls. *Think Think Think* said one; *Let Go and Let God* said another. It didn't look like very sophisticated material. I wasn't feeling hopeful. Rather, I felt insulted. How was *Progress, Not Perfection* useful for the self-hatred that poisoned my mind, or the despair in my heart?

"Today Melvin will share his experience, strength, and hope with everyone, followed by group sharing." He turned to the man seated next to him. "You ready?"

While Melvin spoke, I griped.

I am an achiever, not one of these losers. What am I doing here? I had earned two degrees, a bachelor's from prestigious Cal Berkeley and a master's from renowned San Francisco State. I had read Dostoevsky, Goethe, Dante, Tolstoy, and the Greek playwrights. I had studied the biochemical intricacies of the mysterious DNA double helix. I was succeeding at work; I had a new apartment.

After Melvin concluded, individuals shared anecdotes from their lives. One by one they told stories of putting their lives back together. Some of their honest tales about anxiety attacks, defenseless depression, and thoughts of self-harm resonated with me, which only made me despise them more. I didn't want to be one of them. I sat silently, arms crossed against my chest, slumped in the fifth row, smoking.

Suddenly I realized the meeting leader was looking at me. He had just said, "Are there any newcomers who want to introduce themselves?" Something hard lodged in my throat when I realized he meant me. I had made up my mind not to speak. I was on the spot.

I squeaked out, "I'm Rikki, and I'm an alcoholic. I'm just here to check it out. Not sure yet what I'm gonna do." When I heard myself say *alcoholic*, I got really scared. Did I qualify for membership in the AA club?

After the personal sharing part of the meeting, they gave out embossed plastic "chips" to acknowledge the amount of time people went without drinking. One person stood up to accept a twenty-four-hour chip. That seemed feasible. Another claimed a chip with *30 Days* engraved on one side—thirty consecutive days of continuous sobriety. I had no intention of trying that. Or ever participating in the silly chip ritual.

I did not believe in God; I believed in empiricism, in scientific materialism, in molecules. How could these simple, mindless AA tools help me? I was in the wrong place; I needed like-minded intellectuals, not common drunks.

The meeting ended in a prayer circle that chanted, "Keep coming back! It works!" The worst thing I could think of at that moment was that I would have to keep coming back.

I headed toward those big double doors.

"Hi," a tall lanky woman said, "I'm Patty." She reached her hand out. "Is this your first meeting, darlin'?" She had a lilting Texas accent that made the affectionate term seem natural, though it felt too intimate to me.

"Yes," I said, then fell silent.

"Well, the important thing is to not take the first drink, I can tell you that from my experience," she said, and chuckled so heartily she had to throw her head back, chortling.

"I'm not sure this is really . . ." I tried to cut her off. I felt invaded.

"Of course not." She squeezed my forearm. "But you don't ever have to drink again if you stick around."

My eyes circled the room. People were talking, laughing, even hugging. They seemed a lot happier than I was.

"Here, you take my number and you call me before you pick up that first drink," she said, suddenly quite serious. We fumbled with paper and pen until I got the number.

A few days later, I dialed it.

CHAPTER 25
FELLOWSHIP

On Tuesday and Wednesday that week in June, I went to work as usual. In the evenings, instead of going out for a drink, I just gritted my teeth and watched *Cagney & Lacey* and the Fonz on TV, waiting for the next gay AA meeting. According to my mimeographed sheet from Mrs. Brown, that would be Thursday night in Palo Alto, fifteen miles north of my apartment in Cupertino.

Finally, it was Thursday afternoon. It shamed me to ask for help, but I was craving a drink. I kept thinking I'd just stop at a bar on my way to that AA meeting in Palo Alto. Instead, as soon as I could escape work, I drove to the shopping mall on Stevens Creek and parked near a phone booth. Inside there was a phone directory hanging by a chain, but the number I needed was on a paper scrap clutched in my fist.

I cracked open the booth door so I could smoke, then jingled my pocket change to extract a dime. With shaky fingers, I slipped it into the slot and dialed the number Patty had given me.

"Hello?" A voice answered.

"Hi, is this Patty?" I exhaled a stream of smoke out the doorway.

"Good to hear your voice, my friend!" Patty said, in what I would come to know as her usual earthy tone. "I'm so glad you called."

"I'm . . . I'm just having a hard time," I stammered. I didn't need to explain much for Patty to understand my predicament. Nothing in particular had happened. I just had strong urges to drink, and I was afraid I would succumb. Patty invited me to join her and some other sober friends before the meeting.

"No one wants to be alone with those demons," she said. "You come have dinner with us at the 'Copper Toilet,'" she joked, using her nickname for the Copper Penny in Redwood City. "You can meet Mary Ann and Judy. Around six."

"Okay, I'll be there," I said, with relief and hope. Calling for help hadn't been that hard.

"Just don't pick up that first drink!" she said with a laugh.

Forty-five minutes later, I found Patty seated at a large table with several empty seats and two friends I didn't recognize. Patty introduced me, saying I was a newcomer. The two took an immediate interest in me. They encouraged me to go one day at a time.

"If you don't pick up that first drink, you won't get drunk," Mary Ann said simply.

"Pretty straightforward stuff," said Judy. "And as an added benefit, Rikki, if you stick with us, you never have to be lonely again."

It was a strange thing to say, and it went right to my heart. I didn't even know I harbored the hope of belonging somewhere, of fitting in without distorting myself. Wasn't there a Groucho Marx story about not wanting to join any club that would have him? But a tiny flame of warmth flared in my mind: Might I find a friendly haven in this odd society?

"Find people who have what you want—not money, but peace of mind—and be willing to go to any lengths to get that," Judy added. Those lengths would turn out to be the demanding and fairly rigorous Twelve Steps.

"You guys just don't get it," I said to my new friends. They seemed to be free of the compulsion that gripped me. "You don't have to drink, but sometimes, I really do."

"No, you don't. That first drink is a choice," Patty told me over a chicken-fried steak. She pointed her fork at the faces gathered round. "But all of us here get drunk if we have that first drink. We choose to avoid it."

"But you guys don't experience the intense cravings I get," I complained.

"Not anymore, Rikki, but that's the kind of 'special' thinking that landed me in a mental institution," Patty said. She threw her head back to guffaw at the memory. How had she learned to laugh at that kind of stuff?

Maybe I did feel a little special. I did think they couldn't understand my particular despondence and that I was too educated to get much from their simple steps and trite slogans. But there I was at the Copper Toilet, needing their camaraderie to avoid another drink.

"We all feel like elegant pieces of shit," said a woman named Kay, the tennis player from my first meeting. "We think we are above this fellowship"—she waved her hand at the women gathered together—"but at the same time we feel like roadkill and need to be here."

I remained unconvinced but willing to try things their way. I got through that night and another. Soon I had been sober for a week. I was eager to get back to that Monday night gay meeting in San Jose where they gave out chips for going twenty-four hours without a drink. I had more than earned one of those.

Deborah chose me for her first same-sex encounter. At least, I think she seduced me, but it was all such a blur I was never sure. A long, muscled runner with short black hair and sensual eyes, she had just started to explore eroticism with women. Very secretly, we'd begun seeing each other after we met at the work gym.

Our dating was casual for her but besotted infatuation for me. Of course, we were carefully hiding our liaison from our straight acquaintances, which was pretty much everyone at work. Hanging out at her house one Sunday, I asked Deborah if she wanted to do something Friday night, but she said, without even blinking, that she had a date.

"With who?" I snapped. The tone of my voice surprised me. It was sharp and urgent. Edgy.

"With Patrick from marketing," she said without looking up from her magazine.

My heart stung. I was no competition for Patrick in marketing. I was the forbidden fruit, the lover in hiding, the sideline to a normal life—an invisible person. The thought triggered anger, self-condemnation, and panic—feelings I could not then name. There was a clenching in my gut, a constriction in my throat, and a whoosh of negative thoughts. *You are such an idiot. You should never have asked her. Time for a drink!*

The joke was that when normal people have a flat tire, they call AAA, but alcoholics have to call suicide prevention. The frustrated child in me now had to learn to tolerate breakdowns, loss of control, and things not going my way. To deal with feelings of panic when bad things happened.

Instead of caving to the urge to drink, I turned my attention to my breath and repeated the adage *Let go and let God*. But since I didn't believe in God, my mind scrambled for another AA catchphrase to grab on to: *This, too, shall pass.*

I needed some alone time to process being rejected. Making some excuse, I escaped to my apartment, where I tried to calm my mind. *This is not a crisis. It's just someone saying "no."* AA had a saying for talking yourself down: *Think Think Think.*

"Chew on a hand towel if you need to," Judy had advised me for crises. "Just don't pick up a drink." I went to my linen closet and pulled out a fresh washcloth. Twisting one end, I stuffed it into my mouth and bit down.

There was a gay AA meeting at 7:00 p.m. on the peninsula. I drove myself there at 6:15.

When the meeting got to the sharing part, my hand went up. "Hi, I'm Rikki and I'm an alcoholic." Then, I blurted out my story.

"When she said no, I just started attacking myself," I told them. "I watched the clock until I could come here." Somewhere inside me—a place where it hardly registered—I felt grateful for this gay meeting, where I could talk about dating women without shame.

As I shared, self-hatred drained out of me, and the group helped me laugh at myself. My raw, wounded feelings subsided, and serenity returned.

At those meetings—which I was attending three or four nights a week—I found companionship, understanding, and humor. Soon I earned a chip for thirty days without a drink. According to my new friends, it was about time for me to start the serious healing that would remove the craving altogether.

CHAPTER 26
BORROWING JESUS

By 1982, I had reclassified my teenage LSD experiences as hallucinations rather than revelations. My search for "higher consciousness" had fizzled out.

Hearing about the recovery of others showed me I would have to do some heavy spiritual lifting to stay sober. It would require direct engagement with an active higher power, something hefty I could grab on to when I wanted a drink.

But Cal Berkeley had trained me to trust blindly the unquestioned assumption that our essential ingredient is atomic stardust, not spirit or consciousness. We were merely a collection of cells that churns away like bubbling oatmeal doing biochemistry all day long. There was no little being inside that was my special soul, no connection to the universe that made me belong in the world.

With that mindset, how was I going to follow the AA program, which seemed to rely on a higher power?

Texas Patty came to the rescue. If I had no hotline to a spiritual source, why not use someone else's?

"You just borrow mine, Rikki," she said, as if people did this sort of thing all the time. "You don't have to believe anything." Patty's higher power came in the form of Jesus, as she knew him in the Southern Baptist tradition. Jesus, Patty promised, was there only to help, guide, comfort, and inspire. "You borrow whatever you need until you find your own," she said.

And somehow, I did just what Patty prescribed. I sidestepped all my intellectual baggage to look inward, suspending disbelief while I recovered. I imagined a power for good that could supply courage, wisdom, or calm. I imagined favorable things would happen if I waited patiently. The AA adage that *A bad day sober is better than a good day drunk* began to make sense.

One day at a time, Jesus and I got by without a drink.

But not every day was smooth sailing.

Deborah and I hadn't gotten together for weeks. I wanted to reconnect—and to know if she was dating anyone else. I decided to go find out.

Parking in the lot near her apartment, I couldn't see her front door. I got quietly out of the car and crept to the bushes on the path to her apartment. There I lurked deep in the foliage, wondering if she were home alone. To my surprise, my friend Cathy pulled up in her little Toyota coupe. Cathy Henderson was a lesbian I knew from both work and AA. She knew I was infatuated with Deborah. What the hell was she doing here?

I kept hidden until Cathy disappeared into Deborah's apartment, then slipped off in the dark to my car and sped away. My blood was thrumming hard in my veins as jealousy and anger burst my serenity. AA's advice flew through my mind like a hat in the wind . . . and I grabbed it.

HALT: Don't get too hungry, angry, lonely, or tired. I was angry; I was tired; I was probably lonely. Time to halt, take a moment, and get something to eat. I drove over to a local deli and ordered a corned beef on rye, fuming as I chewed and swallowed. I guessed Deborah was seeing more people than just me and Patrick, and it looked like one of them was my supposed friend Cathy.

The AA literature promised that if I followed their Twelve Steps to sobriety, I would find new freedom and happiness. I would know serenity, and old feelings of self-pity would disappear. But Deborah with Cathy instead of me? The image made me dark with rage and rejection. I felt doubly betrayed. I had to know what they were doing.

I drove back over to Deborah's apartment complex, cruised into the parking lot, and shut off my lights. Cathy's car was where I last saw it. But Deborah's car was gone. *Looks like they went out.* I decided to go looking for them and mess up their date.

There were just a couple of gay bars in the whole southern peninsula, where I lived and worked. Only one catered to women on Friday nights, so I went there first. I scanned the lot for Deborah's Mazda and found it. Steering into a parking slot, I held the wheel with my left hand as my right clenched repeatedly into a fist. If Cathy were in there with Deborah, I was going to punch her in the face. Cursing in my mind, I swore I would knock her down and kick her.

It was dark and quiet in the lot next to the club. I hurried to the entrance with anger pounding in my veins. Pulling out my driver's license to show the bouncer at the door, I rudely pushed past her through the narrow doorway. The clinking, talking, laughter, and music in the bar flooded my ears. I stood still and peered through the smoke-stained air to find Deborah. I found Cathy instead.

She locked eyes with me, then began moving quickly toward me. She read me perfectly and knew why I was there. Behind her I saw Deborah, holding a drink in her right hand and leaning against the bar with one foot resting behind her on its toe. She looked like a poised dancer. I pushed toward her just as Cathy barged into my path.

"Whoa there, sister!" she yelled through the noise.

"Fuck you, Henderson." I took a bladed stance, something I had not even thought about since Dad showed me how to box twenty-five years ago.

Cathy held out her hand to protect her face. "Don't do it. Don't. Get out of here." She was shouting but she sounded as if she were underwater. I wanted to smash her stupid ugly face. "Get the fuck out of here, girl!" she yelled.

I was scared to swing. I had never hit anyone in the face before. I couldn't do it. I grabbed her shirt, and she pushed me off. I tripped, lost my balance, and skipped a step to regain my footing. Our eyes glared into each other's. I took a breath.

The moment had passed. I turned and banged out the same door I had entered seconds before.

In the car, I put my head on the steering wheel and wept. *What is wrong with me? Why do I still do shit like this?*

It was after 9:00 p.m.; the meetings would all be over. I went home and reached for AA literature. I had a copy of *Alcoholics Anonymous*—the so-called *AA Big Book*—which offered me a collection of anecdotes illustrating how to avoid drinking. I read two stories. Then I called Patty.

And stayed sober, one more day. Without Deborah.

Taking responsibility for myself lifted my spirits. I struggled with my demons until glimmers of peace and moments of self-respect grew more frequent. I put together sixty days, then ninety.

After about six months, around Christmas of 1982, I was able to return Jesus to Patty. I had found or discovered my own higher power—a feminine force of goodness and well-being. I imagined what Judy called divine mother: a compassionate, warm, forgiving presence.

When anxiety gripped me and panic rose, I would turn my life and will over to my imaginary divine mother and the anxiety would diminish. If I were struck with anger or resentment and wanted to drink, I would rest in this supportive power until the emotions subsided.

In the AA program, I had to keep it clean on my side of the street. I could not entertain resentment, blame, or self-pity, for they led to a cycle of negative thoughts and a craving for alcohol. And thus, in the service of my sanity, I'd stumbled upon a channel to my own calm intelligence. I could breathe and trust an unknown power to guide me.

But addiction is sneaky; I should never have relaxed into complacence.

CHAPTER 27
FOR NO REASON

In June of 1983, with 360 days of continuous sobriety, I hopped in my '81 Honda Civic hatchback and took an afternoon drive on Highway 84 through Woodside toward the coast.

At the top of a forested hill, where the narrow highway met Skyline Boulevard, nestled Alice's Restaurant. A local hangout, it was named after Arlo Guthrie's infamous ballad. I slowed down and eyed the ramshackle wood-sided tavern. Motorcycles of every shape and color—long black Harleys, bright yellow crotch-rockets, hot red Ducatis, and stable blue BMWs—filled the parking lot. Would it be so bad to go in and have a beer with those guys?

But I didn't. I'd given up that life. I kept cruising westward, feeling sorry for myself. I dialed in some good music, slouched in the drivers' seat, and let myself feel a little blue.

Then I drove past a country liquor store and the thought flashed: *Oh, you should grab a beer.*

To this day I cannot explain why I pulled a quick U-turn and swerved into that parking spot.

Inside, I strode to the cooler, plucked a single Heineken, and stepped to the cashier. "Just needed a cool one!" I said jauntily, holding up the bottle. I forgot about my divine mother and higher power. When I got back to my car, I downed the brew in two swigs. Then I stared at the empty bottle.

What the hell did I just do? I changed my mind. I wanted sobriety more than beer.

I pulled my car out onto the highway going east toward home and safety. At six fifteen, I went to my usual seven o'clock meeting and started over.

This time around I ran straight into anxiety, depression, self-destructiveness, and other remnants of my wild and lonely childhood. Without the alcohol to block out feelings, I began to experience a new kind of emotional turbulence.

Several AA colleagues were in counseling with an addiction therapist. I didn't want to be someone who needed psychiatric help. Hell, I didn't want to be an alcoholic or a lesbian, either, if I were honest. But there they were, a few unpleasant facts.

Patty spoke highly of the work she did in therapy. Borrowing Jesus worked for me, so why not borrow her therapist, too? In August, I started going every Wednesday afternoon.

"Try to identify exactly what the feeling is," my new therapist said. "Pick one: angry, sad, happy, or scared."

Putting my head in my hands, I wracked my brain. We were discussing my fear of dating, especially asking someone out. But it seemed like everything we talked about involved buried feelings about my father. I took a stab in the dark. "Fear?"

"Well, don't ask me. Is it fear?"

We talked about it for a while. I could sense that behind fear was something else.

"I guess it's like I can't bear to be seen." I grimaced as I spoke.

"Shame," my counselor said. "Not your fault. It's toxic shame, transmitted to you by your parents."

I began to understand that I had absorbed warped emotions and destructive thinking from my childhood. I found that my loneliness came from a fear of intimacy. I learned that the years of hiding family secrets had embedded a sense of shame deep in my heart, which got triggered when someone got too close. Knowing that meant I could heal the wounds, maybe reroute the negative thought stream.

I stuck to a routine of several AA meetings a week. After working my way through Step Nine—making amends for harms I caused—I could claim one of the key AA promises: a new freedom and happiness. Even my performance at work improved. I could concentrate for longer periods and absorb more detail. My boss said I was a "good push/pop stack," which in computer lingo meant I could juggle priorities.

In fall of 1983, he promoted me to team manager.

CHAPTER 28
SPRING BLOOM

"What do you think happens after you die?" I asked Judy over a cup of Peet's Major Dickason's. We were lounging on her back deck one Saturday afternoon in the spring of 1984.

I looked up to Judy and followed her advice. She was the one who had taught me to put a towel in my mouth, as long as I didn't pick up a drink. Sitting outside, enveloped in the scent of the eucalyptus that draped over her fence, I had raised the eternal question. Morning light streamed over our shoulders.

Judy stirred some sugar into her coffee, then poured a stream of cream. "I have no idea," she said.

"All the spiritual stuff hints that something survives death, but what could it be?" I had been up late reading *Be Here Now* by Ram Dass.

"I don't worry about it. I just trust my higher power," Judy said, "even though I can't explain everything. That's enough for me."

"If consciousness comes from brains, and brains die, then consciousness has to die, right?" I persisted. The dark scent of my strong black brew filled my senses when I took a sip.

"Rikki, I've decided to have a baby," Judy announced, utterly dislodging my train of thought.

"What?" I said, shaking my head to wake up my hearing. I put my cup down and leaned forward, staring at her.

"I want a family. JoAnn and Jeanette did it. So can I," said Judy with a bright, mischievous glint in her eyes.

"That's great!" A surprised smile blossomed on my face. "What? You're going to find a dad?"

It was a decade before the so-called gayby boom, when it became common for gay families to have children. Adoption, artificial insemination, surrogate mothers, and the use of anonymous sperm donors were emerging as options for parents. A few of our lesbian friends had made unusual arrangements. They had created novel "nuclear" family shapes by asking a friend to coparent a child.

"Exactly! I'm going to ask a man I know to be the father."

"You are so brave! You can make your own version of a nuclear family," I exclaimed. I had just read *The World According to Garp*, in which the character Jenny gets the sperm she needs—from an unconscious, dying man—to have a baby on her own. I was relieved Judy had a better scheme than Jenny. "Who are you going to ask?"

"His name is Steve. You don't know him; he's not in the program," Judy said, referring to the AA fellowship. I thought it wise of her to choose a father who wasn't an alcoholic.

"When are you going to talk to him?" I asked.

"Tonight," Judy said, nodding with firm resolve.

"I've met with Steve and his partner, John, several times now," Judy told me a few weeks later. "We've all agreed on a parenting plan."

"Congratulations! What's next?"

"I wanted to ask if you would be my birth coach. Do the Lamaze thing or whatever it is with me. I'm going to try to do it without any drugs or painkillers."

My heart opened like a blue sky on a spring day.

"I would love that," I said with a wide grin. "What a privilege. Yes! Thank you."

I'd never cared much about children until I reached my early thirties, when suddenly babies delighted and fascinated me. The prospect of a boisterous, exuberant, miniature being entering my life as a tiny friend tickled me pink.

The fathers would have weekly time with the baby when he or she was older, but the first year was pretty much up to Momma Judy by herself. As a godmother I imagined helping care for the new child and running errands. But first, we prepared for birth.

We read everything we could about how couples were doing insemination and talked to all the parents we knew in the gay community. Impregnation seemed pretty straightforward if everything was in working order. We did not need a doctor. We took birthing classes and learned about the labor process, including ways to cope with contractions.

Happily, after just a couple of tries at home, Judy conceived.

We were having a baby.

After hours of breathing through contractions, a tiny, bloody head swelled into the world, as Judy's doctor shouted, "Push! Push now and get it done!"

Judy's lesbian obstetrician practiced at Stanford University Medical Center, and she allowed support teams in her delivery rooms. Two other godmothers and both dads joined us at the birth.

Immediately after Morgan slid into the world, the doctor handed her to the pediatrician. I fell in love with her the moment I saw her scrawny red body and heard her scream. Despite the squalling, I beamed as I watched the doctor clear her throat, nose, eyes. *What a precious spring blossom!*

Of course, I knew about the ideal of unconditional love. My friends and I talked about it as something our parents should have given us, something we were learning to give ourselves. But I had never felt anything like the freight train of devotion and affection that hit me for this tiny child. So innocent, so full of potential. And vulnerable, needing tender care. And happy, making all sorts of facial expressions and noises. And furious! Judy or I would walk her up and down, take her out for drives in the car, and bounce her endlessly in our laps to calm her cries. I never tired of her.

I knew I would simply love her without reservation her entire life, no matter what might happen. It was a strange kind of contract, not based on what I'd get in return, nor on any conditions. She brightened my whole world. I spent as much time with Judy and Morgan as I could, even moving from my Cupertino apartment to a duplex in Redwood City to be closer to them. And I let this little cherry blossom lighten my heart.

CHAPTER 29

I WISH YOU WELL

Judy handed me a small, homemade audiocassette tape labeled "Loving-Kindness" in block letters and smiled broadly.

"Try the visualization on this tape," she said. "It's really powerful."

It was May of 1985; Morgan was a couple of weeks old, and I was over at Judy's house in Belmont chatting with her about the secret to achieving serenity in our Twelve Step program.

In the 1970s and '80s many Americans traveled to India and Southeast Asia to learn the arts of meditation. Several had started teaching from newly established centers on the coasts. Judy had copies of recordings from some of them. They offered guided meditations and short discourses about spiritual practice called dharma talks. *Dharma* was a Sanskrit word that was hard to translate, but I came to think of it as meaning "a path to truth."

"You close your eyes and start opening your heart to someone you love. Easy as pie," Judy said with a laugh. "But then, you move to other people. You'll see."

"Did you like doing it?" I asked her.

"It's challenging! You even have to love yourself."

I looked at the cassette in my hand. "I don't know . . ." It didn't sound that attractive to me. As a recovering alcoholic, the thought of being that kind to myself made me grimace. I hadn't had a drink for two years, but the ability to forgive myself had not yet blossomed.

"You need it," Judy said.

Meaning what? Curious, I took the cassette.

I listened to that bootlegged tape over and over in the ensuing months.

The first time, I sat cross-legged on a little pillow on my living room floor. After slipping the tape into my battery-powered Walkman, I plugged in the headphones. When a soft male voice started up, I closed my eyes. The voice coached me to visualize a flame burning in my chest where my heart lay. Not a wildfire, but a gentle candle-like flame. Then, I was invited to think of someone I loved, whose face brought a smile to my heart. I envisioned my mother.

The next step was to picture inviting that person into the warmth of my sacred cavern where the candle burned. That was easy with my mom; in her fights with my dad, my sympathy had always been with her. When I thought of her, my heart always warmed. I had not yet articulated the ways she had abandoned us to our father's destructiveness, so neither had I acknowledged my buried anger. Paradoxically, that would happen as a result of bringing Mom into my candle-lit heart many times. The first time I did this exercise, though, I felt only a child's uncritical love.

The taped voice went on, encouraging me to completely forgive my mother for any residual judgments or resentments I held, until I could embrace her more fully. I remembered when she grounded me and how she used to tease me about being a hippie. Following the taped guidance, I released these slights and forgave her. Unexpectedly, this tiny shift brought tears of warmth and sweetness.

But next, I was guided to bring to mind a person for whom I felt anger or resentment. I chose a man from work named Mike. We were locked in a power struggle. The instructor's soft voice told me to invite Mike into my heart space. I didn't even like Mike sitting at the table in my office, much less inside my heart. At first it felt like an invasion of privacy. But I slowly relaxed my fears and let myself picture Mike's face near my inner candle.

"I wish you well," I recited aloud, following the tape's guidance. "I wish you happiness." Then came the kicker: The coaching voice told me to wish for the person in my heart the things that I wanted for myself.

I took a breath and, trying to be sincere, whispered. "I hope you get promoted to group manager. I wish you every success. I hope you win the outstanding employee award."

I felt something untwist in my chest, where a little space opened and a kind feeling flowed like warm honey. Loving-kindness, they called it. I honestly wished Mike every success. And wow, did that feel good. A brightness lit up in my mind and I noticed I was smiling. I felt my heart relaxing as if it were a clenched fist opening finger by finger.

The final visualization was the most radical. The coach said to bring an image of ourselves into our hearts. When I brought an image of myself into my sanctuary, I instantly felt I did not deserve to be there. That I did not deserve the warmth of loving-kindness.

"I forgive you," I said silently to myself anyway. "I wish you every blessing. May you be promoted and win the employee award." Slowly, I relaxed. *Maybe I don't have to be so hard on myself*, I thought with surprise.

Judy's tape offered a process I could use with anyone, but mostly I used it with myself. I would flow that loving-kindness into my own body when I felt attacks of self-condemnation. It would leave me feeling kindness for myself, as I might feel for a close friend. The meditation activated a powerful antidote to the self-criticism and painful feelings that I now knew were called shame.

CHAPTER 30
SOMEBODY AND NOBODY

"Some of us are going to a weekend meditation workshop next month," my AA friend Marcia told me after the Thursday night meeting in Menlo Park. Marcia suffered as much from the impact of her parents' drinking as from her own, so she attended both AA and Al-Anon meetings. Al-Anon was a Twelve Step forum for families and friends of addicts. Both programs recommended meditation. "You should come with us," she said.

I fake smiled. I wasn't comfortable with changes in routine. I had found a rhythm with sobriety and daily life that was working for me. Did I want to disturb my equilibrium with potentially disruptive experiences?

"An overnighter?" I asked, hiding my trepidation.

"Just two nights," Marcia said encouragingly. "The safest place in the world, full of meditators and fellow Twelve Steppers focused on their own problems!"

I laughed. I had to admit that if the other attendees were like me, they'd be too self-absorbed to pay much attention to me. I wouldn't have to worry much about their judgments. My only real challenge would be coping with feelings like loneliness, irritation, or anxiety that might arise. I thought I could handle that.

"Okay," I said tentatively. But maybe it would help move the sludge of shame from my head. "Why not?"

"Groovy." Marcia smiled and handed me a flier with all the details.

After parking in the long-term lot, I carried my gear up to the dormitory, following the hand-lettered signs. Then I made my way to the main building and followed another sign to the meeting room.

I found thirty or forty people sitting on floormats and cushions in a large study. A flutter of anxiety hit me; my eyes searched for a spot to put my stuff. Marcia and two others from our Twelve Step community rescued me.

"Come sit with us," Marcia said, gathering her shawl and notebook closer to create space. I plopped down next to her and greeted her friends. Then I settled in my seat and looked around.

One paneled wall sported floor-to-ceiling shelves of books. Large picture windows looked out over manicured grounds. In front of these windows two chairs flanked a small table adorned with flowers. In this pleasant room we would meditate together, listen to dharma talks, and ask questions of the leaders. Our guides for the weekend, Jack and Stephen, were in their late thirties and had studied mindful meditation in Southeast Asia.

"Have you worked with these guys before?" I asked my friends. "I've heard Jack on Judy's tapes, but that's my only exposure."

"Not face to face," said Marcia. "It's my first retreat. I know Stephen is friends with Ram Dass and his Indian teacher, Neem Karoli Baba."

"My first time, too," said Peter. "It's sounds pretty intense." The retreat schedule included only meditation, meals, and dharma talks during our three-day, two-night intensive.

"Glad I'm not the only one feeling a little scared!" I chimed in.

As dusk approached, we opened the first session by introducing ourselves and going over the agenda. Then Stephen led a meditation.

"Allow yourself to rest quietly and observe your breath," he began. "Just notice the gentle rising and falling of the chest." As instructed, I noticed my in-breath and out-breath.

"When the mind starts to spin a tale, let it drop. Gently return the attention to the breath," Stephen continued.

I sat thinking about the pain in my knee and the irritating closeness of the guy on my left. Someone coughed and it bugged me. Okay, that was the mind spinning. I noticed myself taking another in-breath, and then I was thinking about the nighttime arrangements at the retreat and whether I would be able to sleep in the open dormitory setting. *Will I be okay?*

"Notice the sensation of the breath entering the nostrils," Stephen said. I noticed my tickled nostrils, and then that I was hungry. Hungry and a little tired. *What time is this over? Will they have coffee in the morning?*

"The mind is always concerned with its security. It's always asking, *Am I okay?*" said Stephen. "As soon as I meet someone, I'm wondering, *Do they like me? Am I safe? What do they think of me?*"

I almost laughed aloud! That was exactly what went on in my mental background, like an endless jackhammer on a city street. *Am I sitting straight enough? Do I look earnest? How's my hair?*

Stephen was perhaps the most earnest and gentle person I had encountered in my life. His features—rounded nose; saggy, liquid eyes; and plump, pale lips—settled into a welcoming repose when he meditated. When he spoke with someone, his eyebrows lifted gently, and his ear lightly tipped toward the speaker in an invitation to share without fear. I tried to imitate his soft expression and unassuming but focused attention.

"What happens when one defensive mind gets in conflict with another?" Stephen asked rhetorically. He looked around the room, smiled, and closed his eyes.

"There's a little parable from a Zen master called Chuang Tzu about two boats passing each other in a stream," he said, opening his eyes. "Say you have a beautiful new boat"—he gestured the shape of a boat—"and you are so proud of it, and you go out on the river.

And out of the mist, you notice that another boat is heading straight toward you. You get angry and start shouting at the sailor in that boat. You start to threaten him." Stephen shook his fist and laughed at the spectacle of his angry self.

Where is he going with this? I wondered.

"But imagine if the mist suddenly clears and you see the other boat is empty," he continued.

I started to see his point.

"You are no longer angry at someone, because there is no one there." He paused a moment to let that sink in. He was hinting that there wouldn't be so much conflict if people weren't so ready to attribute evil motives to the guy in the other boat.

"But, take it one step further. What if you became an empty boat? What if there was no image of you to defend?"

We quietly let that penetrate. I imagined relaxing my defensive anxieties. *What if I weren't worried about what you think of me? What if I did not feel the need to show off, to be superior?*

"In Zen they say when you shed those fake self-images, you become *nobody*." He paused again. "In meditation, we are relaxing that fabricated self-image, letting it dissolve in open, empty awareness. Essentially emptying our boat of an anxious, separate self. Becoming *nobody*."

While Stephen talked, I peeked at some of the other meditators. I saw one of my friends sitting in a half-lotus, a shawl over her shoulders, her back straight. My back slouched and my knees ached. I unfolded one leg slightly while readjusting the other.

What if I did not need to look good?

Saturday morning, I wanted to ask Stephen a question. After raising my hand three or four times without luck, I switched tactics. At afternoon break I went looking for him outside, behind the main hall. I found him on the rear kitchen steps smoking a cigarette. He'd earlier admitted he was trying to quit; I loved finding him at a vulnerable moment. I bummed a smoke.

"I know you need a break," I said. "Can I ask one quick question?"

"Sure, go ahead," Stephen said, reluctantly nodding at me.

"Okay, basically, as you said, I want to empty my boat and become *nobody*," I said. "But, I'm not like you. You're a kind person. I'm not. I'm kind of angry, arrogant, and fearful. I don't like people that much. You have compassion. I just don't think I'm good enough for this Buddhist stuff." I took a big drag of the borrowed cigarette to cover my embarrassment, bent my knee to steady one boot against the wall behind me, and waited, glancing at him from behind my glasses.

Stephen sat on the step and gazed at me a moment. He took a deep puff of his own Marlboro and looked off into the woods. Then he met my eyes and pointed the cigarette's coal at me. "You have to be somebody before you can be nobody." He blew the smoke away from my face and broke eye contact.

That was it. I stared at the ground, waiting, but there was no more coming. He deserved his break, so I nodded and thanked him. I wandered over to an adjoining schoolyard's swing set.

Somebody *and* nobody? How did that work?

Did he mean I had to become a good person, a holy *somebody* like a Catholic saint? No, that didn't sound right. I thought he meant something more like this: I needed to respect myself. Before there would be spiritual discoveries, I had to believe my existence had value. If I had to do something—the way I'd done the Twelve Steps and therapy—to build my self-esteem, then I would have to do it.

I grabbed the chains and boosted myself into the swing. Rocking back and forth, I got a good movement going. Ralph Waldo Emerson once wrote that a self-reliant person should not follow a path, but should go where there is no path and leave a trail. His words encouraged me to trust my own lights and my personal sense of truth. I pumped my legs and got my swing going as high and fast as I dared.

Blood rushed through my arteries. I began to feel delight and sureness rise in response to Stephen's call to be *somebody*.

On Sunday afternoon, I drove away from the weekend sanctuary deeply refreshed. Ready to be someone who could find her own dharma—a path of truth. I did not need anyone's permission to live. I could stop raising my hand to ask somebody else for explanations, validation, or forgiveness. It struck me clearly that I alone was living my life—nobody else. This freedom gave me an exuberant sense of elation. Nobody could lay out my unique path to happiness and self-discovery. It was mine to unearth, or unfurl, and unleash.

CHAPTER 31

SELF-RELIANCE

"What stops you from asking for a review of the salaries?" my therapist asked from her leather swivel chair.

I'd been sober for two years now. In my fantasies, I pretended I had Emerson's kind of self-reliance, with unshakable trust in my creativity and intuition. But in the real world, I broke out in a sweat when I had to speak up for myself. I could advocate for a position at work meetings, but not for my well-being.

I sat cross-legged in my socks on the middle cushion of her blue couch and thought for a moment. "I don't really feel I deserve it," I said softly. My eyes locked on the carpet in front of me.

In therapy, I'd discovered I was a people-pleaser, which meant I sacrificed my well-being to make others happy—apparently not a healthy thing. From other AA members, I'd learned that my bravado and cockiness were not born of real self-confidence. And my friends said I had a streak of self-pity a mile wide. These attitudes fed my resentments, which made me feel pouty, victimized, and powerless. And at risk for taking a drink.

"Why are you whispering?" my psychotherapist whispered back, tilting her head and raising her eyebrows quizzically.

"I don't know," I said, looking up to meet her eyes as I cleared my throat. "I guess I feel like a phony, trying to pretend I deserve it?" My eyes squinted into a question.

My work colleague, Mike, the one I'd envisioned in Judy's heart-candle meditations, was a peer manager who received a higher salary than me. When I first learned this—he told me his salary during an argument about leadership—I'd resentfully accepted it as the norm. But the more I thought about earning less for producing equal value, the angrier I became. Mike and I had equivalent responsibilities, performance, longevity, and number of reports. We'd both gone to top schools, but he held only a bachelor's degree to my master's. It seemed like a clear case of gender discrimination. When I'd brought all this up in therapy, my therapist had jumped on the issue.

"Why would you not deserve it?" she pressed on.

"I'm not sure. It's just . . . it's . . . I feel so embarrassed." I reached for a cigarette.

"Don't light that yet," my counselor said. "Stay with that feeling." I held the cigarette between my fingers but did not grab my lighter.

"I feel so small, and . . . I don't want to be rejected," I brought out slowly. "What if they tell me I don't deserve a pay raise?" Admitting that made my face flush and my heart whump.

"It's that shame we talked about, Rikki. Toxic shame. You got that from being used and demeaned by a narcissistic alcoholic parent."

"I know," I replied sullenly. My right knee started bouncing against the couch cushion. "But knowing it doesn't take away the feeling of contracting like one of those roly-poly bugs. It's so hard to let people see me. Asking for something gets me seen."

"What do you want as an outcome?" she asked.

A thought flashed. *What would it be like to live for a few moments completely without self-pity? Or without fear?*

My knee stopped bouncing. I sat perfectly still like a Buddhist monk. Looking her directly in the eyes, I said firmly, "I want equal pay."

"Are you going to get that for yourself, or just complain?"

"I'm going to try to get that for myself," I affirmed, nodding to generate some conviction.

"In next week's session, let's role-play you talking to HR," she said.

We practiced a few times; then I submitted my petition to human resources. The inquiry found in my favor. HR increased my salary by 22 percent to match Mike's, effective April 1.

This seemed like the sort of thing Stephen meant by becoming *somebody*. I wanted more of it.

So, one evening in late June, I drove fifteen miles up the peninsula to the nation's then-largest metaphysical bookstore, East-West Books, on Castro Street in Mountain View.

The scent of sandalwood spiced the air in the warmly lit store. Images of Buddha, statues of Hindu deities, and well-tended plants perched artfully among the bookshelves, mingling with shawls, cushions, and incense.

In the Buddhism section, I found books on Japanese Zen, Chinese Ch'an, Southeast Asian Vipassana, and *The Tibetan Book of the Dead*. Among the Hindu literature, I picked up illustrated tomes on the Indian philosophy of yoga and translations of ancient scriptures like the Upanishads and Bhagavad Gita. A thick volume contained the translated text of question-and-answer sessions with a recently living Indian sage called Sri Nisargadatta, which surprised me because I thought Indian gurus were a thing of the past.

I found Stephen's publication, *Who Dies?,* Displayed with the collection of self-help books. Reading the paperback cover, I learned that the focus of Stephen's work was conscious dying. He had written a spiritual guidebook to serve both people facing death and those giving support. To me, it looked like a master training manual for becoming *someone* who could remain calm in the face of big fear. Inside, Stephen told the stories of people who found enough courage to share their experiences of dying.

I glanced at some exercises for working with people in discomfort.

These were particularly interesting to me because of the AIDS epidemic. I'd lost my first friend to AIDS two years ago in 1983, in the early days of the outbreak. Ted had gotten sick quite suddenly, as if from the flu. Within days, his illness had progressed to pneumonia. When he'd arrived at the hospital, the staff quickly identified his symptoms as what people dismissively called "the gay plague" and isolated him immediately.

By the time Texas Patty and I'd gotten over there to visit him, the hospital had jury-rigged an insulated cell for Ted in a negative pressure room, with plastic sheets draped over curtain rods around his bed. We'd had to wear booties, face masks, gowns, and head covers. His disease had advanced so deeply into his lungs that he'd barely been able to speak. Patty had kept up a cheerful banter by gossiping about our mutual friends, and I'd offered my wishes for his comfort. All three of us were helpless, heart-stricken, and shocked.

Ted never left that isolation room. I hadn't made it back for a second visit. In the years that followed, dozens of young, previously vigorous men in our community became deeply ill, with death looming over each of them. Everyone in my circle wanted to help. Various kinds of spiritual, psychological, and physical therapeutics became key topics of conversation. We all knew the healing work of Louise Hay, Marianne Williamson, and Elisabeth Kübler-Ross. Stephen's *Who Dies?* fit in that genre.

As I perused the first few chapters, I saw Stephen was also exploring the general nature of suffering—fear of death being one particular kind of anguish. The book asked how it would be if we could stay open, compassionate, and unafraid in the middle of difficulties. I glanced at a practice exercise for allowing fear to "float freely in the heart."

Standing in the store with the book in hand, I closed my eyes and recited to myself, *Allow everything to be as it is.* At that moment, everything included the spicy air, a tingling feeling of quiet excitement, the pressure of the wood floor against my feet, and high hopes for the power of meditation. All these experiences were easy to accept without resistance. But how would it be when I got to the harder stuff: irritation with other drivers, resentment of success, or anger over a minor slight (which happened every time my boss commented on my shaved or unshaved legs, and how many buttons were undone on my shirt)?

The thought of my boss sparked a tiny kick in my belly and my breath caught. *Allow it to be exactly as it is*, I thought. The tingle grew into a ripple of irritation, then roared into a wave of rage that tumbled through me in a matter of seconds. I always hated being disrespected by that guy, but I had never noticed it the way I did in that simple, clear moment. The thought *I demand respect!* rose in my mind like a line of women warriors, enraged and ready for battle.

I armed myself by purchasing Stephen's book and a round black meditation pillow covered in gold dragons. I took the paperback over to Judy and Morgan's house and read passages aloud while we took care of the baby.

After the retreat, I tried to keep alive the potent sense of vitality, worth, and well-being that I'd known while I was there. Most mornings, I sat on my dragon pillow for fifteen or twenty minutes, training my mind to relax with whatever was happening in my daily life. To my breath-counting, I added the simple practice of *letting everything be as it is.*

Of course, the shininess faded. Like most people I knew, I didn't meditate every day. But I had found a secret to deepening self-reliance. Sometimes my thoughts did quiet down in meditation. Then serenity and happiness would emerge without effort. Along with those moments came the natural composure and self-assurance of a contented *somebody*. I couldn't always summon her, but now I knew she was in there.

CHAPTER 32
BREATHING

On a damp winter morning at the end of February the following year, 1986, the clang of my home telephone startled me. I was sitting cross-legged on my dragon cushion, where I'd lost track of my breath count and drifted into silence. Creaking up from my half-lotus on the floor, I stumbled over to the bedside table on tingling legs.

"Hello?"

"Hi, Rikki." My older sister's voice sounded dead flat.

Linda now lived in Los Angeles with her husband and the two kids. Rick had left the university in Minneapolis to do research at the RAND Corporation, and Linda served as a vice president at the Federal Bank downtown. I glanced at the clock—6:40 a.m. She was calling before work.

"It's time," she said. "If you want to say goodbye to him, you'd better come now."

She meant our father, who had continued to struggle with depression, poverty, and drinking over the past decade. I had not paid close attention, but I knew that a couple of years ago, he'd been homeless and had gone to stay with a friend in Chicago. Then he'd been struck with lung cancer after a lifetime of chain smoking. Linda and Elizabeth, both in LA, had arranged for him to come back to California and enter the Veterans Medical Center on Wilshire. He had been there for a week or so and his prognosis was very poor.

I left a voicemail for my boss requesting family leave, packed a bag, and dashed off to the San Francisco Airport. It was easy to find a flight to LA. I bought a ticket and waited by the gate to board. Sadness permeated my chest like foul air. The tendons in my throat were taut. I needed to meditate for a few minutes.

Setting my bag on the floor between my feet, I sat in an erect posture, folded my hands in my lap, and shut my eyes. The blurry background thrumming of airport noise made me a little sleepy. I could not focus on my breath. Instead, I tried to let everything be just as it was.

My dad was only sixty. I'd held high hopes for him getting sober and finding peace. If I could do it, so could he. Half the reason I so desperately wanted sobriety was to prove to him there was a way out of the strangling darkness of his addiction. Now it was too late. Anger, regret, and loneliness churned within me like molten yellow lumps in a glowing red lava lamp. I gently observed them come and go.

I had told my father about AA, but the approach never worked for him. Maybe he never tried, I didn't know. He kept drinking. Elizabeth had cared for him in Chicago, where he expected her to clean up after his binges, comfort him in his helplessness, and take him to rehab. The ways he bullied Beth into putting his needs first and dismissed her life as inconsequential mirrored how he had treated our mother. A red blob of angry lava roiled in my luminous lamp.

Yet I resented everything—the whole universe—for ending his life this way. My dad was a generous, big-hearted, creative man who was eaten by inner demons. To my mind, that was not right. The higher power I wanted would not let that happen to him. His fate seemed so unfair. To tell the truth, I resented *reality*—which, I remembered from Stephen, was an attitude that created even more suffering.

Sitting at the airport, I kept breathing and let everything be as it was, magma lumps rising and falling. I was scared. What would it be like to be with someone who was dying? Fortunately, Stephen's book had prepared me. I understood what to do and how to be. I knew how to breathe along with a dying person, at their rate and depth, silently. And I knew to let our time together be about his death rather than my needs. I had practiced being an open, accepting, compassionate space so I could stay present in difficult moments. It was my daddy's time to die, and I wanted to support him as best I could.

Today, nearly four decades later, I marvel that I loved that man enough to open my heart to him. I'm surprised it was so important to me that I treat him with compassion. I cannot explain why I loved this abusive person. Like the child who once begged God not to punish her daddy, I just wanted him to be free and happy. I was not alone. My sisters both shared the intention to provide him a gentle, loving exit from the trials of this world, despite the scars we all carried.

The next morning, my sisters took me to the VA to see Daddy. We stepped into his room quietly, tears flooding our eyes and spilling over.

"Hi, Daddy," I whispered. "It's Rikki."

The shrunken figure wrapped in white sheets in the hospital bed opened his eyes. "Rikki," he said, not quite making eye contact.

Elizabeth nudged Linda. "Let's give them some time," she said. They left the room.

His eyes had closed again. The room was nearly empty of color. On the bedside tray next to a clear plastic water cup lay an open blue-and-white packet of Parliaments, which surprised me, but at this point, it made no difference.

I reached over and took his hand in mine. His fingernails were long and well-shaped, giving his hands a graceful line. Blue veins stood out starkly against his aging, mottled skin. His hand was dry and warm.

I closed my eyes, and as I brought him into my heart, I waited for emotions to race through me. But instead, I felt peace. I opened my eyes, and sitting there in silence, I began to breathe with him as I had learned from Stephen. Watching the rise and fall of my father's chest under the sheet, I found his rhythm and matched my respiration to his. After a few moments of this simple togetherness, on each exhale I allowed an "ahhh" to escape my lips. Just an exhalation, a relaxation, a letting go. I didn't do or add anything.

The complex feelings that I experienced at the airport on my way down to LA tickled at the edges of my mind while I kept my attention on our shared breathing. Then it dawned on me, watching my father's labor, that we are all in the same boat. Not just about money and success. We have the same psychological challenges with fear, envy, and so on. My father and I both struggled with secret, inexplicable shame. I was lucky enough to get sober and join a community, while he never found his footing.

I felt sorry for him, but I also felt so close to him that pity melted into grief for our shared human predicament. Our common search for happiness. Breathing in, breathing out, just hanging out with my dad, all my thoughts dissolved in the quiet rhythm. Dad and I had a good twenty minutes of uncluttered intimacy.

When my sisters came back in, we were just sitting there. My mind was still. No more bubbles in my incandescent lamp. Dad's hand was resting in mine, and we were breathing shallow, short, uneven breaths together. I had completely forgiven him, wanting only for him to be released from pain.

That night, our father passed in his sleep. Where did he go?

When the hospital called the next morning, my sixth sense said that some part of him had flown to freedom. It seemed like an invisible curtain had been pulled back for a few moments to allow his essence to pass from the world made of things to another realm made of thinner, lighter stuff. Perhaps it was all my imagination. Science told me only what happened to his physical body. It didn't even acknowledge the inner experience that was my father. Did *that* go out with his brain?

My rational mind fought the notion of a disembodied after-death awareness. All existence was supposed to be demystified by one of the sciences: Cosmology covered the emerging universe, biology detailed the workings of cells, psychology explained the behavior of individuals, and so on.

Yet I couldn't help but think the physical picture was incomplete if it didn't explain simple awareness. To my knowledge, science did not yet offer a theory or hint of one to explain how it is that we experience the sound of music or the feeling of freedom, rather than nothing. Although the scientific community assumed that brains generated this miracle, no one had the slightest clue how that could happen. I had the persistent hunch that something about my father's aware being did not die with his body, but I could not explain my intuition to myself.

The family gathered back at Linda's house and her in-laws came to sit shiva with us for that first day. We ate and lamented and told funny family stories. I wept with frustration and disappointment for the curious, creative, witty comedian who set me on my troubled path in life. And I realized that when I cried about losing my father, I was also mourning the family I almost had, the one that might have been. A family that could decorate a Christmas tree together in peace.

The next morning, I packed my bag and flew home, feeling nearly orphaned.

When I pictured my dad, as I did often in the months after his death, I yearned to talk to him about everything. How I'd been trying to write some short stories. How he'd been so cruel and demanding and needy and eventually pathetic and how he didn't have to live that way. How Buddhism offered hope of freedom. But I could speak to him only in my heart. There, I promised him that I would discover the secret of happiness for people like us, Richard and Richarda. And if I ever did find him in other life or world, I would tell him all about it.

CHAPTER 33
POSSIBILITIES

As a trained scientist, I didn't really think I would find my actual father in another realm. Still, I could not escape the intuition that there was something more to us than physicality and brains. I asked people around me if they thought any part of us survives death.

"Nope. Nothing. Nada. Gone with the last breath," said my sister Linda.

"Of course," my neighbor Lucy affirmed. "Heart and soul are totally independent of the body!"

"I don't know," said my brother-in-law. "It probably depends on what consciousness is, whether it comes from brains or exists on its own."

"We just will never know," my stepfather Hank said. "But I don't expect anything after death. There's nothing left when our bodies die."

"Maybe," I said to Hank. "But I just wonder if awareness might exist independently of brains. If there is any room in science for the idea that consciousness just exists."

"You're fooling yourself," Hank muttered.

I decided to look into it. On a Sunday morning, after I got home from my father's internment ceremony at the National Cemetery in LA, I took a bike ride down to my local bookshop. I expected that the huge Kepler's bookstore in Menlo Park would carry a good selection.

I steered my Schwinn road-bike toward the busy section of El

Camino Real. The warm spring sun had me sweating in my polo shirt and cutoffs by the time I arrived. After chaining up outside Kepler's football-field-sized bookstore, I went inside.

Brisk air conditioning cooled me quickly as I glided past histories and biographies to the science section, which, in recent years, had grown from two shelves to three full racks. I took some time, thumbing through nearly a dozen volumes before choosing three: Stephen Weinberg's *The First Three Minutes*, Richard Feynman's *Surely You're Joking, Mr. Feynman*, and Paul Davies' *God and the New Physics*.

At home, I stacked the books on my desk in the living room. On the worktable sat my new Macintosh computer, its rectangular box looking very much like a stereo speaker. I played *Zork* while I ate dinner, then picked up the Weinberg book. Later, I took it to bed with me.

This quickly became a habit, because what I was learning in that spring of '86 rocked my understanding of the world.

Slowly a picture emerged: quantum science offered a very strange view of our reality. A deep look at matter shattered the idea that it is made of atoms. Feynman and Davies taught me that, to my astonishment, in reality there are no *things*. Intricate, exhaustive experiments with tiny particles like photons, electrons, and protons throughout the twentieth century revealed that the imagined atom and its parts are not actual entities. A particle is just a mental picture invented to explain phenomena observed in experiments.

No atoms? Then what are we made of?

According to quantum studies, we appeared not to be chunks of matter, but some other enigmatic stuff that obeyed different rules than classical physics. I read that Niels Bohr, a founder of quantum mechanics, famously claimed that what really exists are *fields of possibility* that might manifest something, such as location or velocity, time or energy, and particle or wave characteristics. Because Bohr's laboratory was in Copenhagen, these ideas were later called the Copenhagen interpretation.

All this was so challenging to understand that my eyes often glazed over. I grasped just one thing in the rich, complex, and mind-boggling story: Whatever is the substance of our world, it is not *stuff*. We sense things like trees, phones, rocks, and dogs, but what they are made of is described by modern physics as a field of possibilities. Since that field manifests matter, light, and energy, could it not also manifest awareness?

I felt excited, skeptical, and flabbergasted, but I couldn't help asking: Could the world be made of a non-material, self-aware substance of some kind?

My AA friends made fun of me, always carrying a book and sneaking off to read when I got bored. None of them shared my esoteric interests. I thought that Robin and Brian, two friends at work who were exceptionally well-read, might share my excitement for these ideas, so I cornered them at lunch in the cafeteria one day.

"So what?" Robin asked, after I told her what Bohr said about reality.

My jaw dropped.

"But this changes everything!" I answered. Although these quantum discussions were over half a century old—they had been around since the '20s—they were not common knowledge. They were too disruptive to common sense, too fantastic, and almost too metaphysical to gain popular support. What I'd learned was not new, but it was completely fresh. Couldn't they see it?

"This is not some new age stuff. This is Schrodinger, Bohr, Heisenberg!" I pointed out.

"Noticeably not Einstein," Brian said.

"Like, what does it matter, though?" Robin challenged me, chewing a bite of a chicken sandwich.

"Well Jesus, Robin, if we're made out of a non-material substance, what are we? If we are not really chunks of dead matter, it leaves open all kinds of possibilities. Maybe awareness is part of existence. Maybe we aren't just these bodies." I squashed my cigarette coal into the ashtray, crushing it.

"Whoa, don't go off the deep end," cautioned Brian. "Quantum mechanics is just a theory. We're still here paying bills." Brian was my boss and an avid reader. He often talked about some French philosopher's latest ideas about sexual identity and social roles being "constructed," not given. Robin and I couldn't always follow Brian, but we both respected him.

"But quantum mechanics is a damn good theory, and it works under every circumstance," I countered. "It must be saying something about our reality."

"The equations work—they are useful mathematical tools. But you can't assume they represent some real thing," Brian said. He took a sip of his coffee and looked at me over his glasses.

"Of course, I can!" I exclaimed. "That's the whole point of science in my mind. Not just to do engineering, but to describe reality!"

"You burden science with too much ontological responsibility." Brian raised his eyebrows and shook his head. "You just told us Bohr himself said we can't know the real entity. Fine. But there's absolutely no evidence of other-worldly existence at all."

There was an irritating bit of food or fluff stranded in Brian's lengthy beard. I tried to ignore it and focus on the matter at hand.

"But what about the mind itself? That's not a material substance," I countered, my confidence slipping.

"What about it? It's what brains do. Seemingly miraculous, perhaps, but hardly evidence of a transcendent reality," Brian said

"You are always doing this, trying to prove some crazy metaphysics," Robin added dismissively.

That hurt my feelings. I was not trying to prove anything; I was grappling with the disconcerting facts.

"Do you know the root of the word 'enthusiastic'?" Brian asked me. "It means to be possessed." He winked and nodded at me.

I felt the sting of being judged and dismissed. "OK, but you have to admit our ordinary non-quantum notions about reality are just wrong!" I said, trying to recover some dignity.

"But are they? Yes, engineers use quantum mechanics in rocket ships, lasers, motherboards, and MRI scans. But does that mean reality is non-material? Of course not." Brian said, closing the conversation.

But it didn't end the conversation in my mind. I now knew that some of the smartest people in the twentieth century thought that our world might fundamentally be made of something insubstantial that can appear as the characteristics of matter, energy, light, and maybe awareness. If so, Buddhism might be onto something real—even if none of my science-minded friends thought so.

I kept meditating and letting things be as they were while I continued to read up on developments in cosmology, evolution, and the physics of tiny things.

CHAPTER 34
FAMILY

"I'm promoting conservation and preservation for Woodside," my friend Susan told me. She was running for mayor of the little town on the peninsula, northeast of Silicon Valley. "People with big money are moving in, tearing down homes, and putting up humongous mansions."

"I'd hate to see Woodside turn into Cupertino," I agreed. Woodside remained a quaint, hilly, wooded village with one streetlight in the Santa Cruz Mountains. Cupertino had become a crowded suburb of four- and six-lane boulevards.

"In this economy, you should get in on real estate," Susan told me.

"What does that mean, 'in this economy'?" I asked her.

"It means that right now, the fastest way for you to make more money with the money you have is to invest it in real estate," she explained.

"I don't have any money," I admitted. "I haven't saved anything."

"But you have stock options, right?"

"Yes . . . " I said hesitantly.

One of the great things about working in Silicon Valley was getting stock options as part of my compensation. My performance was always well-rated, and three promotions had raised my pay grade. Options accumulated without me paying attention. I ignored them because I didn't quite understand them, and my work associates said to leave them alone.

Maybe it's time to figure this stuff out, I thought. I was thirty-seven; if I was going to have a child of my own, it was time to get started. The idea had been growing quietly in a corner of my mind since Morgan entered our lives, but owning my home was a prerequisite.

I checked later that week and was shocked to find that my options were worth over $40,000. That would be a 20 percent deposit on a $200,000 home!

My realtor soon found a comfortable two-bedroom bungalow with a charming backyard in Redwood City on the San Francisco Peninsula, halfway between Morgan's house and work. The perfect place for me to start a family.

I moved in at the end of 1987. I had a secure job, owned my home, and could afford childcare. I began to formulate a plan.

On Morgan's third birthday in April 1988, she and I played hide-and-seek all over Judy's balloon-and-streamer-decorated house, crawling under tables and behind chairs. It might have been the most fun I'd had in my adult life. We laughed and screeched and covered our eyes while counting to ten. Several of Judy's friends, including two more godmothers to Morgan, had come over to celebrate with cake and ice cream.

"You love playing with her so much," godmother Pat laughed at me. "When are you going to have your own child?"

I looked at her with a bright and mischievous smile. "I've been thinking about that," I said. "Now that I have the house."

"Really?" Judy and godmother Sue chimed together. This was the first time I'd said anything out loud.

"Yeah. I have this friend at school," I said, "and I'm thinking of asking him."

"School" was San Jose State University, where I sometimes took classes in the evenings. The friend was Nick, a gay grad student I'd grown close to in the last year. I was nervous but determined to at least ask him.

In May, I gathered the courage to raise the idea of parenting with Nick. We met for dinner before classes on a Thursday evening.

"Nick, you know I have a goddaughter, right?" I asked over Vietnamese noodles. I felt a nervous jitter in my chest.

"Yes." He tilted his head and squinted at me. "And?"

"And I'm ready to have my own child. Do you think I could do it?" My heart started to thud.

Nick set down his fork. "You'd be a great mother!" he said, and held the eye contact.

"Really?" I looked away. My palms were sweating.

"Of course! I mean it, Rikki. You are very loving and tuned in to children," he said.

"Well, that's good because, I wanted to ask you." I looked up and made eye contact again. "Would you consider being the father?"

Neither of us moved for a good five seconds.

Then Nick's face opened in a brilliant, shy smile like a little boy's. "Me? Really?" he said.

I beamed in reply. "You're sensitive, smart, handsome, and good. Of course, you!"

Nick grinned from ear to ear. He promised to talk with his partner and think seriously about it.

A few weeks later, Nick and I got together with Robert at their apartment to talk about how it might work. Robert was the dreamer in the relationship, and he was thrilled.

"I think it's a wonderful idea!" he exclaimed.

Nick was more practical than idealistic. "And a big responsibility," he said. "I want to be sure we can give this child a good start." He had been a schoolteacher in earlier days and knew a bit about child development.

"But a responsibility we will relish!" Robert said. He grinned at Nick and got a smile of appreciation in return.

I tried to make clear my intentions about the parenting roles. "I want to be responsible for all the costs. I don't want anything from you guys." Nick was a student and Robert worked part-time. It made sense for me to cover the expenses. They looked at each other, then back at me, and nodded. "Let's put it in writing to show my intent."

"We're still legally accountable," Nick pointed out.

"Yes, but if we ever get in a dispute, this document will show my intention to be the sole provider," I replied. I took a breath and looked away. "And I don't know how to say this, but I want to make all the decisions." Then I met Nick's gaze. "About school, daycare, doctors, and so forth." I waited.

"I trust you," Nick said slowly. "You are obviously so committed. You are the one taking on all the risk and all the work."

I nodded. It was true.

"If we had serious disagreements with you," he continued, "we would discuss it."

"That sounds good," I said.

Robert looked on. "What about visitation?" he asked.

"Oh, you guys would have visitation rights like any parents," I said. "We'd work that out when the baby is older."

"This all sounds beautiful," Nick said, leaning back in his chair and exhaling. "It's just, I want to be sure I'm ready."

"You'll be a wonderful father, Nick," Robert said.

Nick's face brightened again and a smile pulled at his lips. "You really think so?" he asked Robert softly, a full grin emerging.

There was a bottom-line issue I still had to bring up: If I started drinking again, I knew I would be a danger to my child.

"One more thing. I want you or my sister Linda to take custody of the child if I ever start drinking," I said. "Okay?"

Robert's eyebrows shot up in surprise. He and Nick both knew my history with alcohol and that I'd been sober for five years.

"I can understand that," Nick said gently, using his validating, therapist voice. "But I can't imagine that would ever happen."

"I agree," put in Robert.

"Thank you. I appreciate that. Addiction is unpredictable though. I don't want my child exposed to a drunk parent," I said.

And thus, we came to our agreement . . . we were going to have a baby!

It took only two tries; in November my pregnancy began.

The hormones released in my body to support the growth of the tiny fetus aroused feelings of well-being, pleasure, and general happiness. The thrill of starting my own family brightened the blue in my eyes and put a blush on my cheeks. As my belly rounded and my condition became obvious, people at work and strangers on the street treated me with extra consideration and kindness. I loved it! I enjoyed being pregnant more than any other period in my long life.

Our Lauren Catherine (who nicknamed herself Magnolia) was born in August 1989, four years and four months after Morgan Lise. We were made to go together. A perfectly formed tiny person, she fit so snugly against my chest that it was obvious she was mine. She drank all the milk I could provide, grew pink and chubby, loud and beautiful. I was able to take a sabbatical from work and spend three months at home with her before we had to use child care. Then I made arrangements for her at a work buddy's house a few miles from my office. Two friends and I hired a fourth to watch our babies from nine to five. I bicycled over during lunch hour every day to feed her and play with the kids.

I had my own little clan! Our nuclear family was the four of us: three parents and a child. Daddies Nick and Robert saw Lauren every week, and we all became closer friends. We were happy chosen kinfolk.

For a little while.

Just a month after Lauren's birth, Nick was diagnosed with an astrocytoma. The doctors described it as a slow-growing brain tumor. He underwent surgery to remove it from his cerebellum in December. Afterward, we thought we were in the clear, but two months post-recovery, in February 1990, Nick had to endure another craniotomy. I asked my nurse friend Caroline about the prognosis for astrocytoma. She grimaced, then tried to recover with a hopeful smile.

"Some of those are benign," she tried, "but . . . it could be a glioblastoma." *Glioblastoma*, I learned, was a very bad word in the world of brain cancer.

I prayed that it was benign.

A few weeks later, in October, I was nursing Lauren in my living room, watching the five o'clock news, when the television began to shake. I jumped off my bouncing couch, held my baby tight to my chest, and ran out to the middle of the backyard, far from telephone poles and wires.

For another ten seconds, the ground beneath me churned. I sat down on the grass. Through the plate glass window, I saw my television and its cabinet tip over, smothering the blanket where I often lay Lauren. My favorite art deco dancer slid off the piano and books dropped to the floor.

I waited outside for aftershocks. After a few minutes, I crept carefully into the house, avoiding the broken glass and debris on my floor. Lauren started to fuss.

I was still dazed when the trill of my doorbell clanged in my ears. *Who could that be?* I wondered. I bounced the bundle in my arms as I went to the door.

"Hi!" A smiling Robert stood outside in khakis and a loose jacket, his hands in his pockets.

"Oh, hi, Robert!" I was delighted to see a friendly face.

He came into the front hall and looked around. "Are you okay?" he asked. His face, pale with pink cheeks, was creased with worry but his soft brown eyes were unafraid. He was here to help me. "Nick's at work."

Nobody ever showed up to help me like that, except my sisters.

"Yes, well, things are a mess, but . . ." I rubbed Lauren's tiny body. And standing there viewing the debacle, I felt a shift, though I did not understand it fully at the time. I wasn't a sole survivor anymore. Somebody had my back.

"Well, you take care of little Lauren while I get this cleaned up," Robert said.

Lauren was less than three months old, already embraced and protected by three loving parents. Now I knew she would never lack for family.

Nick recovered, and the following year we celebrated Lauren's first birthday at Nick's family's favorite vacation spot in Pajaro Dunes on the coast. We all felt so full of love and promise that happy day. But weeks after, Nick again began to feel dizzy and confused. He didn't want another surgery; he tried to ignore his symptoms. In September 1990, his headaches and vertigo were severe enough that Robert and I asked Nick's older sister to take him to the hospital. We knew Nick would listen to her.

A surgery was scheduled a few days out while the doctors put Nick on a regimen to reduce swelling. But Sunday, the day before the surgery, he had a severe stroke from the tumor pressing on an artery.

I called a friend to watch Lauren while I raced to the hospital to meet Robert. Nick's sisters were already there.

"He's in a coma. The doctor says he cannot survive off the breathing machine," Robert told me in a broken, shattered voice.

"What happens next?" I asked, whispering.

"We need to agree to let him go," Robert said through streaming tears.

I had to wait a moment for my breath to come back. "Oh my god. Are you okay? Is Nick's mother coming?"

"She's on her way," said one of Nick's sisters.

"I'm all right," said Robert.

Together, as Nick's family, we agreed to give the order to disconnect the machine. Robert and I, along with his dear friend Kitty, stayed by Nick's bedside as he disengaged from his body.

In the small treatment room, the three of us stood close to Nick's bed and touched his hands and shoulders. His nurses saturated his blood with oxygen so he could easily live several minutes without a breath. Then they turned off the breathing machine. We stood by him quietly, waiting. He would breathe, or die. He did not breathe. Tears streamed down our faces as we gently gave Nick our blessing to leave. In twenty minutes, a doctor pronounced him dead.

We remained by the body for a while, talking softly to Nick and releasing him to the other side. Or to nowhere. Or, as I hoped and increasingly suspected, to home.

In November, Robert's sister invited Lauren and me to the Thanksgiving gathering. With unexpected generosity, his brothers, sister, and mother soon became our extended clan. I especially bonded with his mother, Jean, my "mother-out-law" and good friend, who fully acknowledged Lauren as Robert's daughter. We spent many a holiday at her home in Palo Alto, and Lauren would accompany her Grandma Jean in Lake Tahoe during the summers.

Our newly shaped nuclear family limped harmoniously along. Robert's cheerful disposition and supportive nature proved more important to me than I ever imagined. At thirty-nine I'd found my place in the world, as Lauren's mother and coparent with Robert.

I had everything . . . except the perfect woman to share it all with.

CHAPTER 35
DANCING IN THE UNIVERSE

"Welcome to the way the world should be!" rang a woman's voice outside my berth's portal.

"Woo-hoo! The line was so long I thought we'd never get on," laughed another.

"Hang on, I know that voice," cried my bunk mate for the week.

My old buddy Cathy, whom we all called by her last name, Henderson, dashed out of our room into the hall. We were going to be great roommates: Henderson was an extrovert who knew everybody and loved to entertain with her quirky humor. I was an introvert who'd forgotten how to socialize since quitting drinking eight years earlier.

When Lauren turned two, I decided I needed a break from the cycle of full-time tech manager/full-time mommy/no-time Rikki. My body craved sleep, and I yearned for adult company. So, after delivering my toddler to the adoring hands of her Aunt Linda, I'd headed to San Diego, ready to sail on an all-women's cruise and have an adventure, make some new friends, maybe meet somebody.

"What's going on out here?" I smiled, peering out the doorway.

Henderson glanced over at me. She'd been regaling four young women in shorts and tank tops, who shared the corner suite, with stories of past travels.

"Meet my fellow rabble-rouser, everyone." She pointed to each woman in turn: "Kali, Megan, Terri, Rosalie. This is Rikki."

Hundreds of lesbians from all over the world had gathered on this cruise ship hosted by Olivia Travel. Most were at least partially in the closet. No one I knew ever did anything gay—like hold a lover's hand—in public. But on the boat, we would be free to be our natural selves, without fear of judgment or violence. We could dance, hug, and flirt. We could share our usually forbidden and repressed women's energy.

We all hugged each other, after which Kali pulled us into a laughing group squeeze. But only one face interested me—Terri's. I recognized her strong jaw and full, wide mouth of straight teeth. Bright, wide, sea-blue eyes with crinkly laugh lines. Short blond hair brushed as if she were running in the wind. Our employer, Tandem Computers, used her image on posters to promote healthy activities like family runs and baseball teams.

Once I saw her, it was all over for me.

Terri was a fresh orange in a bowl of walnuts. And when we locked eyes, I felt a click, a resonance in my whole body.

Terri's companion on the cruise—a short, adorable dark-haired woman named Rosalie—clocked me right away. She gave me a challenging look that I ignored. I was sure Terri and I connected—she gave me *something* in that first glance.

Back in my berth a few minutes later with Henderson, I unpacked my clothes in a daze. What I yearned for without naming had happened; in a matter of minutes, I'd found a new home for my heart. I wanted to sing like Tony after he met Maria in *West Side Story*.

"Aiyee!" Raucous screams rang out behind me the next morning at the beach, but when I turned to look, I lost my grip on the slippery, writhing banana boat and splashed into the churning waves.

The six of us—Terri, Rosalie, Megan, Kali, Henderson, and I—had teamed up for an all-day onshore excursion. Morning in the ocean, afternoon in the jungle.

"Oh no!" I screeched, gurgling. "Bye!"

I bobbed about thirty yards offshore in a warm, calm bay off the Baja coast. Was it possible to laugh out loud and swim for land at the same time? I gave it my best shot.

"Let's do the Jet Skis," Megan shouted as she ran toward me on the beach, her feet sinking into the white, soft sand.

"Yeah, where's the rental guy?" asked Rosalie as she joined us.

Terri sat down on a towel. "We should all wear helmets," she said. A seasoned mother, she tended to look out for her friends' health and safety.

"Will do, Mama," teased Rosalie.

By the time we finished Jet Skiing, we were all exhausted and starving. We ate our picnic lunches, made from the breakfast buffet on the ship, sitting on our towels. Kali went off to arrange a guide to drive us to the interior rain forest. Around two o'clock, we piled into a dirty white van with questionable tires.

Plants with leaves the size of bicycles crowded the rutted trail through a dense jungle. After bumping along for an hour or so, the van stopped. Our driver got out and opened the doors.

"Okay, out here for rope swing," he said. He pointed to the ledge overlooking a still, deep pool in the middle of a rushing stream.

We piled out and crowded round the jump point. Hanging from a huge branch that arched over the pool, we spied a twenty-foot rope knotted every couple of feet near the bottom. The tour guide jumped into the river and grabbed the rope, swimming it back to the muddy hillside where we clustered together in awe.

"Do we put our feet on those knots?" I asked, looking out at the river and back at the rope. Fear tingled in my throat and my limbs went slack.

Shit, I have to do this. Terri's watching.

Grabbing the upper knots, I leapt off the cliff. When the rope swung out above the water, my grip gave out. I dropped. Cool water shocked my skin, and I sank in over my head. A frisson of panic rushed through me; I swam quickly to the river's edge and crawled out.

But I did it!

And she saw me.

The cruise ship itself was a hotbed of onboard activities: swimming, dancing, card games, gambling, and live entertainment. I didn't care what we did. Having Terri nearby energized me.

I tried to keep her within sight without being obvious. Henderson provided a good daytime social cover, with her gregarious chatter. Most mornings around seven o'clock, I fetched first-round coffee for everyone in Terri's suite, just to be able to see her early in the day.

"Thanks, Rikki," Rosalie said coldly.

"Thanks, Rikki!" Terri gave me a brilliant smile and sat down on the bed across from me. "I heard you have a daughter." She asked me, "How old?"

"Oh, she's just two, the little pun'kin." I felt the glow that always arose when I talked about Lauren.

"Mine are four and six," Terri told me. She got up to fetch her wallet where she kept their photos.

All I wanted for the rest of the cruise was to get Terri a drink, listen to her laugh, and study her charmingly animated hands while she talked.

One evening, when the boat was cruising off the Baja coast in an endlessly dark sea, our troupe joined a gathering outside on the bar deck. The night glittered with deep-set starlight. Most of the ladies were drinking; Henderson and I were the sober holdouts. R.E.M. and Bonnie Raitt flooded the salty air and blackness that surrounded us. I caught a contact high from my friends as our dancing and singing got rowdier and more sensual.

I found Terri in the circle of dancers and pulled her to my spot on the floor. She laughed as our bodies rocked and rolled to Genesis's "I Can't Dance." Her athleticism gave all her moves a natural grace that made me ache with yearning. I was careful not to make contact, fearing my touch would burn us both. But when the music faded, my hand reached out to brush her sweaty bangs away from her eyes. We smiled at each other.

Suddenly Henderson yanked on my arm and pulled me away.

"Hands off, girlfriend," she told me as she positioned me next to a long, curved glass bar.

"What? Why?" I complained in my whiniest voice. I turned to see where Terri had gone.

"She's with Rosalie. They're a thing."

Of all the lesbians in all the world, she had to be the one to tell me. *Why is Henderson always in my way?*

"I don't care," I said.

I glimpsed Terri in the crowd a few yards away. I saw—and more importantly felt—the glow of her wide smile, ivory teeth, and full lips. A warmth inside me throbbed in response. When her eyes connected with mine, I knew we were already intimate. Just dancing with her out in the universe on the deck of a wild and crazy vessel somewhere in the sea had given me a clear glimpse into her soul, her deepest dreams and values.

"Cool your jets," Henderson said. She ordered two Cokes and spelled it out for me. The South Bay lesbian community was small—perhaps a few hundred people. We knew each other by one or two degrees of separation. We could date the women our friends broke up with, but—like honor among thieves—we had an unspoken code to respect active relationships, even though she had broken it years earlier.

While I didn't let Henderson keep me from Terri during the cruise, once back at home, I pulled back, vowing to bide my time.

"This is circuit training," explained our coach, Trudy, to the noon weight lifting class. "I'll set up a series of stations, and you will move from station to station."

During my pregnancy, I had gained thirty pounds that still clung to my small frame nearly three years later. But recently I'd made up my mind to work out, shed fat, and reclaim my agility. Tandem offered two on-campus gyms. One was in a building adjacent to mine, and the other was about a mile from me. I chose that more distant gym; which happened to house Terri's office as well.

"At each station you'll do thirty seconds at one weight, then increase the weight, do another thirty seconds, then increase and another thirty," Trudy continued. "Then switch stations. One minute rest."

Lifting looked easy when she demonstrated it, but when I did the reps, my arms or legs or abs burned like hell halfway through the second set at every station. I took cheater breaks, hoping no one noticed.

And then, during the second week of weight training, Terri walked through the door. Some hormone like adrenaline or dopamine flooded my system. I felt suddenly alert and energized. My skin tingled as if I'd just emerged from a hot shower. My biceps and shoulders puffed up with fresh power.

Terri lifting weights was the image of vibrant energetic health. At five-foot-four and less than 110 pounds, she seemed always to be in motion, with her swept-back hair, Adidas runners, and muscle tank top. A pink blush rouged her features as if she'd just finished a 10K. The muscles in her swimmer's shoulders and runner's legs bulged and relaxed as she pumped the iron. When she did crunches, a six-pack appeared on every lift.

I concentrated on appearing strong, smooth, and powerful—*make it look easy*—while trying not to say anything stupid. But it was a Kimmy Gibson situation all over again—my crush on Terri made me into a bumbling fool.

Noticeably so.

After class, my friend Tim jabbed me with an elbow. "What got into you today?" he asked with a teasing smile.

"What?" I frowned at him as I walked into the hallway.

"Just can't take your eyes off her?" He leered and sang a line from the popular tune.

"Shhh!" I blurted. My eyes looked furtively around, and I pushed him back into the gym. "Quiet!"

"Good luck," Tim whispered, wearing a lascivious grin.

"Henderson." I'd called her from my desk at work after the workout session. "It's been over six months. Is she still seeing Rosalie?"

"Is who still seeing—oh! You mean Terri," Henderson answered. "They broke up from what I hear. But be careful, feelings might still be raw."

I didn't hear the last bit because a shaft of bright, happy energy shot through my whole body.

"Yowza!" I jumped up from my desk and sat down again. "Yes! Okay, yikes, I'm going to ask her out."

"It's a little soon, Rikki," Henderson warned. "You're gonna look like a shark."

I drove over to Terri's building the next morning and dropped by her office to talk about my sudden new interest in the fonts we used in our customer manuals. Terri was the graphic designer on one of our department's projects. What fonts did she plan for the operating manuals? What graphics had they developed to illustrate technical ideas?

"These are my latest," she said brightly, bringing up a window on her Macintosh. I leaned over her shoulder and heard my heart hammering. I couldn't focus on the screen.

"They look great," I said, with my face locked into a shy but probably flirtatious smile.

We stumbled through nervous chatter, until by some miracle—was it my higher power?—she invited me over for dinner.

Dinner turned out to be magical. Everything clicked for us. Soon I got babysitters on evenings that Terri's kids went to their dad's. After dating exclusively for a few months, we decided to spend time together as a fivesome. We looked like a perfect family: Terri with her girls aged seven and five, and Lauren the youngest at three. We fit together, all of us average height, with the same light coloring and similar builds. I loved the kids, the trips to Great America, the big dinners, and the feeling of belonging. Everything I wanted was coming to life. Spring unfurled into summer and fall. We celebrated our first Christmas together. Terri dressed all the girls in white dresses with red hair ribbons, and we went to Mass.

Another year passed, and another. After three years together, in the fall of '95, we started looking for a home with four bedrooms. My career had grown along with Tandem's success. As a technical program manager, I now made a $100,000 a year plus stock, and I had equity in my Redwood City home.

Thank you, I breathed to some invisible something. *Please don't abandon me.*

On a planet of five billion people, I wondered how many enjoyed blessings like mine. What did I do to deserve it all? Was something watching out for me?

"I can't do this anymore," Terri told me on the phone one December evening, about two months into our house-hunting.

"Do what?" I said, as a dull roar flooded my ears and adrenaline slammed into my arteries. *What can't you do?* I panicked, knowing Terri did not want full-time kids. Terri's girls lived half-time at their dad's. So, to Terri, Lauren was a problem: a full-time six-yar-old, and not a quiet one.

"I need my own life," Terri said, getting to the point. "I'm sorry. I love you, but I can't deal with a full-time child."

What? My brain scrambled to grab on to something that made sense. All the air had left my lungs. *What? When did she decide? Is it really over? What can I do?*

I knew she wanted me to discipline my daughter more, but it wasn't my style. I was feeling my way through parenting, not wanting to repeat the neglect of my early life. I had gone to parenting groups, read books, and talked to other moms. It was not easy. How could you get your child to cooperate without destroying their spirit?

I loved them both dearly, Lauren and Terri. There had to be a way forward.

"Can we try therapy?" I asked, unable to hide my frustration.

We hired a therapist, Marlena, who had recently published a book about undefended love. The three of us had met on the cruise ship years ago. As soon as we got started, Terri complained that Lauren manipulated me.

"If she disobeys you, you let it slide," Terri stated.

"What am I supposed to do? Hit her?" I glared at Terri with steel eyes.

"No, of course not." Terri looked to the therapist. *Help!* her eyes pleaded.

"Maybe you could bring Lauren in so I could observe you together?" Marlena suggested.

"No," I said, bristling. Suddenly I felt angry and defensive. "Under no circumstance am I going to let my daughter become the identified patient. No."

"Hmm. That's an interesting response." Marlena waited, staring at me in silence.

"If we don't change something with your parenting, I can't go on," Terri repeated.

I froze. I was trapped. I couldn't do things that I thought would hurt my little Lodi. Yet I couldn't bear to lose Terri.

"Well, I'm open to new techniques," I said, betraying my desperation. A poisonous fear leaked from my gut into my veins.

"We're out of time for today," Marlena interjected gently. "Rikki, why don't you pick one thing to try and experiment with it this week. Set a clear boundary around meals or bedtime. How does that sound?"

It sounded as if I had little choice but to nod.

"Okay," I mumbled.

"Lauren, I'm going out to the car now. I'm going to get in and drive away."

In a popular book about strong-willed children, James Dobson made a convincing argument that you had to make sure your child knew you meant business. So, I experimented. When it was time to get Lauren, now in first grade, into the car for school, she dawdled intentionally. Transitions were hard for her. I made up my mind to be strong like Dr. Dobson recommended.

Tuesday morning, I went to the front door, opened it, and stepped out. "C'mon, get in the car," I said and waved her out the front door.

She stood staring at me in the hallway, unmoving. Steeling my nerves, I walked out to our Honda Civic and got in. I buckled my seat belt and turned the car on. No sign of Lauren on the front porch. I slowly backed out of the driveway into the street, and, taking a deep breath, drove away.

This is insane, my mind screamed at me. *The front door is open and my child is alone. What am I thinking?*

But this is exactly what Dobson had suggested. Maybe not the open door, but the basic scenario. I drove quickly around the short suburban block, taking maybe two minutes. On my return, I found my most precious little person sobbing on the front sidewalk, nose running and shoulders shaking.

What an idiot you are! I hollered at myself.

I pulled quickly into the driveway, got out, and gathered her in my arms.

No more Dr. Dobson and his authoritarian bullshit.

I went back to therapy and explained that parenting my way was number one.

I stuck to my guns, Terri to hers, and the relationship crumbled. I went to her house one more time to beg, but it was too late. She had already moved on.

CHAPTER 36
SANATANA DHARMA

"Come with me to this alternative church I found," Henderson suggested.

Before falling for Terri, I hadn't even known how much I wanted a little family with several children. How much I loved being in love. Now that I'd lost both, they seemed essential for survival. I felt excavated; an empty pit lay in my heart. It wasn't just about a lover; it was that another life dream came very close to being real before it slipped away.

"I don't know. I don't see how it would help," I resisted, too blue to lift myself.

Months after the breakup my grief dragged on, twisting in me like a chained ghost. I was such a bummer to be around that Henderson was the only friend who would still put up with me.

"C'mon. You need to do something. Try this."

She was right. I accepted.

Henderson's sanctuary was in the back of an ordinary brick-and-mortar professional building off Winchester Boulevard in San Jose. Though I was disappointed with the inauspicious setting, I figured if God were going to suddenly appear in my life, what better place than a stripped-down office space on one of the busiest commercial streets in Silicon Valley? I was lucky to make it to the service at all. Six-year-old Lauren didn't want to get up, dressed, or in the car, so our Sunday morning went worse than a school day. By the time we pulled into the lot, my pursed lips and hard grip on the wheel betrayed my irritation.

Opening the rear passenger door, I looked at Lauren in her child seat and sighed. Getting from there to the building wasn't going to be easy. I unbuckled the straps.

"Okay, Peanut, let's go." I reached across her to grab her backpack, and she pushed me into the front passenger seat. I lost my balance and banged my head. "Ow!" Then I absorbed the insult with a sigh, not sure how I could respond without making a scene. "Out." I pointed to the ground outside the car.

Pulling Lauren one foot after the other, I cajoled her to the entrance where Henderson waited. We could hear the mellifluous tones of an unfamiliar chant in multiple harmonies calling to us from the other side of the door. Loosening my jaws, I exhaled to decompress.

The three of us stepped into a space filled with about fifty people and twice as many folding chairs. We found seats a few rows from the front. Spicy incense enchanted my senses, and I looked down the center aisle to see a raised altar where a burning brass bowl sat on a table between two tall white candles. The crooning choir of a half dozen men and women stood on the left side of the dais. I later learned that the hymn's words, "Om Namah Shivaya," meant something like "Praise to the name of the great being."

The Center for Spiritual Enlightenment was unlike any religious place I had been before. Rather than exhibiting familiar Christian symbols, the altar was adorned with five two-by-four-foot cloth panels displayed on five small easels. On each dyed sheet, an icon for one of the world's major religions blazed in gold on a purple background. I recognized the shape of Om, the Hindu syllable for all creation; a Christian cross; a Jewish star; the crescent moon of Islam; and a yin-yang symbol that might have represented Buddhism or Indigenous religions.

The minister sat on the right side of the altar, draped in a purple robe with a white surplice. When the chanting ended, the choir members took seats in the hall and Reverend O'Brian walked over to the pulpit, front and center. I dug out Lauren's toys: My Little Ponies and a coloring book.

"The king or queendom of heaven is within you," Reverend O'Brian began. "Shining like a precious gem hidden in a cave, the priceless treasure of our own wisdom awaits our discovery." I trotted a green-haired pony across my lap to entertain my daughter as the sermon continued. "The longing each of us feels for love and partnership is really the same as our longing to discover our inner treasure," she said.

I looked up from the toys in my lap. I had that longing.

"We yearn for completion, wholeness. We look for it in other people and things, but fulfillment and happiness are already within. You could even say that the hunger we feel is our inner treasure calling each of us home."

I liked the idea of being called home to some safe and comforting place where I belonged.

To illustrate her theme, the reverend read not from a scripture, but from *The Gift,* a collection of devotional Sufi poems by medieval Persian writer Hafiz. One selection, called "This One Is Mine," told of an enslaved person finally being found by a loving friend, who promised to go to any lengths to free her and bring her home.

Something deep within me cracked open when I heard the short poem. In that moment, the incense, the Sanskrit chanting, and the purple robes took me back to the Latin Mass of my childhood. I used to feel great joy singing hymns to God with my grandmother. When I heard that poem, I also heard a promise that lit me up inside. The Ineffable seemed to be calling me home. Me! Tears spilled from my eyes.

Like a bee buzzing near a blossom, I felt pulled toward this haunting unknown. It seemed so close I could almost hear it whisper my name. As the minister read, warmth and relief penetrated my bewildered heart. I wept like a rescued child, bent over in my third-row folding chair in a strip mall in San Jose. Cathy patted my shoulder and handed me a nearby box of Kleenex. Lauren looked up at me from the floor, then crawled up into my lap.

"Why are you crying, Mommy?"

"It's nothing, sweetheart," I whispered. "Tears of happiness." I smiled through contortions on my face and scrunched my eyes into a laugh. "Whoever cries for happiness?" I asked. We both whisper-giggled.

My visceral reaction to the Sufi poem made me think that the loving presence I experienced was somehow real. The minister certainly thought so. As she wove together quotations from Christian and Hindu traditions, she concluded that these religions all pointed to the same inner wellspring of peace and happiness. "When we connect with that," she said, "we experience love."

Is that what just happened to me? I wondered.

At the end of her talk, the minister led us in an extended Om chant. Two or three minutes of the group invocation left me with a refreshing tingle after the flush of crying.

I wanted to slip out unnoticed when the service concluded, but Henderson dragged me over to meet Reverend O'Brian.

"Welcome to the Center," she said as we shook hands.

"I was very moved by your talk, Reverend O'Brian," I said.

"Please call me Ellen."

I daintily dabbed my nose and tried to present myself. "What is the name of the religion you are teaching?" I asked her.

Ellen paused. "Sanatana Dharma," she said.

"Sanatana Dharma," I repeated. "What does that mean?"

"It means 'the Eternal Way.' And it leads like a labyrinth to what we call the One Truth Known by Many Names."

That was interesting. To find the shared truth rather than the many differences among conflicting religions seemed like a truly worthy venture. Despite my intellectual resistance, a thought flashed in my mind like skywriting: *This woman is going to lead me straight to God.*

Maybe the idea of God was a comforting fantasy, or maybe it actually referred to a brilliant light within my own being. I honestly couldn't tell. I wasn't even sure if my religious impulses were positive or destructive. The truth was, I had a deep urge to disappear into something larger than myself and escape my loneliness once and for all. Was I seeking death or transcendence? I decided to trust the yearning for a while and see what happened.

During the winter of 1996, I went to CSE every week with little Lauren in tow. Each Sunday, Reverend Ellen invoked inspirational literature and songs from varied sources and periods around the world. She made it seem as if there was a glowing secret at the heart of human experience that people wrote about from every possible perspective. The idea of One Truth seemed both profound and simple. The core of yoga, Reverend Ellen said, could be summarized in just nine words:

It is.
We are It.
We forget.
We remember.

Part of me wanted to trust the possibility of spiritual sanctuary and belonging. But I worried I was conning myself, taking the delusional way out instead of facing the harsh realities of bodily existence. As a scientist, I wanted my spiritual and scientific views to support rather than contradict each other. Still, throughout that winter, I listened with an open mind to Ellen's sermons.

She shared with us the mystical visions of Christian saints, the prayers of yogis hungering after Brahman, the ecstatic poems of Sufis, and the sutras describing Buddha's freedom. Each week she found ways to remind us that there is only One Being, and we are It.

"Hi, Terri?" I asked. We hadn't talked for months; I grimaced with the thought she might not want to connect with me.

"Rikki, good to hear from you," Terri's cheerful voice said. "How've you been? How's Lauren?"

"I'm great, doing fine," I lied, "and Lauren, too. Listen, I got word of an interesting one-day women's retreat next Saturday." I should have left it alone, but I wanted to share this exciting abundance with the person I still loved.

"Yeah?"

"Yeah, it'll be led by the minister at the Center for Spiritual Enlightenment. Her thing is bringing together poets, visionaries, and mystics into one story."

"Henderson told me about her. It sounds interesting . . ."

"I think this would be right up your alley," I said.

"What's the theme?"

"Integrity as spiritual practice."

"Hmm. Chauncey will have the kids. I could come."

My heart banged in my throat. "Okay, yay, I look forward to seeing you. Let me give you the details."

We met at the retreat venue the following Saturday. I introduced Terri to Ellen, then we took our seats in the main hall. Each attendee began to withdraw into her personal space for the day.

When we broke into small discussion groups after Ellen's morning presentation, I made sure to join Terri's. Later at lunch, I found her at a picnic table after I went to the ladies' room. But she was chatting it up with another person and we didn't get a chance to talk.

At one o'clock we gathered in the main hall for another presentation. I sat with a friend when Terri stayed with her lunch group . . . and a tiny shiver of anxiety ticked up my spine.

Is she avoiding me?

During the afternoon session, Ellen asked us to write about personal integrity; she called it at-one-ness. We all took our journals outside, where the sun was warm and the grass dry. Women scattered across the lawn in front of the retreat venue; I spied Terri sitting alone on a little bench, her notebook in hand.

I smiled and started to stride across the lawn. But the curve of her shoulder and the tilt of her head struck me like a gong. Something wasn't right.

She didn't come here to see me. She's here for the retreat.

As if a filmmaker had changed the focus of the lens, I suddenly saw that I'd been trying to entrap her, not really share the riches. I didn't want to investigate integrity; I wanted to rekindle a fire with Terri. And my ploy didn't work.

That day was the last time I spoke to Terri for seventeen years.

In 1996 I took up meditating on the One Truth, trying to find a sweet spot in the silent moments of my own mind. With the new inspirational input and the community of spiritual friends, my grief burned itself out. Finally, I was ready to make a fresh start.

First things first. Lauren and I were going to move to the mountains.

CHAPTER 37
THE ASPECT REVELATIONS

The Virago 750's narrow tires gripped the warm pavement as we careened around hairpin curves on Highway 17, the roadway to the coast. Lee kept us in the right-hand lane; I clung to her waist, letting my weight follow hers, as she lay the bike into the turns. The road snaked up into the mountains, where we entered a dense redwood forest.

Ferns unfurled in the spaces between trees, forming a lush green embankment. On both sides of the highway, deep ravines plunged into that dense foliage; but sometimes a hillside rose straight up from the edge of the road. I couldn't believe people really lived here, in what seemed like a state park or nature preserve. Warm spring air blew over our legs, bringing the scent of green pines and eucalyptus, while the sun glared down on our black leather jackets. At the feet of mossy trees, wisps of ocean fog curled up and lay still. I wanted to live there more than anywhere else I could imagine.

I'd grown up surrounded by forest preserves west of Lake Michigan. My childhood friends and I had splashed through creeks while pretending we were explorers hunting bear deep in the woods. We played outside nine months of the year, riding bikes or hiking in the forest when we weren't climbing trees or playing football. I wanted my daughter to know that kind of freedom, to live in a safe woodsy neighborhood instead of a cement suburb. I'd put my eleven-hundred-square-foot starter home on the peninsula up for sale, and after I'd found a great listing in the *Mercury News*, my friend Lee had offered to ride me up there on her motorcycle.

Following directions from the newspaper, we maneuvered through the forest to a rustic two-story A-frame nestled into a hillside with a little black-bottomed pool in the side deck. The house stood partially on stilts, and the driveway seemed too steep to ride on the motorcycle. We parked the bike off the road and walked up.

"It's beautiful in here!" I said softly, looking around at the towering redwoods.

"No kidding," said Lee. Through the trees beyond the driveway, we could glimpse the play of light on water.

"What's in there?" she asked.

I grinned. "I think that's the pool."

"Cool!"

We climbed the stone staircase to the first level of the home and knocked on a red front door.

"Welcome to your future mountain chalet!" said Jack, the owner. A tall, bearded, muscular man in his early forties, he wore an easy smile.

"Greetings, Jack," I said as we shook hands and I introduced Lee. The open doorway revealed a hallway and living space with high-beamed ceilings and solid-colored walls painted moss green and pale burgundy. "I love the entryway!"

"That's good to hear," Jack said pleasantly. "The colors were my wife's idea. Shall we start our tour at the top?" We walked up the stairs and past three bedrooms to the end of the hallway. Jack pulled on a rope handle that lowered a ladder from a trap door in the ceiling. "This would make a great rec room; we just never got around to it."

Up the ladder I found a carpeted room with windows on both ends, mostly filled with plastic bins and sealed cardboard boxes.

"Great space," Lee said, looking around. "Wouldn't you have loved this as a kid?"

"Put in a stereo and a hide-a-bed, and you'd have an extra room up here," Jack said.

We walked through the upstairs bedrooms: the primary had a fireplace and full bath, and another room would make a great office for me. Lauren could take the corner "treehouse" bedroom—outside, redwoods crowded its windows.

The main floor (on stilts!) included a dining room, kitchen, huge breakfast room where I could put a Ping-Pong table, and a living room with a wood stove, skylights, and windows on three sides.

"I love the openness of the space and the way light comes in from every angle," I said.

"Wait till you see the basement garage and the pool." Jack smiled, waving us out the back door to the deck.

I want this place, I thought, taking in the wood paneling, picture windows, and warm pool set into the redwood deck. It was the epitome of mountain living.

Jack wanted to sell it to me directly, without a real estate agent.

"Agents get up to 5 percent, split between us. That's close to $20,000 each."

"Really?" I did some mental math. "Wow."

"Yeah. Big savings for both of us."

"What about issues that might come up after we initiate the sale?" I asked him.

"You'd have to trust me, but we could make a ladies-and-gentlemen's agreement. The house is in good shape, as the inspection book shows you. I could cover all minor repairs until we hand over the key. For the following three months, I'd be willing to split the cost of any unforeseen issues."

I looked at Jack and checked my gut feel. *Trustworthy, a family guy.* I thought about it for a short minute.

"Okay, Jack, I see you've thought it through. How about we put it in writing?"

In June of 1996, Lauren and I said goodbye to our first home and moved to the coastal Santa Cruz Mountains.

When my stepfather Hank called on a summer Sunday, I was reading articles online using my new Mosaic browser.

"Hi, Hank. How's it going?" I looked out the window onto a cascade of redwoods and the small waterfall splashing into a rock koi pond.

"Your mother asked me to call and tell you she found the recipe for chicken paprikas. Do you want her to send it to you?" Hank asked.

"Oh, great. Yes, please, I'd love it." In my mountain chalet, I'd created a home office in the upstairs guest room. In a corner sat a small table with a candle and incense. Next to it on the floor lay my meditation pillow. I sat at the desk.

"All right." The line went quiet. Hank was a very shy man, not one to chitchat.

"What are you reading these days?" I asked, hoping to spark a conversation.

"My son sent me a book about the science in *Star Trek* by a physics professor." My stepfather had been an aeronautics engineer—literally a rocket scientist. He had a passion for the physics of gravity and Einstein's spacetime theory. "It's okay. How about you?"

"You know I got my modem going?" Near the phone outlet on the desk sat the black rectangular box that connected my computer to the world. "I've just been online getting more evidence for you that tiny particle/wave things don't obey physics." Hank and I had a running argument about quantum mechanics.

"Argh." A strangled croak came from the phone. Hank was an Einstein devotee, and Einstein had long insisted that observed quantum phenomena would someday be explained in terms of spacetime physics. These new experiments proved Einstein wrong.

"I read that a French physicist named Alain Aspect proved that tiny entities like photons really communicate instantaneously over long distances," I crowed. On the little table next to me lay a sandalwood mala. I picked it up and fingered the soft wooden beads.

"That means faster-than-light travel, which is forbidden by classical physics," Hank said.

"Well, I guess there's stuff that exists outside classical physics," I said, making a spinning lariat out of my Indian rosary.

"Harrumph," grunted my stepfather.

"Whatever it is that we are really made of, it obviously shows up as matter, energy, awareness, thoughts, feelings, gravity, black holes, guilt, love, understanding, stars, and all the phenomena of existence, right?" I replied.

"Okay . . ." he said, knowing it was a trap.

"And Aspect's rigorous work proved that there is room in science for nonphysical phenomena. In his case, instant communication at great distance."

I could hear my friend Robin saying, *So what?* So, I answered.

"So perhaps there is room in science to include the awareness that experiences everything," I proposed.

"I don't like it," Hank complained.

"I love it," I countered. Physics had proven that the fundamental stuff we are made of is not hard matter as we'd learned. Reality was richer, more mysterious and marvelous, than we'd even imagined. How could anyone not love it?

Wrapped in leather with a piece of foam and plastic on my head, I did not have much protection. An oil slick, a crack in the road, or a misjudgment on a curve, and I would be down. I'd heard about a fellow biker who cruised into a damaged, low-hanging telephone wire and was thrown fifty feet to his death. Riding focused my attention.

After Lauren settled into third grade at our local school, I'd taken a motorcycle training course and gotten my license. A 1994 Honda

Magna 500 showed up nearby in a Craigslist ad and I snatched it. The cruiser had a low seat like a Yamaha Virago—suitable for a five-foot-four rider—and plenty of gumption to get me zooming up and down the hills on the sinewy mountain roads. It was my training bike.

I named her Bad Betty. Each time I mounted the bike, I focused every iota of attention on what I was doing: the sound of the engine, the feel of it vibrating, the touch of the tires on the road, the visual signals streaming in, the delightful sway of my riding body as I swung my weight and leaned. Nothing but my awareness and this motorcycling; the thrill of racing down the road in open air, confronting intermittent fears of death. Exquisite.

Who needed Terri?

I waited for the winter rains to dry up before I took out the brand-new 1998 blue-and-black Magna 750—named Big Bertha—I'd bought in January. Grabbing the handgrips, I threw my right leg over the saddle and planted both thick-soled leather toes on the cement. Straightening out the fork, I pulled the key out of my jacket pocket and slipped it in the slot.

The pine and cypress air carried a faint scent of smoke, but the valley was still. Sunlight streamed through the trees and the dew on wild grasses sparkled here and there. I put on my helmet and gloves, then flicked the key to "on." I squeezed the clutch, downshifted to first, and pressed the start button. The engine grumbled sweetly. Four chrome pipes streamed exhaust from the powerhouse braced between my knees. The bike rumbled down the driveway and out onto the two-lane tarmac. I rode away into the morning.

Big Bertha and I cruised up and down the rolling hills through the woods, snaked round turning bends, and broke out of shadows into sunlit stretches of pavement. Leaning deeply into turns, I felt uncountable vibrations rise from my toes to my eyebrows. Cool air blew hard against my face shield and chilled my fingers on the handgrips. Strips of sunlight stippled my black leather jacket and the smell of ocean salt wafted up from the coast in intermittent breaths. Not a thought intruded on my focus.

Who needed meditation?

In March I called an old friend of mine: a recruiter for high-tech positions. That first year of the new millennium, jobs were flying off the shelves as investor money kicked off startups or funded fresh avenues of research.

Within a few weeks, the recruiter found me a wonderful, highly coveted, impossibly great position. Nokia had just opened a plant in the small mountain town where Lauren and I lived—Scotts Valley. They had recently acquired a startup that gave them the technology for a network traffic security control system for cloud computing. I had only a vague notion of what that might mean, but I knew I could figure it out in real time. Signing on as director of software engineering, I led a small group of twenty engineers.

The campus was surrounded by redwood forest and was fifteen minutes down a country road from my house. I passed Lauren's junior high school on my way to work. The landscape looked like a state park and the company had gyms with racquetball courts. Within six months I was promoted to site manager, which added quality assurance to my portfolio as well as general management of the Scotts Valley campus, comprising several hundred people. Stock options and other perks came with the promotion. Life was very, very, good.

Everything seemed to be humming like a Magna 750. Lauren was doing well in junior high, there were no leaks in my roof, my stock portfolio was so strong it astonished me, and I was proud of my accomplishments. I was in excellent health; I'd even become a vegetarian like my daughter.

If happiness actually could come from money, possessions, success, and family, then for a few moments I had it. I had it all.

CHAPTER 38
THE OTHER SHOE

"When things are this good, I wait for the other shoe to drop," Hank said grimly.

Hank, my mom's second husband, had emigrated to the States as a young teen from Graz, Austria, in 1939. Fleeing Europe with his parents and no other relatives, he'd escaped Nazi persecution via steamship out of Trieste. He was not a pessimist exactly, but he had no illusions about the world. After I told him about my new job in the mountains, he'd hinted that my luck was a bad omen.

"What other shoe?" I asked him. "The first one hasn't even dropped yet. Let me enjoy this!"

But his words set off an alarm in my mind. Of course, he was right. Good things did not last; everything changed in time. How *much* time was the question.

Both shoes hit the ground firmly the following summer, August 2001. On a Friday evening, I received an email telling me that my badge had been disconnected and that I should report to the lobby at 10:00 a.m. the following Wednesday for a meeting with my vice president.

Shitdamn! My heart sank to my knees. I sat down and dropped my face into my hands. Hank was right; my perfect life was too good to be true.

On Wednesday morning when I arrived at the corporate lobby, I found ten or twelve other Nokia employees. John, a marketing colleague, touched my arm.

"Alas, you too as well," he said with a commiserating smile. "Were you surprised?"

"Totally," I answered. I felt ashamed to get the boot, but John's camaraderie eased my discomfort.

"Not me. I heard rumors, so I started taking real estate classes to prep for a new career. My wife's a broker."

I felt like a fool again. I'd not only missed the warning signs, but had also failed to prepare.

The meeting with my VP took five minutes. A gofer came into the lobby and called my name. He walked me inside, then knocked once on a door and opened it. My boss perched on the opposite side of a small table set in a narrow office. I sat down, facing him.

"Nokia is cancelling the network edge security project," he told me. "We've closed the Scotts Valley site."

I looked at him with flat eyes. Nokia had promised us so much when we left our old jobs to join the new venture. Now they dumped us like used parts. We had been snookered.

"All positions have been eliminated, though a handful will be hired back to join the Mountain View office. A $5,000 severance package is offered for those who sign this waiver."

Less than two weeks' pay. Hardly even a thank-you.

"Thank you," I said, and retaining my composure, I stood up and left.

I had two months of cash on hand and was eligible for unemployment insurance. I still held Nokia stock and assets in my 401(k). I had solid equity in my home. I'd be all right.

Of course, I was disappointed that my dream job ended so abruptly. And I knew its short duration was not going to look good on my resume. But I'd gained a lot of experience in both engineering management and politics at Nokia. I felt confident I would land another position soon.

And I might have, if the dot-com bust had not been well underway by summer of 2001. Programmers were getting laid off by the thousands. A lot of talented people were out looking for work, and I did not yet understand the impact of that on my employment prospects.

A couple of days after the 9/11 attacks, I resurfaced from the fog that had engulfed me since the first images hit the airwaves. Among the envelopes and fliers that had piled up on my kitchen counter near the wall phone was a card with a blue-lotus logo. I pulled it out and discovered an invitation to a spiritual course of study at the Center for Spiritual Enlightenment: a twelve-week program on "Living the Eternal Way," grounded in the theory and practices of yoga.

I looked at the blue-lotus flier in my hand, but I saw images of fire and smoke in my mind. A high-rise exploding in flames.

What really caused this conflict? My mind search for understanding. *Politics, economics, religion?* When I looked from a psychological perspective, the deepest cause of the tragedy seemed to be hatred. We would not be capable of blowing each other up without it.

What causes hatred? I'd pondered this many times. My answer was always the same: fear. Fear of losing resources, status, and security. Fear makes others appear to threaten your happiness. Fear triggers hate.

There has got to be a way to end irrational fear, I thought. *We've got to see how connected we are. Like the survivors in New York feel right now, only all of us.* I wondered if the CSE flier might be a bit serendipitous—like a hint from the universe. Could the disciplines of yoga open a human mind to love instead of fear?

I called the number on the invitation.

"Good afternoon, CSE. This is Lynn," said a woman's voice. I hadn't been to CSE since I'd joined Nokia. A generous donor had gifted a beautiful multi-building property in San Jose to the center. They now had a main temple, several buildings, three ministers, a labyrinth, and a spiritual book store.

I took a deep breath and said, "Hello. I am calling to learn if there is still room in the Eternal Way course?"

"Yes, certainly. We can fit you in," she told me. "You've missed the first session, but you can catch up."

"Oh, good. Thank you."

"Just so you're aware, in this course we ask participants to engage with the fundamentals of yoga. We will meditate, study, fast, and practice the virtues of an ethical life."

Fast? Ethical life? My eyebrows scrunched down in a frown. Uh-oh.

"Virtues? Like what, being truthful?" I asked. I'd been living by the ethics of Alcoholics Anonymous for twenty years. Hopefully that would be good enough.

"Yes, like that," Lynn laughed. "The course will go into various habits that promote spiritual awakening."

"Okay . . ." I said slowly.

"And we also ask that you attend every remaining session. Is all that acceptable to you?" Lynn asked me.

I hesitated. I hadn't anticipated that the class would demand so much personal commitment. Still, I needed to know if yoga offered insights that could actually help heal our human wounds. I decided to keep my eyes open and go all in.

Exhaling slowly, I said, "That sounds great. Thank you so much."

"See you next week," Lynn said.

When we hung up, I felt a little pang of anxiety, a contraction around my heart. With all these rules, I couldn't help thinking of the strict, ritual-laden Catholic Church I grew up with.

What am I getting myself into?

CHAPTER 39
HOMECOMING

I was running late. I parked on the street, then hurried down a path toward a high-roofed building with stained-glass windows. A small group stood out front talking quietly, and a smiling face pulled the door open for me.

Inside, I found a sanctuary filled with hundreds of people in rows of wooden pews. A few folks in the last high-backed bench scrunched together to make room for me. Even from the rear of the temple I recognized on the altar the familiar purple and gold religious symbols from CSE's previous makeshift church. Above them, a screen suspended from the ceiling glimmered with a PowerPoint slide. Reverend O'Brian stood at a podium explaining the projected image. It was a multi-petaled flower labeled "The Eight Limbs of Yoga."

I learned that each petal had a Sanskrit name such as *pranayama*, *asana*, or *dhyana*. They represented various tactics yogis used to help them connect with their serene inner nature. One petal was about breath work, Reverend Ellen explained. Another focused on yoga postures, a third on meditation. A fourth recommended virtues to cultivate, and one stood for good spiritual habits such as contentment and study. Each week, the course would delve into one of the eight practices.

Reverend Ellen then summarized the teachings of yoga in nine words, which I remembered from my first visit to CSE five years before:

It is.

We are It.

We forget.

We remember.

"It," Reverend Ellen explained, "is the one, universal, conscious being. Each soul, each of us, is a unit of this consciousness. You and I, we are It."

The reverend's simple statement sounded similar to the fundamental premise of all the Eastern religions I'd encountered: that there is something behind the multiplicity of appearances. That whatever It is, It's a single, aware whole and we are an intimate part of It.

My eyes began to tear up, surprising me. What had moved me? Maybe it was the simplicity and accessibility of an eight-step program to God-consciousness. I'd been through Twelve Steps to sobriety; surely, I could master eight new techniques.

Deep in my heart, hope was waking up. Discovering my own godlike nature might not be that far away. Everything about CSE felt harmonious, as if I was in the right place at the right time. My skin even tingled with anticipation that I'd finally found my path to liberation.

"As we go about daily life, we get distracted from our own being," the reverend went on. "We forget what we are."

That sounded honest. Every time I'd experienced the freedom and happiness of my own self—maybe while motorcycling or laughing with Lauren—I would all too soon drop back into my normal thought patterns made up of judgments, self-criticism, and fears. I would leave my expanded self somewhere in the dark.

"And, luckily, we remember again," smiled Reverend Ellen. "That is what yoga is for—to help us remember."

After the short lecture, we broke into small discussion groups of six. My team gathered in another building, so a CSE assistant named Jill showed me where to find them. We took a path that ran along a fountain and past the bookstore to a small chapel.

"Welcome, come in and get settled," said Pat, my group leader, after Jill introduced me.

"Greetings, Pat, everyone," I said as I looked around with a self-conscious smile. I sat cross-legged on the floor atop a little round pillow like the others. The small room was decorated with statues of Hindu deities and soft lighting. In a circle sat three women and two men, aging from their twenties to seventies, who looked like ordinary people I might meet in a grocery store.

Pat asked each of us to reflect on what drew each of us to this study of yoga. One by one, people shared their private yearnings.

"We need more love in our family, especially dealing with a teenager," said a middle-aged man with blond hair that fell over his ears.

Amen to that, I thought.

We sat in silence for a moment. A residue of incense permeated the room, lending a rich, dark, wood scent to the air.

A dark-skinned woman, with dreadlocks pulled back into a thick ponytail, cleared her throat. "I've been meditating for years, looking for God. After listening to Ellen's Sunday sermons, I think yoga might be my sacred path," she said. Her eyes reached inward to some private vision, and her words struck a note in my own heart.

Pat let the silence linger until more people felt ready to speak.

A woman about my age, wrapped in a white woolen shawl, raised her hand. "I agree with both of you. The world is so filled with strife, and I'm afraid I'm part of it. I get triggered all the time. I'd like to find and keep that peace Ellen talked about."

It was my turn. "I came here to see if yoga could transform my fearful mind into one filled with love or understanding. But what is this It? I guess I'm hoping yoga will deepen my intimacy with whatever It is." The pun got a smile from my new friends.

After half an hour, we brought our discussion to an end. The small groups returned to the main temple to learn our homework for the coming week. The first assignment was to write down our understanding of yoga's four short principles. Then, we could contemplate behaviors in our lives that could use a little more self-discipline and jot them down in a journal. I guessed I could be a little less harmful—to creatures, to earth, even to myself.

CHAPTER 40
COMMITTED

"It doesn't sound right that understanding yourself, your own being, should be an extraordinary experience like falling in love," Jill said to me.

A few weeks had passed since my first Eternal Way session, and we were getting a latte and a caramel macchiato at Starbucks. Since last week, I had refreshed the meditation altar in my home office with a statue of Kwan yin, an Asian icon of compassion, and begun to get up each morning at five thirty. I'd make a cup of black coffee, then sit on my round cushion decorated with gold dragons.

After lighting candles and incense to help filter out the busyness of the world, I'd sit in a half-lotus for forty-five minutes, experimenting with breathing techniques that we were learning in the twelve-week class. Between sips of coffee, I'd sit very still, hoping to experience a rare moment when my mind wasn't busy with thoughts and perceptions. I'd ask myself, *What is still present when the chatter stops?*

"We're talking about this ordinary, simple awareness happening right now that lights up the taste of this drink," Jill said. She held up her cardboard cup. "Not something airy-fairy that exists out there." She waved the air above her head with her free hand.

But the idea that we shared our conscious being with an all-encompassing awareness *out there* was everywhere in the spiritual literature. As the course recommended, I'd started reading spiritual texts after meditating, such as the Bhagavad Gita and the late Upanishads, about the unity of our personal souls with a kind of universal oversoul.

"It's interesting you would say that," I said. "All this spiritual stuff makes it sound like there really is something airy-fairy out there, and I have to purify myself to connect with it. Even Jesus said, 'I and my father are One.'"

"That doesn't make any sense," Jill said. "You can't have it both ways. If we are already one with God, why would we have to purify ourselves to be one with God? Liberation must be just a matter of seeing clearly, not getting purified."

I gave her a deeply confused look. *What*? Jill had the knack of making you stop dead in your tracks to question some basic assumption. *We don't have to purify ourselves?*

That was a profoundly refreshing idea.

I loved talking about these things. I could go on like this for hours. But in the physical world, I still had to find a job. The stock market continued to tank; my investments had lost 50 percent of their value, and I had to keep selling off shares to pay the bills. Naturally, I spent most of my afternoon hours searching for employment.

I scoured the electronic job boards for any work that I thought I could do, then redid my resume to show off the appropriate skills. Every day I combed through the openings at tech companies in the Bay area who hired people with my background. I tracked down friends in the industry who might connect me to opportunities. When I found a potential job, I'd use email to locate a friend at the company who might recommend me. Many days I could process four or five applications, each with a unique cover letter.

Words from the old Grandmaster Flash song often piped into my mind: *It's a jungle out there, and I wonder how I keep from going under.* But I kept going because behind my solar plexus I felt a growing certainty that I was not here on earth to suffer. Rather, happiness seemed like a puzzle for me to solve. Happiness was my birthright, if I could just figure out how to find it. I believed in my journey. Good things were coming to me.

Weeks went by. Then months. I kept working on the "petals" of the Eight Limbs of Yoga: virtues, spiritual habits, meditation, yoga postures, and breathing techniques. And I applied for dozens of opportunities. Nothing happened. Not a callback, not an interview, not a "No, thank you." The universe was silent.

How could that be? I felt terribly abandoned: Did this higher consciousness I chased not love me? Yet still—and this is a blessing—I held a conviction that things were going to turn out. Somehow, if I stayed the course, I knew I'd find my way.

"Any luck with job hunting?" Jill asked me one Sunday after CSE's morning services.

"No, it's deadly quiet out there," I replied. "Am I doing something wrong?"

She shrugged. "The job market is really tough right now. My friends tell me companies aren't hiring anyone without an engineering degree."

I had two degrees, but neither was in engineering.

"I just thought that my life would improve if I got into harmony with the truth. In AA, we used to say our higher powers had great plans for us."

"You never know what might happen," Jill said.

"I'm as sincere as I can be. Am I crazy to expect a job to show up in my life?"

"Well, you might have to look in other industries until tech stabilizes," Jill suggested.

I took that advice to heart. At the end of 2001, I expanded my job search to include education, public service, and genetic science. And

I began to look outside the Bay area, realizing we might have to move for me to find employment. Meantime, I continued to pour myself into my spiritual practice. It was the only other thing I could think of to do.

When the twelve-week Eternal Way program was over, I signed up for the next series.

"We're becoming serious yoginis," said my friend Kathy, laughing, to a group of devotees hanging out near the bookstore after Sunday services.

"And yogis," chirped Michael.

"Is anyone taking the yoga series?"

Ellen led an eight-week study of ancient text written by a sage known as Patanjali. The written teachings were as old as Christianity, while the yogic traditions dated back thousands of years BCE.

"I am," said Kathy, and six more hands went up.

"How about you?" Jeff asked me.

"Absolutely. I just have one question though," I added. "What exactly are we trying to accomplish?"

Seven pairs of eyes stared at me. The question seemed out of place. Then my friends all spoke up at the same time:

"Well, union with God . . ."

"Peace . . ."

"Higher consciousness . . ."

"The end of suffering . . ."

I wondered if I were making progress on those things. I could sit completely still in a half-lotus for an hour. I could do six different breathing techniques and create dreamy states of tranquility. I easily fasted for a day, cleansing my physical system and clearing my head. I practiced the virtues and avoided dangerous habits like gossip or use of mind-altering substances. I rarely lost my temper or patience.

When I felt lost, confused, angry, or sad, I redirected my mind with spiritual chanting, breath work, or giving service to others.

Surely God was close.

CHAPTER 41
GURU BLUES

"Have you read Stephen Mitchell's book, *The Gospel According to Jesus*?" asked Kathy, a friend at the CSE temple. She had an ingenious mind that often gave her fresh insights.

Our Patanjali class met on weekends in the upstairs rooms of a historic mansion that CSE was renovating on its beautiful San Jose campus. Since we couldn't bring drinks into the newly carpeted rooms, we finished our cups in the downstairs kitchen. It was a Saturday morning, and four of us were standing in that small, tiled room, chatting over coffee.

"He quotes Luke 17:21," Kathy went on, "where Jesus taught that 'the kingdom of God is within you.' It reminds me so much of yoga."

"I haven't read it yet," I admitted. "But did Jesus really say that? I mean, my takeaway from Catholicism was that God is up there and we are down here, groveling." I thought for a moment. "I don't remember anyone saying God is within me."

"That's what Communion was all about!" said Michael, a fifty-something man who made his living as a life coach. "You take the symbol of Christ into your body, physically confirming your deeper unity with him, all being, everything."

"I never thought of it that way," I said.

"I wasn't a Catholic," my friend Lynn, a Reiki practitioner, said, "but I read the Gospels. Jesus spoke often about the kingdom of God. He compared it to treasure, pearls, a mustard seed . . ."

"That stuff never made any sense to me," I admitted.

"And Jesus also said you can't find the kingdom of God when you look for it, because it is already within you. You just can't see it," said Michael.

"That's very interesting," Kathy said. "Because yogis claim divine consciousness is already within you. It's just hard to perceive it."

"So, wait, we're back to 'I and the Father are one,'" I said, "but if that's true already, why do we have to do all this spiritual work?"

"Yogananda wrote beautiful plaintive hymns about searching for God, waiting for God, inviting God into your heart," said Lynn. "It is clearly not that easy to find this kingdom."

Michael said, "It is, we're It, we forget, we remember." He took his cardboard cup to the garbage can. "Drink up. We gotta get upstairs, it's 8:56."

Reverend Ellen was a follower of Swami Paramahansa Yogananda, who came from India to Los Angeles in 1925 to share his metaphysical philosophy. Ellen, as a disciple in his tradition, had been authorized to initiate others into its secrets.

Most of us regarded Ellen as our guru, the term for a spiritual teacher in India. Gurus play the role of a master in a master-disciple duo, in which the disciple must be a faithful and obedient apprentice. I, for one, had too eagerly fallen into that dynamic.

As a spiritual director, Ellen guided the lives of students and ministers in her community. She was the authority on what to wear, whom we could date, what we should eat, and how to speak to CSE members. That seemed to make sense in the context of a spiritual group until it didn't. I began to wonder.

Had I given up too much of myself in order to belong, to blend in, and to benefit from community? I ate Indian food and chanted devotional bhajans when I was in my car. I had spent my tech career wearing jeans and polo shirts. Why was I now wearing Indian saris and flowing pants? And why did I regard eating as an indulgence? How was all that moving me toward self-realization?

And for the life of me I could not figure out how I could make money again. I was still out of work. I'd been unemployed for three years, making do with a small stipend from the center, odd jobs, and my 401(k). I had some money for Lauren's college set aside, and we could go maybe six months more without an income. Then I would need to sell the house.

Nothing I did blossomed into an opportunity. Despite the calming effects of meditation, I reached a tipping point. Whenever I thought about money or work, my eyes would fill, my heart would ache, and my head would spin. My attentive daughter did her best to make things easier for me. She took a liking to inexpensive, used clothes and retro styles and never asked me to spend much on modern teenage necessities.

But as a single mother, I was the sole provider for my daughter. I had to manifest a home with basic amenities, healthy food, medical care, and clothing. I feared I would soon be unable to do so.

"Linda, I have something important to talk to you about," I ventured to my sister Linda with some trepidation. We were taking a walk while Jill ran an errand. Jill and I were in LA for a family visit.

"Okay," she said. Linda was a brisk walker. My breathing came a little strained.

"You know I've had some financial challenges," I started, sick with shame but desperate.

"Yes, of course I am aware."

"I'm running out of funds, and I'm concerned I might get into a situation where I don't have a home for Lauren." To have reached the place, in all senses of the word, where I had to beg for help, I'd walled myself off into a tiny corner where I felt almost nothing.

"Hmmm." Linda kept walking. I supposed she heard me.

"If it came to it, would you take Lauren if I can no longer provide a home?" It was one of the hardest things I'd ever done, asking for that backup help.

"No. No, Rikki, we couldn't do that. You'll have to figure it out yourself," she said.

I instantly turned my face away, heartbroken and burning with shame. I felt as if I'd fallen out of a spaceship, lost in emptiness. We never, for the rest of her life, said another word about my struggles. But I now knew something I'd never admitted.

Linda didn't have my back. No one had my back. Not even, apparently, the Great Being I pursued in yoga. At least not when it came to money. I had to admit that chanting the Sanskrit names of God might bring me joy but did little for my status in the material world.

Janice grabbled my arm outside the sanctuary the following Sunday.

"You're looking for a job, right?"

I stared at her without responding.

"You're a project manager?"

"Yes, yes. I am," I said, sorry to be reminded of my situation. Of course, I had alerted everyone I knew to my predicament.

"Because my brother is a VP at an antivirus company, and he's looking for a part-time contractor to start a software quality program."

Holy smokes, could my luck be turning? I was afraid to get my hopes up.

"Oh my God, Janice, really? Yes, I can do that. Right up my alley."

"Good! Send me your resume and I'll call him tonight."

When Janice's brother called me Tuesday evening, I was stunned. I'd stopped hoping for callbacks. After a quick phone screen, he said he didn't usually do business favors for his family, but my resume looked solid and he liked our conversation. He said he'd have HR call me to set up interviews. And that was that.

I aced the interviews and was working at MicroSafe the following week, in December 2004. My pay was small, but it was enough to cover our immediate needs.

My financial hysteria was over.

"I'm making good progress with these guidelines for small group leaders," I told Ellen at midday lunch with the CSE staff one day. "I'm feeling really good about the work I've done so far."

She gave me a funny look. "Don't start to think you have something to offer," she said, and turned away to someone else.

What? Did I hear that right? Surely, she meant the ego has nothing of real value to offer, not the whole of me? There was something wrong with her erasing me like that, though. Being a devoted yogi didn't mean I became nothing.

This wasn't the first thing Ellen had said or done that made me chafe. Obedience to any kind of leader was not in my nature. I'd been acting the role of a devotee, but I also wanted my freedom. I could make every effort to obey the Eight Limbs of Yoga, but not to obey a person. With a guru at the helm, CSE had begun to feel more like an oppressive cult than a spiritual home or source of inspiration.

I'd also begun to question aspects of yoga that did not quite make sense to me. As Jill suggested, if we were one with God already, why were we always acting like separate, isolated souls praying to be accepted or attuned enough to receive grace? It felt untrue. Somehow the endless seeking for what was already present seemed "off."

It was probably sacrilegious to think this way, but I'd grown tired of endless seeking. Could there be a more immediate way to see into one's actual present self? To see directly the qualities of your inmost being, without having to starve yourself or go into trances?

Maybe I'd misheard or misunderstood Ellen. But at that moment, whether I said it out loud or not, I knew I needed to get away from the center. Out from under someone else's control. I needed to find my own way.

But I was on the CSE board of directors. I was a volunteer program manager and a leading yoga student. Ellen had taught me so much, and I felt I owed her something. My life was supported by a wonderful circle of happy friends, and I had a purpose. Yoga connected me with myself, my inner contentment. I was using my skills in service of goodness of some kind.

How will I ever leave?

CHAPTER 42
SLIPPERY SLOPES

A blast of freezing air hit my ski mask–covered face. I tucked my chin and gripped the safety bar with both mittened hands. Afraid to look down, I gazed out at craggy peaks cascading into a sky flecked with faraway clouds. My whole body tingled with exhilaration as my blood gave its heat to the chilly wind. I'd been on a chair lift only once before, in my late forties, and had ripped the ACL in my left knee attempting to get off. Now, I was trying again because I felt young, larger than life at fifty-four, adventurous, and in love.

Dangling thirty feet above huge boulders and ice thrilled me with both fear and excitement. Under my ski mask, a smile shaped my face. I was flying near the top of my world with a beautiful woman.

Last night, an innocent touch had changed everything. We were up at the Palisades ski resort in Lake Tahoe, California—my daughter, her best buddy Lindsay, my friend Jill from CSE, and me. Jill was the first person I'd met when I went to the Eternal Way course at CSE over four years ago. We'd become friends, but then she and her husband moved to Arizona. Recently, Jill had returned alone to her Los Gatos house. She didn't talk much about her family life but it seemed like the marriage had come to an end.

Jill volunteered occasionally at CSE, and we worked on some projects together. I got to know her informal, irreverent side. She had a unique sense of humor about our spiritual endeavors—she made me laugh at myself for trying so hard to be perfect. Most of us yogis were too "spiritual" to have fun, but rather than trying to act like a holy yogi, Jill enjoyed life. She played golf, hiked in the redwood forests, rocked out at concerts and parties.

It was January of 2005, and Jill had invited Lauren and me on this ski trip to Tahoe. We drove up the mountain from Santa Cruz on a Friday afternoon after school. Jill took us to a fantastic little one-bedroom ski condo she'd rented, right in the Palisades Olympic ski village. We could walk out our door to the lifts.

We piled into the tiny lodge with all our gear—Jill brought extra skis and snowboards—and pulled out the hide-a-bed in the living room for the kids. Jill and I put our stuff in the bedroom. We all got dinner, then Jill and I decided to venture out through the snow to one of the outside hot tubs at the Olympic ski village. We went in search of a steamy plunge in the icy air.

Twenty minutes later, huddling indoors and in a bathing suit under a terry robe, I peeked through a glass door at the steaming spa about twenty feet away.

"Go for it!" Jill said, and pushed me toward the door. I pushed back.

"You first!" I waved her ahead of me and laughed.

Jill opened the door and we both hurried out in our bare feet, careful not to slip on the icy surface. Very quickly we were knee-deep in 103-degree water, then in up to our hips, then to our chins. We smiled at each other as blood rushed to our chilly faces. I forgot my financial losses and still-uncertain future. All my limbs were warm and cozy while my head and face tingled in the 45-degree air. I felt terrific! We were on a vacation, and everything was going to be all right. I let everything go, let everything be just the way it was.

Soon after, back in the condo, we all snuggled into our jammies, and everyone went to sleep so they could get out on the slopes early.

❦

On that Saturday morning, I stayed behind in the village, sipping hot chocolate in the cafe and catching up on background reading for my new job at MicroSafe. While Jill skied, the kids took boarding lessons in the morning and spent the afternoon gliding and tumbling down the mountain.

I was a little bored when around three thirty the three of them toppled into the cafe covered in fresh powder, laughing about their antics on the slopes. I was envious but reticent to give skiing another try. *What if I fall and hurt myself again? I'll ruin everyone's fun.*

Jill, Lauren, Lindsay, and I ate mediocre pizza for dinner, then bundled up to sit outside in the freezing cold around giant campfires in the village. We looked into some of the shops, then turned in around nine thirty. I fell easily to sleep. Until I woke in the middle of the night, alerted by an unfamiliar sensation. Jill's leg brushed mine and lay there against me. I froze. My skin burned where she touched me, and my heart raced with an unexpected urgency. Out of nowhere, I felt the strong urge to wrap Jill in my arms and kiss her. I quickly rolled to the edge of the bed, away from the heat.

Where did that come from? Jill and I are just friends, I thought with a touch of panic. But then I remembered how our legs, feet, and arms bumped gently in the hot tub. I'd ignored it, pushed it out of my mind. After all, Jill was straight, married to a man for years. I slowed my breathing—a habit from yoga—and then remembered that almost everyone was straight once. There definitely was something between Jill and me, a warmth and an easy laughter. I suddenly smiled as a queer thought struck me: What if Jill had been flirting with me and I was just too dense to get it?

When we got up at 6:30 a.m. I said nothing to Jill about what I experienced during the night. What could I have said? But the feeling of affection was strong, and I felt certain she returned it.

"Jill, take me along today, will you?" I asked. "You guys made it look fun yesterday, and I'm feeling brave this morning. I wanna give it a try."

"You got it!" Jill said. "I've been skiing my whole life. I'll show you what to do, and this time you won't fall off the chairlift." She touched my arm and smiled.

Good heavens, I thought, *she really is flirting with me.*

"Here, put these base layers on first. Then this fleece, and these ski pants. This jacket should fit." Jill laid her extra pieces out on the bed; we were almost the same size. She had planned ahead.

At breakfast, we all sat in a booth, where Jill's thigh somehow kept touching mine under the table. While the kids headed for the lift, Jill helped me rent boots and skis for the day. Fully equipped, my face was covered with hat, mask, and goggles; my hands were buried in clumsy mittens that gripped ungainly skis and poles. My stumbling feet were jammed into inflexible ski boots. The entire ensemble was covered with baggy pants and puffy jacket. I slowly clomped along on the ice behind Jill. We made our way to the gondola that would carry us to chairlifts for all the trails.

In my Charlie Brown get-up, my heart hammered so hard I couldn't think. Finally, the gondola door slid open and it was our turn to plod into the little capsule. I dropped a pole and then banged my skis into someone when I turned to retrieve it. Jill recovered the pole for me and pushed me toward a little bench by the window. I didn't look out; I stared at my feet and counted to thirty over and over. *I can do this,* I thought. Close space, heights, falling in love, and the freezing cold all challenged me to lift my courage and derring-do. *I am already doing it!*

After we clambered off the lift, we got out in the snow and prepared me for our first ride up and run down the gentle "green" slopes for beginners. Jill showed me how to get off a chairlift, and I slid easily off the chair into the snow on our first try. We practiced the same basics I had learned in my knee-wrenching adventure nine years ago.

Jill skied effortlessly, constantly shouting for me to lean this way or that, to do the S-curves instead of pizzas, to point my skis and go. I was terrified and quickly became exhausted.

My legs started to shake, and of course I began to cry as I struggled against my body's insistence on doing pizzas to slow me down. Every time I got moving, I feared I would fly over a cliff. I couldn't steer. Somehow, I scraped and clawed my way down, Jill calling out praise when I did something right. Suddenly, I got a little rhythm going and felt a tiny jolt of happiness. Wheeee! It was like motorcycling!

So, we did it again. And thus, it happened that I found myself dangling above the boulders, high in the air with a beautiful woman. My face was freezing behind my mask, and I never expected what happened next. I was shocked when I pulled down my ski mask and heard my voice calling above the wind.

"I don't know if you are feeling anything like this, but I really have the urge to kiss you." *Oh no! What did I just shout?*

But Jill smiled. She smiled! She said, "What's stopping you?"

That was all I needed to know. Jill and I were on.

When we got home from the ski trip, we started to see each other frequently. Jill would come over to my house after I'd finished evening calls. Together, we'd help Lauren with homework, watch TV, or just hang out. My calendar was dominated by work and parenting, but we found time to laugh and discover each other.

Jill had no shame about her sexual longings in the ways I'd always had. Her self-assurance and natural confidence had an impact on me, as would so many things about Jill over the coming years. I tried to imitate those qualities. I learned to relax during physical intimacy in a way I had never before experienced. We laughed and played in pursuit of orgasm, which with other partners had always been a bit of a performance for me. With Jill I discovered how to just be myself while being intimate with her.

Back at CSE, a group of members were finishing the renovation of the historical mansion on campus. Volunteer teams came in to help with odd jobs such as painting and trash removal. Jill came nearly every day. We flirted secretly like giggly school girls, sneaking eye contact when we thought we could get away with it. But CSE was sadly not the right place to celebrate.

The problem was the ethical standards that advanced students were required to follow after they took their vows. The rules were clear: no yoga leader could get involved romantically with a member of the community.

"The advanced yoga students are supposed to take vows at the end of March," I told Jill. "I can't do it."

"We're not doing anything wrong," Jill said. "We're adults."

"But you were in the community. I'm not supposed to get involved with you."

"I left the community," Jill pointed out.

"Not really. You still volunteer," I said.

As we talked, Jill and I realized that if we were serious, we would have to end our membership at CSE. I would have to withdraw from classes and resign from the board.

"What do you want to do?" Jill asked me.

"I have to talk to Ellen. I guess we really should leave CSE. Honestly, Jill, I've been uncomfortable about taking vows for months. The whole idea creeps me out."

Besides, I thought, *aren't I secretly looking for a way to escape the CSE culture?*

Maybe our blossoming relationship was also a pathway to freedom.

CHAPTER 43
CRUISING ON HOME

Jill and I went to talk to Ellen about the ethical problem. We had to wait on the white couch outside her office. *Why are the people behind the closed door always late?* My mind was a tumult of hope, defiance, and uncertainty.

"Come in," Ellen said as she opened the door, her face impassive and unwelcoming.

We sat on a couch across from Ellen, and I felt an increasing chill as I explained our situation.

"We understand we are breaking an important rule for ministers. But we've been seeing each other for months and are pretty serious about moving forward," I summarized.

"Could you try a period of separation?" She raised the question like a school teacher asking if I could try getting my homework done on time.

"I don't see why," Jill said, a bit testily. "After all, we're both adults, Rikki hadn't taken vows, and I wasn't a minister when we started seeing each other." Her voice was sharp. "And I wasn't even living here at the time; I had moved to Arizona."

"Still," Ellen went on, "to the community it appears inappropriate because you both are well-known leaders."

I understood that community members had to feel safe and be able to trust that no one in an influential position would ever take advantage of their sincerity. But Ellen's proposal was a nonstarter.

"We're not going to take a period of separation," I said, angry and apologetic at the same time. Ellen had found her husband in a neighboring spiritual group. Was it really so different?

"I have to stand by the ethics standard for our community," Ellen said, unmoving.

We rose. It was clear there was nowhere else for the conversation to go.

"Thank you for your time," Jill said.

We each hugged Ellen awkwardly on the way out, and it was over.

After that meeting, though it hurt, I had no second thoughts about leaving. Jill, meanwhile, was relieved to put CSE behind her.

We were done.

"What was it like to leave the community?" a yogi friend named Chris asked me privately over coffee. We were sitting in a booth that Jill and I had often used.

"It was like ripping my skin off, Chris," I told him. I sipped a caramel macchiato through a plastic lid. "I was embedded in that organization. I feel a little lost without it, and sad."

"Do you miss the people?" he asked. He leaned forward on his elbows, his clear green eyes locked on me. Chris was one of the most earnest students of yoga I knew.

"Yes, the spiritual kinship, the shared vision," I answered. "I miss the meditations and rituals. But I had to move on."

Chris knew Jill and I were a couple now. I was embarrassed, though I knew I shouldn't be. I kept my head high.

We'd ordered scones, and Chris swallowed a bite of his.

"I'm not sure I believe the ethical standard applied to you guys," he admitted. "Anyway, I'm going to miss you both. Why quit yoga, though?" His eyes stayed on me.

"I won't stop meditating and stuff." I took a sip of coffee. "But I never got comfortable with the guru thing, the whole lineage-of-gurus concept."

Chris sat back and nodded. “I don’t understand the emphasis on gurus in Kriya Yoga either,” he admitted. “There’s a lot I don’t quite agree with. But still . . .”

I sighed. “I don’t know what to tell you, Chris. Emerson said not to follow a path but to leave a trail. I have to follow my inner compass. So do you.”

“I’m so close to becoming a minister,” he said. “I want to start a spiritual gathering place like this in Mendocino. I can’t quit now.”

“Well, keep going and do that!” I said, meaning it. “You’ll offer a great ministry, Chris. And don’t worry about me. You can take the yogi out of the center, but you can’t take the center out of the yogi.”

“Let’s pull over and roll the top back!” Jill said.

I opened the window and put my hand out. With the sun streaming down on us in Jill’s silver and black Porsche, the coastal air felt wonderful.

Pulling briefly off the Pacific Coast Highway, Jill rolled the top down. Then we continued south across the Bixby Bridge to Big Sur. We cranked the music up so we could hear it over the wind.

After we parked in Pfeiffer Big Sur State Park, we hiked inland, climbing up creeks and over fallen trees and boulders. We spied a dead-still possum hiding at the bottom of a shallow pit, but on the return trek it would be gone. My legs got tired and my feet sore as we pressed on in search of the waterfall that fed the current in this part of the Big Sur River. I would soon learn that with Jill, we would always go the extra mile, or around the next bend, or to the top. As we tramped through the woods, I thought of the many years I spent alone in my house or apartment, studying or meditating or whatnot. Now I would have to get new hiking boots to explore the adventure and beauty of the world with my newfound love.

In the spring of 2006, I had to face the financial facts.

"I can't keep draining my 401(k)," I told Jill. "I've got to get my expenses down, and that means selling the house."

Jill nodded.

"It's a good time to sell; real estate prices are high. You'll get rid of the mortgage payments and realize a lot of cash you can use for Lauren's school or your living expenses."

I put the house on the market. Some people might see that as just another bump in the road, but not me. I felt as if I were hanging in space, adrift like the time Big Bertha hydroplaned on Highway 9. Selling my place, my space, my shelter left me untethered, with no place to set my feet. I knew this was a one-way door; I would never own my home again. I didn't want anyone to see what was happening to me. How many people did I know who had actually *lost their homes*? None. *Except my father, the great loser.*

I soon got an offer above my asking. But I walked through it like a bad dream, half in shock. I hid my regret and grief from friends and family, while Jill made the sale sound like a smart financial move. Meantime I emptied my home. I hauled my furnishings to Goodwill, threw out boxes of accumulated stuff. My Ping-Pong table went to a youth center. Photos, keepsakes, and my life with Lauren went into cardboard boxes for storage.

All the while, I quietly hoped Jill would invite us to live in her house, but her mother was living with her, and no invitation came.

Lauren and I found a one-bedroom rental in the woods just outside the city limits of Scotts Valley so she could stay in the same school district until high school graduation.

"Where are you going to sleep?" asked Jill, when she saw I'd given the bedroom to Lauren.

Selling my house made something in me crack into pieces and die. I'd lost everything. Afraid I sounded whiny, I didn't share my real feelings with anyone. I kept up—I tried to keep up—a positive demeanor, but I felt bereft to my core. Even as I faked an upbeat mood, I knew renting this cottage signified a major downshift in my life status. I'd hit bumps with permanent consequences that I hadn't navigated well.

"I'll put a mattress on the floor in the little mudroom off the garage." And Lord, didn't my heart hammer hard when I had to say that.

But then I hit a bit of luck.

In June of that year, my manager quit and I accepted a promotion to fill his position as director of global quality engineering. I feared the responsibilities were a little over my head, but my boss had been certain I could handle them. I needed the money. In my new role, I would need to travel quite a bit, but I'd have a livable salary again.

I set up a little office on the glassed-in porch where I held Skype calls at odd hours with my groups in Asia. I now managed teams in Tokyo, Manila, Nanjing, Taipei, and Cupertino.

Jill visited me at my house when I was free in the evenings, and we'd binge on *24* or go out for frozen yogurt. I was more than ready to take the next step: live together and become one family. But I didn't want to seem needy. I broached the topic one evening at my place.

"You know that old joke about lesbians? What do they do on the second date?" I picked up my coffee mug. It was cold. "What?" asked Jill, not quite catching on. She sat next to me on the leather couch I'd brought from the house.

"Rent a U-Haul."

Jill guffawed. It was gay legend that lesbians rushed into cohabitation.

"Seriously though," I said carefully. I didn't want Jill to feel pressured. That would make her pull back. "We've been together for two years, right?"

"It's true," she said thoughtfully.

Since selling the house, I felt particularly vulnerable and unsettled. The assurance of belonging to Jill and having a place in the world was important to me. Jill had a good financial situation; I knew she didn't need me as much as I needed her.

"Don't you get tired of all the driving?" I asked her, hoping not to sound clingy.

"It's not so bad. Just a few miles across the summit." Jill sat forward and took a sip of water.

"Well, what I really meant was . . . I mean, maybe we should live together instead of maintaining two households." I appealed to practical considerations rather than my need for security. "Why am I paying rent to a stranger?"

"I've been thinking about that, too," Jill said, settling back into the couch. I snuggled against her and she put her arm around me.

"We could spend nights together," I said.

Jill smiled and kissed my cheek. "Yeah, baby!" she cheered. "Lauren's a senior now. She could commute from my house."

"What about your mom?" I asked. I wondered if Jill worried about how it would look, moving in with her lesbian lover.

"She was planning to move soon. Staying with me was just temporary."

"Really? Were you thinking ahead?" Sometimes Jill kept things private to the last moment, leaving her options open.

"Maybe."

"So . . . ?" What was she telling me? Was it safe to get excited?

"Yep. Let's do it. Early next year?"

I turned and wrapped her in a big hug. "Baby, that's terrific!" *Not just me alone in the world. I had Jill.*

I was scheduled to take a tour of my company's Asian sites in January. We decided that we'd wait till I got back from that trip, then Lauren and I would move into Jill's house in February 2007.

But I still had not told Jill about the ominous hearsay that a friend in Nanjing passed on to me. It seemed my job might be evaporating like damp footprints on hot blacktop.

CHAPTER 44

A RECKLESS CHOICE

"So, do you think I could quit MicroSafe?" I asked Jill on a Saturday afternoon in April 2007.

I posed the question casually, but it rolled out like a palmed grenade falling from a combatant's hand. We were changing the tan cotton bedsheets on the California king in the master suite of Jill's home in the Santa Cruz Mountains. Just the mention of me quitting altered the air; you could almost hear the shatter of dropped champagne flutes.

Both the north and south windows were open to the spring breeze blowing off the bay. Shafts of warm light streamed into the room. Jill did not look at me. I watched her fit the corner of the fitted sheet over the mattress and smooth out the wrinkles. We tucked the ends of the crisp top sheet, then lifted the white down comforter and fluffed it full of air before dropping it on the bed.

"If that's what you think you should do," she said, turning to the bundle of used sheets. She picked them up and walked toward the hamper in the bathroom. Her back had so much to say, if I'd been able to hear it. Things like, *Only if you have a better job lined up already!* And *Only if you are a total idiot.*

Instead, I heard, "Sure."

Because I wanted to hear "Sure." I needed to know I could quit.

I'd just returned from a business trip to China for an annual meeting with the twenty-seven people on my team, who were sprinkled across Nanjing, Taipei, Tokyo, Manila, and Cupertino. In March, we'd held our annual face-to-face gathering in Nanjing.

I'd arrived in China with a briefcase full of statistics on software defects and process proposals to discuss with my group. But before I met with them, I had drinks with a friend who worked for Oscar, MicroSafe's engineering VP in Taipei.

"You understand, this is all political," Robert told me. "Oscar and Kevin want your headcount. And they don't like you telling them what processes they should follow." Kevin was the regional VP in China, as Oscar was for Taiwan. Robert was Oscar's executive assistant, and he knew the lowdown. A little bubble of panic started to tickle my upper chest.

"I don't like hearing that. I'm here in Nanjing meeting with all twenty-seven people to put together our annual and quarterly goals. We're expecting to stay resourced at this level," I told my friend. "Should I expect layoffs?"

"Listen, honestly, Rikki, Oscar and Kevin want to break up your group. Reassign your people to the VP in each country."

"Shit," I said. That move would eliminate my position. This would never have happened to Samuel, the man I'd replaced, who had earned a master's in engineering plus several Taiwanese national awards for design. The directors and VPs had treated him with a respect I could never command.

"Yeah," Robert said. "You're gonna have to make yourself seem really useful to even have a job," he said, taking a long swig of his bourbon and soda.

I stared at him while my guts contracted and fear knotted my throat. I tried to swallow my sparkling water. Then I thought of my boss, Mahendra, the company's COO, and felt a glimmer of hope.

"Maybe Mahendra will put up a fight for us."

"Maybe," said Robert, making a face that said, *Not a chance.*

And he'd been proven right. Not long after coming home, I learned that my team had already been reassigned for the next quarter starting June 1.

So, there I was, a few days later, in Jill's bedroom—our bedroom—pulling the coverlet over the bed and fluffing pillows, terrified I might be fired any day. I wanted to quit before that happened.

In retrospect, I wish I'd waited to be laid off. There would have been unemployment compensation and severance pay. But I was overwhelmed with anxiety. I was fifty-six, supporting myself since I was seventeen. I'd never been fired, and I did not want to face the shame of it. I'd been suspended once, the most crushing experience in my career, but I had never been fired. I wanted to walk out on my own two feet, before the executives could push me out.

"Okay," I said to Jill's back. *Okay, I'm going to quit.*

I'd already written resignation letters several times. After Jill disappeared into the bathroom, I turned and went directly into the office with my computer. I logged into my email. The date was April 26, 2007. I typed my regrets and appreciations in an email to Mahendra, gave two weeks' notice, then attached the latest version of my resignation letter and clicked send.

A thrill of empowerment made me smile. At least I had taken action for myself.

I was sure I would have a new job in weeks, a month tops. My resume looked strong. The stock market was healthy, people were making money and starting new companies or growing old ones. Silicon Valley enterprises were reaping huge revenues.

How hard could it be to find a job? Surely my old streak of bad luck had ended.

"I don't know what's going on," I told Jill over veggie stir-fry. "It's dead out there."

After resigning, I'd quickly put together two resumes: one

highlighting team leadership, the other highlighting my project management skills. After posting them both on the Indeed job site, I updated my LinkedIn profile to display both skill sets. I'd sent an email to my contact list, letting them know I was looking. Then I'd made a list of all the tech companies I could think where I could check for job postings.

For the past couple of weeks, I'd scoured the job boards every day while Jill managed her home furnishing shop in the beach town of Capitola. I'd enthusiastically invested eight-hour days in job-searching. But the market was stone-cold.

"I'm seeing the same thing in retail," she said. "It's this real estate bubble. It's causing a contraction of money, so tech companies have probably stopped hiring." She scooped up some broccoli and rice.

My throat contracted with fear.

"That could go on for a long while," I said, frowning. I got up to get hot sauce from the refrigerator. "Want some of this?" I asked, waving the bottle as I sat back down.

"No, thanks. Yeah, recovery could take years." We ate in silence for a few minutes. "Maybe you should look for part-time or one-off work until things open up again," she suggested.

Observing the descent of my career into odd jobs for a few dollars an hour made me feel completely defeated. But I didn't want Jill to see that. I urged myself to perk up.

"I'll do that. I saw some ads in the *Mountain Network News*. I'll check the *Santa Cruz Sentinel* too."

While Jill did the dishes, I took out my laptop to get started.

I worked various gig jobs that I found through friends, the local paper, and posted ads. But my anxiety hit the roof at times. If I could not pay my own expenses, how long would Jill let me live in her house? Some nights I would weep quietly in my pillow, terrified. My father had been homeless at the end of his life. The same thing could happen to me.

If it comes to living in my car, where will I find a bathroom? Where will I park to sleep?

"Jill, I've run out of cash in my savings," I said. I had waited for a quiet time when nothing else was going on. "I've still got assets in my 401(k), but I hate to sell them right now."

"Okay," she said cautiously. "So, what does that mean?"

"It means . . ." I started. "It means I've got to cut back on my rent and restrict my spending to essentials. I can't do lunches or movies anymore," I explained. Each word felt like a cut from a knife.

Jill didn't respond. My words hovered in the air between us.

I had once seemed Jill's financial peer. Now I began to see that working or not, I was a less than equal partner to Jill. The imbalance set up a palpable power disparity that would persist into our future, putting a profound strain on our mutual trust. Resigning from MicroSafe had made it even more difficult to build the bond, love, and intimacy we both sought.

I wondered if this is how it was for my father when he could no longer find work, alone in the world with no recourse. And now this was happening to me—*what the hell was wrong with me? With our family?*

Months and years wore on. I lost faith in a benevolent universe. No higher power seemed to be watching out for me. No one but Jill, who stuck with me for some unknown reason. Was it love? I didn't know how much longer that would be true. I was grateful, and at the same time I knew at any moment I could lose her.

The spiritual teachings that I had studied, if I understood them, affirmed that all of my needs would be met. Even Jesus, according to Matthew in chapter 6, told his followers not to worry about food, drink, or clothing, but to seek first the kingdom of heaven and these things would be provided. But the universe did not manifest what I thought I needed. Was I a fool to still hope in my heart that there was good to come, that all this loss was taking me somewhere rather than nowhere?

There were a lot of stories in spiritual circles about how difficult it could be to follow truth, or the call of spirit, or the narrow path. I'd heard spiritual teachers joke that God did not have many friends, since he led people to goodness or love rather than, say, comfort and wealth. Would my obsession with finding spiritual truth force me to face the isolation and abandonment I most feared? I did not know what to believe anymore. I just wanted to work.

CHAPTER 45
A ROOM WITH A VIEW

On an ordinary morning in late May 2009, I sat down amid the exercise equipment in our upstairs workout room on my crescent-shaped purple pillow and looked out beyond the south gardens.

When I'd been a practicing yogi at CSE, I'd kept a small altar in the office with a candle, a statue of Kwan Yin or Buddha, and incense. Candles and incense had been the sine qua non of spiritual ambiance since I was a kid in Northbrook, where altar boys at high Mass wafted censers of smoking frankincense in somber, costumed processions to taper-lit altars. But now I had dropped the spiritual trappings. I no longer cared about looking holy or following sacred rules. With the simplicity of a Zen student, I merely took a cushion into our workout room and sat on it.

It was a bright clear day with a wide sky. A huge forest of redwoods, live oaks, and eucalyptus promenaded for miles down the steep mountain to the Monterey Bay. Far away, the edge of the sea melted into a misty, curved horizon. Tiny sailboats scuttled about Santa Cruz Harbor close to shore, and I could even glimpse the gleaming red curve of the roller coaster at the boardwalk. But it was really my inner landscape that I wanted to explore. I closed my eyes.

As usual, I sought the experience of oneness with what Yoga called universal consciousness. What Zen called one mind. What Christian mystics referred to as grace and what the Sufis named the presence of God. I imagined, should that union occur, I would see a kind of welcoming light into which I would dissolve, as if falling in love. I'd read numerous accounts of extraordinary experiences like that. No such thing had ever happened to me.

For over two years now, Jill had watched me scramble for money and contribute what I could to our home. While she ran her business in Capitola, I did laundry, grocery shopping, gardening, and chores. I applied for all sorts of jobs outside my wheelhouse: barista, gardener, deck builder, textbook editor. Small gigs like delivering newspapers, writing proposals, filing news clippings, and substitute teaching brought in a little cash. Jill had begun to trust me. She knew by now that I was not a bum looking for an easy ride. Rather, she saw me as "a smart, capable person who got squeezed out by young talent. You aged out of the job market," she told me. "It's not your fault. You'll be fifty-nine soon!"

Only rarely would her frustrations about money burst out in an otherwise heated argument. "It *would* be really helpful if you could come up with something each month to help with household bills," she might blurt. The jabs would make me cringe with self-condemnation. All the good energy I'd accumulated in meditation would dissipate like a faded dream.

At some point I started keeping a daily journal, where I worked out how I was feeling and coached myself to keep going. After a few months, my daily outpourings revealed an unfortunate but persistent theme. Much like the narrator in T. S. Eliot's poem, "The Love Song of J. Alfred Prufrock," who laments that beautiful and magical mermaids will not sing for him, my emotions turned out to be streaked with self-pity—the feeling that I was a pathetic and broken person, uncannily similar to my father.

But some impulse in me fought tooth and nail against that image. I didn't want to echo my father. Intuition and AA training kept telling me I wasn't born to suffer; I was supposed to be happy. Daily scribblings and meditation helped me stay in touch with that happiness hunch and its positive energy.

This morning, as my sit bones pressed into my purple pillow, I held a half-lotus and began my effort to make myself disappear so I could witness universal consciousness instead. But quite suddenly, unexpected emotions flooded my mind. Anger. Disgust. I was fed up with trying to eliminate myself. Instead, the vital presence of *me*, right there, feeling and thinking and perceiving, startled me like a knock at the door. Then as my disgust faded, in its place a powerful sense of my own buoyancy and power flowered. It was as if I were listening to inspiring and uplifting music.

The inner brightness reminded me of my first Buddhist retreat back in 1986 with Stephen and Jack. But, if that had been a bubbling glass of champagne, this was a cascading Whitewater River.

By contrast, it struck me that my notion of God was merely a flat idea. A mental image that had none of the vital, vibrant aliveness of what I was immediately experiencing as my own shining, beautiful self. Relief tingled through my body. Little tensions in my neck, cheeks, and wrists released. My toes unfurled, jaw opened, and eyes softened.

I rocked back and forth to relieve pressure on my spine. My eyes gently opened. Outside, the back deck, patio, pool, and gardens bloomed into sight, with the bay in the distant background. I felt almost exhilarated.

The God thing makes me submissive and fearful. And dependent, I thought. *I can't do it anymore. I don't need it anymore.*

As I stood up and stretched my legs, another truth blossomed in my mind. No matter how I tried to justify it, I had to admit that the God I'd always imagined tolerated unbearable human suffering and intentional cruelty. I could find no way around it, and I'd been trying for decades. Like Ivan Karamazov in Dostoevsky's story of the four brothers, I really could never understand or trust a God like that. Now I gave up trying.

I put away my meditation pillow and went downstairs to prepare dinner. I took out small red potatoes, green asparagus, and multicolored salad fixings. My life might be challenging, but it was mine. My relationship might have power imbalances and trust issues, but love mattered. Understanding and integrity would bring healing where it was needed. I fetched a chopping board and sharp knife. I might have a meager bank account, but I had Jill and Lauren, a beautiful and safe home, and access to healthy food. I looked out the kitchen window over our flower gardens rich with spring colors, orange and yellow and blue. I would keep finding ways to make money and stay afloat.

One day at a time.

A few days later, Jill found me at my computer. "Let's take Star for a walk," she said, holding the leash to our little black rescue mongrel.

"Great idea. I need to get away from this anyway. Give me two minutes."

I grabbed a jacket and my stash pouch, then joined Jill and Star outside. Ocean fog curled up from the coast, trickled through the trees, and cooled the sinking sun's warmth. The three of us trekked a quarter mile down the wooded lane, then veered off-road onto a curving trail through a redwood grove. Jill stopped, let Star off-leash, then lit the joint I'd rolled with some homegrown weed we got from a neighbor. She took a deep puff, and we kept walking. Star ran ahead and into the trees.

"Something entirely new occurred to me the other day," I began. Jill passed me the doobie, and I took a long hit.

"What's that?" she asked, and scuttled ahead of me down a sandy patch of trail. Rocks and debris studded the ruts cut by winter rains. A dusty scent of pine and warm redwood filled my nostrils.

"I experienced . . . well . . . it doesn't sound like much, but I sat there knowing myself as very alive and vibrant, while God seemed like a distant concept," I explained.

"Huh. Well, that makes sense. We really don't know anything about God, but we can know ourselves." She waited for me and took the joint. "I hope Star doesn't run into any poison oak," she said, and tramped quickly after the dog.

My booted feet stepped more slowly down the rugged trail. I wondered if Jill really appreciated the power of the insight. I caught up to her where she stopped to retie a shoelace and said, "No more pleading. I want to remember my inner potency. No more begging some fantasy for help."

"Everybody prays for courage or whatever in hard times," Jill said. "But you're right, our prayers really tap our own inner strengths."

We treaded to the bottom of the ravine, footsteps crunching. Above, I could hear the wind in the redwood canopy, pattering like rain. An afternoon breeze kicked up wood-scented tree dust that sparkled in shafts of light. The woods, the pot, my happy dog, the comfort of chatting with Jill about these private matters, all colluded to make me feel unusually content, uncharacteristically unworried about my unpredictable future.

"The owl's been here," Jill said with delight. She pointed to the side of a broken trunk, rising some fifteen feet above our heads. Gobs of white bird guano stained its bark. "You can see the nest up there." She pointed to the top. "Do you see any chicks in it?"

I walked over to an old-growth redwood and pressed both my hands to its bark. Its scratchy fibers pricked my palms. I looked up through the branches of the stately column that stood quietly, unmoved by human drama. Redwood debris drifted down from raggedy branches into my face. Everything—leaves, wildflowers, insects, grasses, lizards, mammals—took a breath, each in its own way.

I let go of the redwood and turned to Jill. "After all these years of searching for some philosophy or god to trust, maybe what I need is already here. Maybe all I need to do is trust my own being."

"What are you talking about?" Jill put the roach out carefully on a rock, grinding it with the toe of her sneaker.

I sat down on a long flat boulder and looked out over the meadow sprouting with wildflowers. "My little sister, Elizabeth, tells really bad stories of my father's suicidal despair and helplessness when he couldn't find work. When he was homeless, before he got sick."

Jill sat down next to me. "What stories?"

"When Beth was just a teenager, Mom left him for Hank. Daddy freaked out. Elizabeth found him at a friend's house with one of the guy's shotguns in his mouth, struggling to fire it. And then Mom and Hank didn't have room in their new home for Bethy I guess, so she left LA and went to live with Aunt Margaret in Chicago. But Dad followed her there. He was so depressed he said shit like he would jump out the window of his friend's hi-rise if she didn't take care of him. He expected her—a kid—to find a job and pay his rent so he could drink."

"Your family was messed up." We sat side by side on the rock looking beyond the edge of the woods.

"Yes," I said. "And I'm scared of that despair, that darkness. I want to trust myself, but what if I am really like him? What if that's why I can't find a job?"

"Stop it!" Jill snapped. "Those were his demons. You are nothing like your father, Rikki. You are strong, caring, and sober for how many decades? He was a lost cause. You are just hitting hard times. They will pass."

I tilted my head and squinted at her for a moment, reflecting on her words. "You're right," I said, nodding. "That is exactly what I discovered. I am much more than that old conditioning." We smiled at each other. "And I know there's something in me I can trust."

"That's my baby," Jill beamed. She got up, took my hand, and pulled me to my feet. "Star! Here, girl!" she called, and clipped the leash onto Star's collar. Together, the three of us hiked up the hill toward home.

PART III
GETTING REAL

CHAPTER 46
A FRESH WAVE

I sat on my knees in the east garden that lined our driveway, wearing cut-offs and a tank top. It was mid-September, and even the late-blooming calla lilies had yellowed, curving inward as they drooped toward earth. Over the summer their plump rhizomes had propagated happily in moist and mulched soil, and now pale green stalks crowded into every niche and cranny.

In advance of winter rains and spring growth, my mission was to divide the callas into small well-spaced clusters. I had pulled dozens out by the roots, wielding a hand spade to loosen their grip on the clay-packed soil. The sun was blisteringly hot, making my grim mood worse with every fresh stream of sweat.

I stabbed the earth around some stubborn roots until I could lever my trowel to pry a few tubers out of the ground and yank the tangled roots free. I kept my breathing steady, four counts in and four out, to calm my emotional tumbling. For the past day or two, depression had hovered around me like the wet scent of a coming storm. Now it was descending like a sheet of gray rain.

It was 2010. After three and a half years, I still had not secured a consistent income. Jill now covered all of our household expenses. During the decade since 2001, my seven-figure net worth had melted into five. My AA friends had taught me to keep a gratitude journal, and my daily scribblings often celebrated how lucky I was to have a place to live. I no longer took for granted a comfortable home and healthy lifestyle. I had learned how easily those things could be lost.

But gratitude was tarnished with remorse and anxiety. My belly would contract with hot shame when I thought about the financial burden I was to Jill. Other times my heart would thump with fear that something might threaten our relationship and thus my security.

I'd been sober for more than twenty-five years and knew how to live through a bout of the blues. I recognized the rapid erosion of feeling secure in the world; the steady decay of hope and belonging. Each heavy breath felt thick with a familiar feeling of futility. I had years of practice in not believing the kind of hateful voices that infiltrated my mind. But that hot, late-summer day, I couldn't hold them off. Their darkness engulfed me.

You're such a loser. A cruel harangue hammered my inner ears. *Now you've become a burden on everyone. You were going to help Lauren with grad school and buying a home.* Tears tracked my cheeks. *But no, you have nothing. You are totally worthless.*

I leaned forward into roots and soil, burying my face in muddy gardening gloves.

The world would be better off without you. I pushed the words away, knowing they were shadows of my father's life story. *If you could find life insurance without a suicide clause, maybe . . .* I shoved the thought aside, feeling desperately alone and abandoned.

"Is there no one or nothing for me in this world?" I heard myself howling aloud.

Suddenly a booming voice burst into the air from the deck above the overgrown garden.

"I have always been here for you," it thundered.

Even as my eyes shot up to find the source, I recognized my own tone, resonance, and inflection. My lips had not moved but the voice was mine.

The unexpected audible utterance, both alien and familiar,

shocked me out of my self-pity and desperation. An image of Moses hearing God's call in the desert flashed in my mind, and I laughed aloud. A voice in the garden? It seemed so droll—exactly my sense of humor. Still, the announcement was confident and powerful. *Where did it come from?*

I raked plant debris while ruminating on the strange experience. Slowly I understood that a hidden part of me had revealed itself to me, just as it had on my purple cushion a year and half before. But what did it mean?

After stripping off my muddy clothes, I headed in for a shower. I stood a long time under the hot pellets of water, noticing my mood had lifted. While the tightness in my muscles melted away, I felt slightly buoyed, as if a friend had visited for coffee. *The invisible friend must be my own heart embracing me,* I thought. Inexplicably, the mere recollection of the resonant sound aroused warm feelings of belonging.

As I dried off and dressed, I thought of how I might explain this to Jill. I decided not to try. But I wondered how the booming voice I heard compared to that of Yahweh in the Moses story. Like mine, Moses's "call" must have been a vocalization of his own being. The name *Yahweh*, I knew, could be translated into the phrase *I am that I am*. Or simply *I am*. Or *I have been*—as in the declaration *I have always been here for you*. My garden voice and that of Yahweh in the ancient myth were perhaps not very different.

I sat on our bed and leaned back against the fluffy cushions. Their embroidered patterns vibrated with the same rich hues as our bedroom walls—a burgundy red with a deep gold—which were said to be sacred Tibetan colors. I lay still, resting in my temple of solitude. *There actually are layers in me,* I reflected, *that are unavailable to my perceiving and thinking mind.*

Of course, I understood that most of the human psyche was unconscious. But now I seriously pondered what might actually live in those unseen depths.

What was this subtle energy in me that declared, *I am here for you*? I had no idea what to do with that question. It lay buried for another eight or nine years, ripening like a dragon's egg in a faraway cavern.

About a week after "Jehovah" hailed me in the garden, Jill's brother-in-law Len left me a voicemail to call him back. I punched his number into my landline the next morning.

"Hey, what took you so long?" he half teased. "I'd about given up on you."

"Oh, sorry. Is it time-sensitive? What can I do for you?"

"No!" he laughed. "It's more like what we can do for each other. You do project management, right?" Len asked.

My brain scrambled. Was he talking about work? Len was the chief engineering officer at a software security company called Wave Systems in Cupertino.

"Software projects. That's what you were doing?" he asked.

"Yes, um, actually, ah, I'm really good at that," I stammered. My mind was a stupid blank.

"Perfecto!" Len almost cheered.

Is this really happening? I held my breath. *Is he going to . . .* ?

"I need a part-time contractor to jump in here and take over a project mid-stream," Len said.

I fought to think of something normal to say. "Sure. Great. What can you tell me about it?"

"Send me a resume. Then let's meet at Wave next Monday morning for an interview." We set the time and place and hung up. Blood pounded behind my eyes.

Then a shudder rippled through my body and tears flooded my face. Work! Real work. A big smile took over my entire mien. Self-respect. New jeans. Groceries. Lauren had gotten a Pell Grant for tuition, but maybe I could help her pay for books next semester.

Despite my recent anti-deity insights, prayers jammed all the airwaves in my mind. All I could hear was my voice begging the goddamned universe not to take this away from me. *Please God,* I intoned silently, *yes, I am grateful for my health and Lauren's thriving, but please, you dickwad mother*fucker, *just let this happen.*

The universe let it happen.

Len hired me to take over coordination and management of a web-based digital security product from Roger, an engineering director. He'd warned me I might encounter resistance. I wasn't worried. My career had often exposed me to anxious managers who feared that project leaders like me would step on their turf. Roger was no exception.

In my first week at the company, I joined a meeting of key players in engineering and quality assurance. At some point, I appropriately asked Roger to give us the current timeline for his team's delivery of certain blocks of software code.

"I'm not giving you anything," he snarled. His voice was unusually guttural. Startled, I looked up. He glowered at me; everyone else was suddenly staring at their hands or their computers.

Oh, fuck fuck fuck what do I do? Baba, help me now.

Baba? Why was I asking him for help? I hadn't called on Baba since I quit smoking, decades earlier. In the sixties, Ram Dass, a.k.a. Dr. Richard Alpert of LSD fame, had adopted a local Indian village guru as his teacher. I had a heart bond with his Baba from Neem Karoli. When I called to him, I knew I was really calling to the goodness and love within me, but it helped to imagine a human figure. *Help me here, Baba!*

"Gathering that kind of data is my job," I said to Roger, meeting his eyes.

Show me how to handle myself.

"Not if I can help it," he said. His dark eyes, twisted lips, and husky frame sent my heart spinning.

Baba Baba Baba . . . I kept my eyes on Roger while my mind waited for something. Perhaps a second passed. Then I stood up and left the room. Striding to my cubicle without any idea of what to do, I grabbed my car keys. Once outside, I trekked to the parking lot and found my green Prius.

Safe in the driver's seat, I locked the door. Then I sat up straight, closed my eyes, and let all the air in my lungs flow out. I breathed in for a count of four and held that breath for a count of seven. Finally, I exhaled slowly for a count of eight. Remembering to breathe through my nose to calm my brain, after five or six cycles I still had no idea what to do. But it was not smart to be missing for too long. I did one more breath, locked up, and walked back into the meeting.

Everyone behaved as if I had simply gone to the ladies' room.

Over the next few weeks, I tripped on a few more landmines before I figured out that all three software directors resented my presence. None believed I could add value. I navigated with my best diplomacy, knowing that complaining to Len would just make things worse. Slowly, as I gathered data and pulled the team together, I claimed some victories. People saw that tasks got defined, target dates had estimates, work was staffed, and I tracked weekly progress. Over time, the directors began to work with me constructively. Len was happy with my performance, and the following spring in 2011, Wave hired me as a full-time, salaried program manager.

My ordeal appeared to be truly over. I had made it through to the other side. I was sixty years old, the perfect age for a renaissance.

"I feel like I've become a different person," I told my friends Jan and Illana as we walked barefoot along the beach south of Santa Cruz.

"How so?" Jan asked. A chilly fog swirled around us, rarely penetrated by the fuzzy afternoon sun. We walked in stride on the damp sand. Sometimes a little wave would wash over our feet.

"I've lost so much: money, possessions, status. Yet here I am, starting over."

"You experienced Persephone's descent into Hades. What Christians call a dark night of the soul," Jan said. "During the passage, you shed everything that's not essential."

"Yes," I mused, "exactly. And then, what's left?"

"Shamans go through the same thing to travel in an inner landscape," added Illana. She had worked with shamans while earning her doctoral degree. "They surrender their personal psychological identities so they can receive the voice of the god," said Illana.

"I sure haven't received the voice of any gods!" I laughed with a sarcastic and slightly wounded tone.

"You will. Remember Rumi and the Sufis: the vessel must be emptied before it can be filled with sweet nectar," Illana said.

"Did you see the movie *An Officer and A Gentleman*?"

"Sure," Jan said.

"I remind myself of the Zack Mayo character. A desperate, failing antihero reaches a breaking point when she has nowhere left to turn."

"But then what?" Illana asked pointedly.

"I'm not sure. I know that I don't expect to get happiness from the world. It has failed me or vice-versa—whatever. But it's madness to expect the world to deliver my demands to the front door."

"True enough," Jan began. "And at that point you look inward, toward yourself and your own being."

"Amen." I wanted to connect once and for all with *something* in myself that I could count on, that couldn't be taken away. I'd had nowhere else to go.

I had come a long way from my first meditation retreat in 1985. Had the journey been worth it? The jury was still out on that. Part of me still thought I'd have been pretty happy with a couple million dollars and a planned retirement.

CHAPTER 47
IN LIVING COLOR

"Have you signed up to help Terri?" my old friend Cathy Henderson asked me one Sunday afternoon in March 2012.

We were relaxing in the outdoor hot tub on the pool deck. Jill and I had friends over to celebrate the coming equinox. The pool was pleasant and the hot tub had reached 102. The air was intermittently warmed by streaks of sun that pierced the high clouds. Len, Jill's brother-in-law and my boss, was grilling salmon and veggie burgers on the barbecue.

I hadn't seen much of Henderson since the '90s, but when we got together, she always brought fresh news from our circle of peninsula lesbians. But this alarmed me. My brain skipped a beat, and I squinted to think. Did she mean my ex-lover Terri, from decades ago?

"You mean my Terri?" I asked. A vision of her finishing the Honolulu marathon so many years ago, exuberant and depleted, flashed in my mind.

"Yeah. You don't know?"

"What? What don't I know?" My belly twisted. I hadn't had news of her since we broke up.

"Glioblastoma. She needs rides to chemo."

Fuck. I was pretty sure that was the kind of malignant astrocytoma that killed Nick, Lauren's biological father.

Henderson gave me Terri's number, and I called that day to see what I could do.

I parked at the curb in front of Terri's house, under a magnificent jacaranda tree redolent with purple blossoms. Bright petunias and pansies filled curved beds that nestled along the front of the house and sidewalk. *How did she ever find strength and time for that?* I wondered.

Terri's daughter Monica answered the door of the two-bedroom ranch in Santa Clara. I recognized her immediately, though she was almost thirty now. She shared her mother's round-faced innocence and spark of Irish charm. We embraced, then she took me through the front room into the kitchen where a skinny Terri, wearing what looked like a wired shower cap, sat at a round table eating butter.

"Terri," I smiled, and went over to gently hug her thin and bony frame. "It's been a long time, my friend." She squeezed back and the years fell away. I felt the cozy intimacy of a long friendship.

"I'm so glad to see you, Rikki. Thanks for coming. You look terrific," she said.

Seeing her again made my heart swell. "You look beautiful, like yourself. Even with your electric hat." We both laughed lightly. Her shaved head was tucked into a little bonnet with wires protruding all round that ran to a small box with a shoulder strap, sitting on the floor.

"Sit down." She gestured to the kitchen table. "Do you want a drink? Monica, get Rikki an iced tea."

"But what's with the butter?" I asked, pulling out a chair at the roundtable.

"Ketone diet. High fat, low carb. It might help slow the tumor growth."

Terri wore jeans and a short-sleeved apricot polo that brought out the searing blue in her eyes. Only the left eye could see now, but it wasn't obvious until she told me. Despite the whole catastrophe, Terri's working eye was alert and attentive. And her warmth was authentic.

"How's your energy?" I asked.

"Better than you'd think. I can't run anymore but my wife, Laura, takes me out to the trails to see everyone. It's a little hard to move around with this thing." She tapped the wired black box with a sandal.

"You have to wear it all the time?"

"Just about. Let's get going. I'll explain in the car." She stood up and slung the strap over her shoulder.

We walked slowly, but she was strong and steady the whole way to my car.

We drove twenty miles north to Kaiser Redwood City's cancer clinic. Terri told me that her head device sent electronic pulses to her skull with the objective of creating a magnetic dipole across her head. The dipole would align the molecules in her brain a certain way—positive poles toward the negative, negative toward the positive—which Terri's medical team hoped would have a disruptive effect on tumor formation.

At the Kaiser complex we found our way to the chemo lounge. While Terri sat in the infusion chair with an IV delivering blasts of cytotoxic drugs, we talked. Our conversation flowed from our daughters to our spiritual paths, the books that had moved us, and how we'd grown. Terri told me about painting, and about quitting high tech. She spoke of finding passion both in her art and in inspiring others to find their creative paths.

"Rise up in living color, Rikki. Stay strong." Terri considered herself a peoples' cheerleader. Whatever you aspired to, she wanted you to pursue it. She loved vivid colors and had painted her acrylic fingernails the same rich blue as the walls in her bedroom.

"I want my nails to match the room where I die," she said, though she was not ready to die yet.

Terri was as tough as those nails. After she'd been diagnosed, she'd made up her mind to "go out strong." When she said, "I relish the energy and excitement of finishing with strength," I knew she meant it. She was a triathlete who had done that many times.

Over the next few months, my role in supporting Terri shifted from driver to reader. I visited her home with the delicate flower gardens, now tended by her wife, a few times a month. I sat on a chair across from her as she lay on the couch in the apricot-colored front room, reading aloud from books that caught her attention. She had already followed advice about saying goodbye and closing unfinished business. Now she wanted to prepare emotionally for letting go.

We read Christian testimonials, contemporary Buddhist teachings, and New Age guidance. She shared with me her remaining fears and unconfessed regrets. One day, when she needed bedrest, we sat on the bed in the blue bedroom. She worried that her parents might have been right, that Jesus really wanted her to be a Catholic.

"What if I got it wrong and he's angry with me for deserting?" She looked at me as if I might have an answer.

Baba, help me here, I implored my deeper self.

Terri said, "I followed my heart. How can you know if that's right? You can only do your best."

"Why don't you write Jesus a letter?" I heard myself say aloud.

Terri lit up with a full-on grin. "You know what? I will. Would you get me that spiral pad from the dresser? I'll do it now."

If you had only a few months, the time to write to Jesus was the moment you thought of it.

"Dear Jesus," she penned, "I have pursued my spiritual best the only way I knew how. I tried to follow my truth. If I made a mistake, I am sorry. I found my passion and it felt like this is what you wanted for me. I hope you understand. Love, Terri."

When she handed me the notebook, her whole face had relaxed into a soft smile. In one utterly sincere gesture, she'd made her peace with the universe and inspired me with courage.

Moments like that helped me stay close to her until the end. A few months later, in July of 2013, she suffered a stroke from which she never recovered.

After Terri passed, hundreds of people jammed the Unitarian Universalist Church in San Jose for her memorial service. Vibrant bouquets overwhelmed the altar. During the service, I spoke about her courage in facing life as an artist and athlete and facing death as a young and vital woman. About how she had let everyone feel intimate with her, as if we each were special. "Rise up in living color," I reminded all her friends.

So, when I felt her presence a couple of weeks after she died, I was not shocked, though I could not explain it.

I'd treated myself to a professional full-body massage in my home. In my trusted masseur's hands, I relaxed into deep quiet. His forearms were working on my lower back while my mind drifted on an endless blue sea. Abruptly, there rose in me a warm, easy feeling, a bubble, and then laughter. It felt as if Terri were in the room, and then I heard quite distinctly, in her voice, "Rise up in living color, Rikki, and no whining!"

A wave of happiness and freedom brushed my naked body like a sea breeze. I'd only ever felt one presence before, that of my first adolescent love who passed away in his late fifties. He appeared in my sleep some forty years after we'd dated. In the dream, I was standing in a darkened industrial garage when the sectional steel door flew up and revealed his muscular body in silhouette. From behind his head, the glow of an intense rising sun streamed highways of yellow light onto the empty floor. He said he was passing by and wanted to say hello. In the morning, I Googled him and found he had died of leukemia a few weeks prior.

Whether it was possible or not, I had the strong impression that Terri had safely navigated an after-body passage and was just passing by to say hello. She had aspired to become an angel. Perhaps this was one of her first acts of service.

CHAPTER 48
GRACE

A couple of years before Terri died, in spring 2011, the squawking of my home phone interrupted the planting of asparagus. Jill and I had dug a deep trench and filled it with nutrients before setting the young plants in mud and covering them with compost-rich soil. I stood up and looked toward the house; nobody used the telephone landline anymore except family. I ran down the pebbled path to the garage and grabbed the wall-mounted receiver after the sixth or seventh ring. Struggling to hold the phone against my shoulder, I sank my teeth into the filthy fingertips of my gloves to pull them off.

"Hi, Linda!" I said happily when I heard my sister's voice. She rarely called; especially not on the home phone.

"Rikki, I have some very difficult news."

What? Mom? I put myself in full-competence mode, something I had learned somewhere along the way. I stood ready to hear it and face it, whatever it was.

"Okay," I said firmly.

"I have a type of blood cancer called lymphoma," she said. "It will kill me eventually but for now it is not life-threatening."

Everything drained out of me, right there into a crack in the cement garage floor. I was instantly helpless, a lost child. In that moment, I saw how scared I was to be in the world without my big sister. Panic, palpitations in my chest, scrambled my thoughts.

"Oh," I said.

"It's called indolent, lazy," Linda went on. "Because it grows very slowly. Indolent follicular lymphoma. I'm going to do some chemo and go on living."

I don't recall the rest of the day. The news put me into quiet shock.

But Linda went on with her life, and so did I.

Five years later, in early 2016, my stepfather Hank passed away from an undetected pancreatic cancer. My mother, already enduring many of the ailments and indignities of old age, suffered a series of small strokes as shock and grief rippled through her thin, fragile frame. She lived ninety minutes north of Los Angeles, about five and half hours from my house. Since she needed 24/7 care, my younger sister, Elizabeth, moved in with her while Linda drove up weekly from LA with supplies. They managed to get Mom on hospice care, and a nurse began to visit twice a week.

I was by this point working as a security program manager at VMware in Palo Alto. In late February, the company's executives decided to offload the work in my department to India. All twenty-five US employees were laid off. I was sixty-five, too young to retire and too old for most employers to consider. I submitted my unemployment insurance claim and turned my attention to my mother.

I drove the 350 miles south to see her every couple of weeks. I usually slept on her sofa, but on one particular visit, in May, I stayed at Linda and Rick's home in LA.

On that spring Friday morning, Linda, Rick, and I prepared to take a carload of supplies to Mom's house in the mountains, giving our sister Elizabeth a day off. We packed frozen Costco foods in boxes next to bags of fresh groceries from Gelson's in the trunk of their Prius. Linda went to into the kitchen to fill her water bottle. Preoccupied with my own thoughts, I wandered into the dining room to collect my purse and shoes.

My mother was very close to death. I could not stop contemplating what might be going on in her inner world. I felt compelled to look inside my private haven and consider what she might be feeling. Abruptly, I stopped moving right where I was near the dining room window and shut my eyes. Relaxing my attention, I simply felt into the quiet space of my personal sanctum.

Standing stock-still in my socks on the hardwood floor, I noticed the pressure of the planks against my feet. I heard the water gurgling into Linda's bottle. A bitter, citrusy scent hit my nostrils from the bowl of oranges on the breakfast table. My tongue felt the smooth hardness of my teeth. It occurred to me that each of these different perceptions was experienced in a similar way, in the same interior. Pressure, sound, scent, touch. Different but very similar.

All my experiences, including this thought about my subjective experiences, are known in here, I thought. *Here* seemed like a vast, empty Imax theater in which various events were magically presented to me, the audience. A coffee smell. A humming motorcycle engine. A flurry of thoughts. All these appeared right there in my interior auditorium. *This is where real life is lived,* I thought.

"The inner world is real," I said aloud.

"Uh-huh," Linda said from the kitchen. "Did you get some water?"

I took my bottle to the spigot. I knew it was bad timing, but I couldn't stop myself.

"I mean, we never experience organs, or cells, or neurons. We experience sights, sounds, emotions. In here." I tapped my chest, repeatedly. "That's what's important. The me inside me is more real than, I don't know"—I stood there trying to think of the right words—"than the socially constructed me. Or the biological me," I said to my water bottle.

"Ready? Out to the car! Rick, will you set the alarm?" Linda strode out the front door. I moved my feet and headed out after her.

Rick climbed into the driver's seat, and I sat behind Linda in the rear. As Rick backed the little green hybrid out of the driveway, I leaned into the space between their bucket seats.

"If the inner world of experience is real, why do we act like we are only bodies made of atoms? Like when someone dies, we say their whole experience ends. Why do we do that?"

"What are you talking about?" Rick asked, coming out of his own reverie. He steered the car onto Santa Monica Boulevard.

"I'm talking about the private life, where all the important stuff—understanding, love, creativity—comes from. The inner sanctum, the part of you that experiences things."

"You're talking about consciousness. Nobody knows what that is." Rick, a.k.a. psychologist Dr. Richard S. Marken, studied perceptual feedback mechanisms in living organisms. "But I think it works like a quiet inner control system finding creative solutions to novel problems," he said.

I was eager to talk with him about his ideas. But a blast of Amos Lee's voice and guitar thrummed out the front and rear speakers. Linda had hooked her iPhone into the car stereo.

"Could we just not talk till we get to Mom's?" she said. Her clipped voice spoke pure annoyance. Linda could be demanding and crabby. None of us knew yet that a malignant tumor was growing in her abdomen. Later she would tell me she'd felt a pressure in her belly that scared her.

I sat back in silence, wondering what I had been trying to say. My insight was fading like an eagle's distant cry. I only remembered the gist of it: the inner world is real. But I could not remember quite what I meant by that. Cancer and death seemed pretty real, too.

It would be a few years before I again experienced something vibrant and alive and absolutely genuine inside me—a place where I had never been wounded, where I was always whole, alive, and unperturbed.

My mother passed away a month later, in mid-June at her home, at eighty-nine, under Elizabeth's care with hospice assistance. We daughters felt blessed that Mom was spared months or years of physical and mental anguish. But Linda's tumor had been silently adding bulk while she schlepped Mom to doctors and boxed up household supplies. By the end of June, her pain could not be ignored.

"The indolent lymphoma transformed into deformed large B-cell lymphoma," Rick explained to me over the phone. "They can't kill it with chemo." Linda would not live out the year, her doctors said. "The only known treatment for DLBCL is to destroy all the stem cells living in Linda's bone marrow, then transplant fresh ones from a healthy body. We've registered to find a match."

"I'll get tested, Rick. I'm old, but I'm healthy."

My blood markers turned out to be a perfect match with Linda's, ten for ten.

"It's a go, Linda," I told her. "You're not dead yet!"

All through the process, I experienced the strange sensation that we were destined to go through this together. That the reason I had taken up kickboxing was as much to be a strong healthy donor as it was to cope with work. That Linda and I were being led by some invisible power toward her healing.

In October of 2018 she received, and began recovering from, the brutal stem cell replacement treatment. After four months she was back at many activities she loved, from gardening to square dancing. I loved watching her return from the edge of death—the beauty of her courage and love for life.

One afternoon in early 2019, I was home in the computer room finishing a phone conversation with Linda.

"I'm going up to Lake Tahoe for my book salon's retreat this March," she said. "I haven't been able to go for years." She was still taking piles of pills and immunosuppressants, but she could manage light travel.

"Oh man, Linda, have fun and enjoy your life," I said, feeling nothing but gigantic love for my big sister.

We hung up. As I docked the handset, my eye snagged on a small Tibetan singing bowl with a brass striker sitting on the desk. I picked up the striker and gonged the bell for both of us. The vibration triggered waves of physical and emotional relief.

I closed my eyes and stood motionless, attentive to the vibrating streams I heard within my personal Imax. The tones weaved in and around each other, dimming slightly with every passing second. Finally, the gentle sounds melted away. In their place I noticed the heavy sensation of my feet pressing the ground. Then, an itch on my left forearm appeared like a sparkle of fireworks. There was a slight streak of sharp pain in my right rotator cuff. Each sensation or perception appeared in my awareness, where I recognized it, knew it, *was* it.

All my experiences occur in this same inner space, I thought. *Everything happens in here, not out there!* The lights were on in my inner theater, and I watched events occur here.

This was the same thing I had noticed in Linda's dining room, years earlier. This time, I asked myself a question. What actually was it that recognized, that knew, the thrumming of a gong, the feel of a Waterman pen, the taste of Arabian Mocha Java? What was the magic thing that made it all alive, instead of not? I could only answer, the essence of me. Plain old simple me.

But what was it about me that was capable of experiencing something? What made it possible for there to be an experience, rather than nothing? Consciousness was the obvious answer, but what was that, really?

I did not know what aware presence was, and I did not think anybody else really knew either. But it was peaceful, like a shelter in a storm. It was quiet, even content, and it was right in the heart of me.

I'm going to write a song for Linda, I thought. I had written some simple folk songs before, using my repertoire of twelve or fifteen guitar chords. So, I spent a few weeks crafting a melody—a simple C major progression with a few sevenths thrown in—and the lyrics flowed once I heard the music float out of my guitar.

When you gone through the hell
That life laid out for you.
When you gone beyond and afar.
You come back to the home
And the moments before you
With a grace that might come from above.

Linda wept when I sang it for her in a Zoom call. Years later, I would sing again it at her memorial service.

CHAPTER 49
GOODBYE

"Well, Robert, this is the year we pack it up and leave California," I told Lauren's dad as we sat in his living room sipping sparkling water. Jill and Bob, Robert's husband, were outside on the patio with the dogs.

It was 2019. Jill and I had decided in January to sell her house and home-furnishings business and move to Santa Fe. The retail business was under attack from online stores, and real estate prices were starting to level off, meaning it was a good time to sell. We'd both known this was coming, but it seemed too soon.

Our visit to Robert and Bob, who lived in Palm Springs, was part of our "good-bye" tour of the West Coast.

"Oh, no!" Robert threw himself back on the couch cushions. His palms flew to his cheeks as his face contorted into a worried grimace. "Is that good news?"

"Well, it's the plan, so moving forward on the plan is good, I guess." I half smiled.

"Still going to Santa Fe?"

"Yeah." I swallowed a mouthful of water.

"But?" He heard something in my voice. His hand reached out and covered mine in my lap, and he peered attentively at me.

Robert was my very close friend. I could share anything with him. I took a long breath and exhaled volubly. "But I don't know, Robert.

I've been in California since 1966—over fifty years. Everyone I know is here. I'm going to miss you all so much."

"Oh, Rikki, they have these new contraptions! You can actually fly here in the air."

We both laughed, lifting the mood.

"The distance won't matter. We'll stay close," he smiled gently.

"I'm almost sixty-eight," I sighed. "And life keeps presenting challenges. They're different, but not easier. Right now, I'm losing my home. But," I brightened, "I'm gaining one, too. Our new place will be in both our names."

"Oh, that's good news! I'm relieved for you. It's good to have that security."

I nodded. "But you know what I mean. Everything is going to change in a few years. Our bodies are going down, baby."

"Yeah, but also . . ." Robert hesitated, "this will sound weird, but there is something beautiful about closure, about completing things." Robert had been a hospice nurse for the last decade of his career. He had been with dozens of families at the time of a loved one's passing. "Some people focus on securing their money, or punishing someone in their family at the end. But most people want to heal wounds, find and give forgiveness, bring relationships back to simple love."

"Wow, that's beautiful, Robert. I think you are onto something."

Robert had saved and invested wisely during the decades of his marriage to Bob. Now he had a substantial portfolio that secured a comfortable retirement. He had arranged some sort of trust that ensured Lauren would inherit something. For me, financial security for our daughter seemed impossible twenty years ago. But what I couldn't provide, Robert now could, and that brought me deep relief and happiness.

"What I've witnessed in people who are facing their last days is there might be some flailing around as they try to figure out what's most important," Robert said.

"Well, we've got years. But I don't want to waste them."

"You know, Rikki, I think it is about celebrating life," Robert said. "These retirement years should be for celebrating living itself."

"What are you two gabbing about?" Jill said as she and Bob came in from the patio with the four dogs.

"The way life poses different challenges at different stages," Robert said.

"Finding out what is important in old age," I added.

"Lighthearted chitchat?" Bob teased.

In LA, we stayed a couple of nights at Linda and Rick's. Jill worried that we would be too great a burden. Linda had steadily recovered from the transplant but continued to take many medications. Still, she felt strong and insisted we stay at her house. I wanted to be there, up close to see how she was really doing. Jill and I attended carefully to the cleanliness protocols—Linda was on immunosuppressants—and tried not to be a nuisance.

The big, round, hand-carved table in the kitchen was the perfect place to sit down and chat. Linda set out bread and olives, nuts, and sliced apples. I made a cup of coffee with fresh-ground beans, while Jill sipped a sparkling water.

"How are Robert and Bob?" Linda asked as we settled around the kitchen table. It was chilly, and we all wore warm socks and sweaters.

"They're great; nothing new in paradise. But we got talking about what is the most important thing in our lives right now."

"And what is that, do you think?" She took a bite from an apple slice.

"I don't know," I said, shaking my head as I looked inward. "I kinda wish I'd found God." Linda and Jill both laughed.

"I know you do, Rikki," Linda said. "Maybe you still will. Carl Jung claimed that old age is our opportunity to complete the lifelong process of individuation," she said. "Which means encountering your deepest self, where God is most likely hiding."

"That's fascinating," I said.

"I just want to stay in the now, enjoy and savor every moment. I already escaped death once. This is all extra. I don't want to miss anything, even the bad things," Linda said.

"We're only alive now," Jill said. "I'm with you, Linda. Experience it all."

But there was something more I wanted.

I wanted to understand what we are *for*, why we exist. People told me it was ridiculous to ask, because nobody knew. Maybe it was coming from an unstable family that left me hungry for belonging and meaning in the cosmos, but I just couldn't let it go.

What are human beings, what does it mean to be one, and what the heck is going on?

Would I ever know the answers to those questions?

CHAPTER 50
SCIENCE QUIZ

"Halloo!" called a familiar voice from the driveway below our deck. I trotted down the redwood planks to the railing and leaned out. Two neighbors stood on the blacktop holding towels. A sliver of sunlight gleamed through the overcast morning's foggy shreds.

"Hi, ladies," I hollered with a welcoming wave. Our house was the local gathering spot for swimming and hot-tubbing.

"We have arrived," Lucy sang out, raising both arms in happy salute. Her salt-and-pepper hair streamed out of her straw hat down to her waist. A psychologist, Lucy was my age, single, and lived two houses down the lane. The south wall of her living room was all glass, and her shelves were lined with drums, feathers, bones, and stones. Wrapped in a purple shawl with an ankle-length orange skirt, she incarnated the earth mother for our little mountain community.

"Hey, Rikki!" Melinda said, looking up. "Are we too early?" Melinda lived next door and raised chickens. She was my go-to neighbor for fresh eggs or a cup of flour. She sometimes escaped her life as real estate agent and mother of twin preteen girls to come over and smoke a joint with us.

I gestured toward the back steps. "Throw your towels on a pool chair and c'mon up. Jill's getting her suit on."

"What's going on, girlfriends!" Jill banged out the kitchen door, holding three clear goblets and a bottle of local Cabernet. "I hope this is good. I liked their Zinfandel." She half-filled the glasses. As always, I stuck with a nonalcoholic soda. I enjoyed smoking pot and hanging out with drinkers, but alcohol was simply not in my life plan.

"Thanks, Jilly," Lucy said, choking a little on the smoke from a joint she brought. "Hard to believe you could be leaving our 'hood soon."

"I'm gonna miss you guys so much," Melinda said. Picking up her glass, she turned to me. "How's your sister doing?"

"Oh, I appreciate you asking," I said. A grin flowered on my face as warm blood flooded my cheeks. "Really well!" I almost cheered. "She's able to do most of the things she used to do. Maybe not the square-dancing yet, but . . ."

"It's because of what you put into those stem cells," Lucy said.

My eyebrows furrowed, and I shook my head at her. "You really think all that stuff mattered? The workouts, the diet, following all that advice for boosting stem cells . . ."

"For sure that helped!" Melinda exclaimed. "You gave her healthy, high-quality cells. Lots of mitochondria and ribosomes."

"That's true." I smiled at the memory. "The nurses were amazed at how many billions of plump stem cells I produced."

Lucy sipped her wine, then pointed her glass at me. "It's not just the nutrition," she said. "It's the devotion and love you put into the whole thing."

I nodded. "Actually, I almost agree with you, Luce, but I can't understand how that could happen. How could my intentions affect an outcome inside someone else?"

"It's spirit!" Lucy laughed. "It's the pure energy of spirit, which you, Rikki West, poured into your stem cells."

"See, I have a hard time believing that," I said. I took the little reefer from Jill and inhaled deeply, held my breath a few seconds, and blew the smoke away from the group. Then I dropped the last bit of roach into my empty Perrier can.

"That's because you went to Berkeley," she teased. Lucy studied at Harvard, a liberal arts college, whereas Cal Berkeley focused on science and technology.

"What do you mean?" I asked.

"You got indoctrinated into thinking science has the only and final voice on what's true. What is reality." She took a sip and challenged me over her glass's rim, one eyebrow raised.

Did I think science had the last word on reality? As a body of knowledge, of course, science was profoundly incomplete. Still, its methods seemed to me the best means we had of determining facts about the world.

"Well, science isn't done yet. There are many unexplained phenomena," I said. "Did you know that they've detected something throughout space, even here on Earth, that interacts with gravity, but not with light? So, they call it dark matter. It's supposed to make up more than 90 percent of what's here, but you can't see it."

"That's unnerving!" Lucy laughed. "What else don't we know?"

"Exactly. So, science isn't quite *true*," I said. "It's evolving. But you're right, I do expect explanations about the world to be consistent with what we know so far. And I can't explain how the love within me could help create healing in another person."

"And yet, we all know that's what happened," Lucy confirmed, smiling at each of us.

Jill emptied her glass and set it down. "It sounds like science is good at how *things* work, but not so useful for how *spirit* works," she said.

"Right!" I nodded. "Do you remember Stephen J. Gould? I think he was an evolutionary biologist. He said the same thing. That science and religion explore two different kinds of truth—he called them non-overlapping magisteria. Science deals with quantities: frequency, length, temperature, so on. What he called the religious side deals with qualities—warm, red, sweet, loud—and values like truth, goodness, and beauty."

"Great minds." Jill nodded.

"Well, no offense, but I think Gould is full of crap. In company with Plato and Aristotle, I want a philosophical theory of everything." I shaped a single imaginary globe in the air with my hands. "All of it. World, awareness, body, and mind."

"So do you think science will ever give us that complete picture?" Melinda raised her eyebrows and looked around the group.

"Probably not," ventured Lucy. She stood up and picked her glass off the table. "But let's get into that hot tub anyway."

We took our drinks and went down the back stairs to the jacuzzi.

"I think science will get closer and closer to reality," I said as we walked down the steps to the hot tub, "but scientists need to study awareness itself, not just the physical brain."

"That could get interesting," Melinda said. She sat down on the ledge and dangled her legs, holding her glass aloft. Jill plunged all the way in, dunking to her chin and whooping. Both Lucy and I, at least a decade older than Jill, eased in slowly, standing hip-deep and keeping our arms high out of the steaming water.

"Anybody want to take a dip in the pool?" Jill said. She sat on the ledge between the pool and hot tub and reached into the water for the thermometer. "Sixty-eight degrees! C'mon, it'll feel so good to get back in here." She put two feet into the pool. "Brrr!"

"We used to do that all the time at Harbin," Lucy said, referring to the clothing-optional natural springs north of San Francisco. "The cold plunge/hot springs shock was fabulous!" She looked at me. "So, if you know science hasn't got all the answers, why do you doubt your healing power?" Lucy asked.

"Yeah," I nodded. "I'm not sure what to think," I admitted. "Maybe I'm not brave enough to bear the scorn of science-minded folks if I affirm there are nonphysical realities. They call you woo-woo and snicker."

"Nobody really knows what is going on," Jill said, "and I'm not sure many people care. Most people just want to cling to any belief that makes them feel secure."

"You can be so cynical, Jill," Melinda laughed, "but I agree there's something more to me than my body and my social life." She slid into the water from her perch. "Something spiritual, I guess. But I think each person has to find their own way, their unique path to wisdom and happiness or whatever it is for them."

"Amen!" cheered Lucy, and stretched her glass across the water to clink with Melinda's.

I smiled at Jill. "What do you think?"

"I think you made your own miracle happen, Rikki. And none of us can explain that really," she said.

Later that evening, I burrowed into the leather recliner in the office with the lights out. A blob of waxing gibbous moon filtered through the east-facing bay windows, casting a thin yellow light on the carpet. The pot we'd smoked had got my mind racing, leaping from one thought to another. They boiled down to a basic question: *Are we merely one-lifetime biological entities, whose interior life is determined by brain cells doing biochemistry—or is there something deeper within us, something that connects us metaphysically?*

Like Melinda, I was pretty certain I was not merely my body. I could not deny the vivid brightness of my own aware self that I'd become familiar with during meditation. I knew I was something alive and present here and now. But did that presence really exist, or was it a trick of my brain?

I looked over to the woods across the lane that hid my neighbor Connie's house. Seasonal rains had carved ruts through the wild grasses in our yard. The twenty-six rosebushes that lined the sidewalk to our front door were producing their spring canes. I knew about that world because perceptions of light, sound, scent, and touch from it were fed to and processed in my brain. But it was the magic of awareness that somehow turned sense perceptions into genuine experiences like taste and smell.

I wanted to explore that awareness. But all the pathways to the inner world that I knew about were full of cultural and religious baggage—senseless rules, dogma, and questionable leaders. I couldn't bring myself to trust another spiritual teacher or another vague metaphysical concept.

I had to keep finding my truth in my own experience, for myself.

Suddenly the standing lamp snapped on. "Hi, baby. Why are you sitting in the dark?" Jill asked from the doorway.

"Hi, honey. No reason," I said. Then I remembered a Zen koan about the meaning of the Buddha's teachings. "'Vast emptiness, nothing holy,'" I quoted, amusing myself with a little joke about my presence. Vast and open, but completely ordinary.

"Come watch a show with me," she said.

We held hands on the way downstairs.

As I moved through the house, I said a quiet goodbye to the things I would miss—the wooden bannisters, the rooms opening onto the back deck, the view out the kitchen window.

"Goodbye, Tibetan prayer wheel," I whispered and we passed the living room where the ancient hand-painted wooden wheel stood.

"We're taking that with us," Jill said.

CHAPTER 51
HATCHED

April 2019. I woke just after 5:00 a.m. and peered into the unfamiliar dimness of our room at the Santa Fe Inn. Jill lay curled under the queen-size comforter breathing slowly. I folded back the bedclothes and stepped out in my T-shirt. A thin carpet offered little warmth against the freezing hardwood floor.

We had flown to Santa Fe, New Mexico, to find our retirement home. The previous day we'd gone house-hunting with a local agent. We'd developed a good feel for the small, four-hundred-year-old Spanish city surrounded by Native pueblos. Today, we planned to hike among the naked aspens in the Santa Fe National Forest.

The brochure on the table said there would be fresh coffee in the lobby at 5:30 a.m. Out our window, across the roof of the inn, a thick swirl of tiny snowflakes filled the air. I quietly pulled on the sweatshirt, jeans, thick socks, and down jacket that I had set out the previous night. Gathering my journal and fountain pen, I went downstairs.

The lobby of the inn replicated a classic New Mexican hacienda, its white ceilings held high by thick round wooden beams. Seven-foot tapered columns held up wooden arches. A Native American *horno,* already bright with a welcome wood fire, sat at the center of concentric red ceramic tiles.

I found the canisters of black coffee and filled a thick white mug. Across the room, wrought iron cafe tables lined a glass wall that looked into a small inner courtyard. There, darkened sculptures of a Navaho family scene faded from gray to blue in translucent morning light. I sat down and peered out at them. White snow edged the shadowy tree branches with a pre-dawn chiaroscuro, and streaks of rising sunlight sparkled on each tiny snowflake as it fell in the Santa Fe Inn courtyard.

Would Robert or Lauren really come this far to visit me?

I uncapped my pen. "Jill, Linda, Robert . . . they all want to cherish the fleeting moments left to us in life," I explained to my notebook. "But personally, I need to face my *overwhelming questions*."

That idea came from Eliot's "The Lovesong of J. Alfred Prufrock." The narrator is struggling against deadness, timidity, and inertia. The line I remembered said something about life leading you to an overwhelming question. But the antihero of the poem does not want to hear it. Instead, he'd rather go and make a social visit. He'd prefer to turn away from pressing inner questions.

Not me.

Suddenly I remembered a burning question I had buried like a dragon's egg nine years ago. What was the source of "Yahweh's" voice in the garden? I had never explained to myself what happened on the morning in 2010 when I heard my own vocalization calling to me from our back deck. The voice that asserted it represented a continuing presence in my life.

I'd lodged this memory, and the mystery of my own faraway depths, in a far corner of my heart. Now, peering into my imaginary cavern I beheld that buried riddle. *What is in these depths?* Before my inner eyes, the egg hatched into forbidden, fire-breathing, earth-churning questions that flew out at me. I scribbled quickly:

What has always been there for me?

How deep do I go? At some point, do I meet with trees and stars? Other beings?

Am I alone?

Will I die when my body dies?

Where do I belong? What am I for?

Is there any point to my life?

Does anything care about me?

Since I've come into existence, is there something I should be doing here?

As I unloaded each query onto the page, my chest expanded and my breathing got easier. I'd been trying to understand the human condition in various ways since I was a tiny kid. Were we children of God? Bundles of atoms? Spiritual souls? Reincarnating bodhisattvas? Physical automatons? Brains-in-vats, as told by philosophers, or gravity and randomness, per cosmologists, or emptiness dancing, like the New Agers said?

You weren't supposed ask these questions, because everyone acted as if they already understood these things. But I did not understand them. I'd never been able to accept the explanations for life I'd ever heard. And my thundering heart would not rest until I had plumbed my depths and found truth in my own experience.

Would I live long enough? I looked at the fire in the horno and the snow outside on the gray-blue statues. Would the city of Saint Francis's faith nurture my quest?

CHAPTER 52
I WANT ANSWERS

When Jill and I got home from Santa Fe, we began prepping the house for sale. Jill organized everything—sanding the hardwood floors, updating three bathrooms, repainting interior walls and cabinetry, remodeling the TV room. While I did part of the chores, I inwardly remained preoccupied with my "overwhelming questions."

I was completely done with spiritual practices, rituals, teachings, and trainings. It made no sense that I would have to perfect my character before discovering my authentic self. I am what I am already. As Mary Oliver said in her poem "Wild Geese," I did not have to be good. I did not have to crawl on my knees through hundreds of miles of wasteland to earn something that I already *was*.

Rather, the reality of my being should peek through in ordinary human experiences. For example, absorption in music, awe in nature, and even grief seemed to be hints, or flashes, of deeper layers. They were like random notes from a philharmonic performance that leak into a noisy bar from the concert hall across the street.

I wanted to get into that concert hall and sit down.

Snowmelt fed the wild grasses, sedges, swathes of lupin speckled with asters, and tiny bright wildflowers. Surrounding us rose vast ancient redwoods. Beyond them the Sierra Nevada thrust upward from our altitude of 8,600 feet to great heights, hovering over us in majestic silence.

For some of the interior house work, like the floors and repainting, we had to vacate the premises for days. We used the time to continue our good-bye tour of beautiful places on the West Coast. This week we were camping in Tuolumne Meadows, deep in Yosemite National Park.

After eating a pasta dish heated over our little gas stove, we watched the sun retreat into nothingness (random notes from the philharmonic). Then we snuggled into our sleeping bags in our rented tent cabin and slept in peace.

At first light, I crawled out to make hot coffee over the camp stove. Crouching, rubbing my hands over the tiny flames, I breathed the same cool, thin air as the hidden mice and badgers, chickadees and nuthatches, mosquitos and frogs. I felt completely at home with them. We sat together in silence as the majesty of light consecrated the meadow.

I had an hour or two to think and write before Jill woke up. Crawling back into my sleeping bag, I mounted my headlamp and pulled my down jacket over my head. When I clicked on my light, it illumined a tiny circle in my lap. I opened my journal.

You need to challenge all your existing assumptions, I wrote. No concept was sacred; everything was open to question. I was keenly aware that both Einstein and Darwin had ushered in profoundly new paradigms about our world by challenging long-held assumptions. If I wanted answers, I would have to look at things in a completely fresh way.

One: Don't assume consciousness comes out of brains. Maybe it's built in to the universe. Or a quality of the ultimate substance we're made of, I penned. Research had hit endless roadblocks because of commitment to that assumption.

Jill rolled over and murmured in her sleep. I tucked in the edges of my jacket to hide the light from her eyes.

Two: Don't assume the world really is the way it appears.

My body used five or six very limited senses to gather important survival information from the world, but the picture I formed from that data might have little to do with the reality out there. My nose served mostly to enhance flavors, not sensitive enough to notice the stream of chemicals that wafted through the environment alerting other species like plants, dogs, and ants. I could react to only a tiny spectrum of electromagnetic light; I heard only a thin strip of sounds and was oblivious to the vibrations central to tarantula and bull snake survival. Astronomers claimed that the sound of a vibrating black hole was a B-flat thousands of octaves below middle C. That sound would never register in my mind. What else could I not perceive?

I was taught that humans are complex organic life-forms comprising a zillion living cells, walking on a planet formed from exploding stars, socializing in a world dominated by technologies that could manipulate those star-born atoms. But was that really true? I never *experienced* those atoms or cells. I experienced *qualities*, like the scent of pine, the taste of lemon, the sound of my dog barking—a small range of colors, scents, sounds, pressures and so forth. Maybe the world was somehow made of qualities or experiences that get recorded in our bodies.

Jill moved again, and her head popped out of the covers.

"Morning," she smiled, and disappeared.

Three: Don't assume that love, or Plato's ideals of truth, goodness, and beauty are made up by human minds. Maybe they exist somehow or somewhere on their own.

"I made coffee. Want some?"

"Hm-hmm," came the muffled reply.

Smiling, I closed my notebook and packed away my headlamp.

❦

"We should get married before you start at Tesla," I told Jill as we lay in bed one morning.

The house was finally ready for buyers to view, with remodeling complete and new furnishings from Jill's store installed. The gardens were weeded, mulched, raked, and watered. While we waited for an offer, we took a few more trips, including a weekend in San Francisco and an RV tour of Olympic National Park in northwest Washington. In July, Jill had accepted a job at Tesla for the interim until the house sold.

Getting married would simplify putting me on Tesla health insurance as well as buying our new home as a couple. Gay marriage had been available to us for several years, but we had never bothered. Now it seemed practical. As a lesbian, I never expected to marry. I had always intended to care for myself. But given how things had worked out financially, I had no security if I lost Jill.

She looked at me with her mouth in an "oh" shape and her eyes wide. "Today's the eleventh of July."

I didn't quite get the connection, but she was excited and happy so I didn't interrupt. I hoped she would say yes.

"Seven and eleven are my lucky numbers; eleven-seven is my birthday!" she cried. "Let's do it today!"

We printed out the required forms and asked our neighbor Lucy to witness our signatures. Then we called our friend Illana, a licensed minister, and asked her if she would officiate a little ceremony at her home with just ourselves and her spouse, Jan. We ran the papers down to the Santa Cruz County office and filed them. Then we got blessed, fed, and celebrated at on Illana's back porch in the woods. In the evening we drove down coastal Highway 1 to Carmel for a honeymoon weekend.

It had taken years to build enough trust between us for Jill to want a legal marriage. But by marrying me, she instantly gave me a safety net. The relief in my mind and body was palpable. My breath came easily, as if I'd been given a clean bill of health after a long, scary, struggle.

But I also felt something more that I didn't expect: a deeper bond, greater intimacy, more solid trust. Jill was no longer my girlfriend or partner; now she was my family.

Once Jill started at Tesla, I was home with household chores and no idea what to do with myself. All the spiritual pathways I'd explored were useless to my current quest. None of my stale insights were going to help me. They had shown me how to *have* experiences like compassion and meditative dispassion, but not how to recognize in my own gut whatever-It-is that is *having* them.

What I'd left out was understanding the *knowing*, the witnessing element in every experience. Not the psychology or thoughts of the knower, but the witnessing itself, the consciousness. Without that, there would be no experience. Yet every teaching I knew about was steeped in mysterious concepts, local culture, ancient value systems, and totally confusing language. After forty years of exploring ideas from India, Tibet, Japan, China, and Southeast Asia in their American translations, I'd gained familiarity with many refined ideas; but they were just ideas! Useless to me in pursuit of my own intimate and immediate self-knowledge.

Google found many websites related to "who am I," "self-inquiry," and "what is aware." I combed through pages of what felt like spiritual hyperbole and unsubstantiated truth claims. From my home library I dug out a couple of science books about consciousness that actually avoided the topic, focusing instead on the activity of the brain. Conversely, I listened to a neuroscientist explain on YouTube that consciousness did not arise from neurons, period. He joked he could squeeze neurons forever and never get a drop of *experience* out of them.

But what consciousness was, and what was conscious, no one could say. Then I found Rupert Spira's intriguing book on Amazon. *Being Aware of Being Aware*—as in, *knowing* the *knowing*. It was a slim gray volume by a Western student of Eastern philosophy who claimed to offer direct, nonreligious, immediate self-insight.

I approached the work cautiously, not wanting to get bogged down in another spiritual practice. But the question the author posed was relevant to my search.

"Am I aware?" I read aloud.

Yes, clearly, I answered myself. I didn't have to think about it.

But here's where the writer took an unexpected turn. He asked how the reader discerned the inevitable answer that they were aware.

Well, it's apparent, I thought. *You look. You notice yourself, and you also notice that you are noticing yourself. How is that important?*

Because, the little book claimed, the part of me that is doing all this knowing is aware being: unchanging, always present, always at peace. The content that is known—all my experiences flowing one after another—changes constantly. Thoughts, feelings, sensations, and perceptions continuously flow, never repeating. But aware being remains constant, ever-present. Spira simply called that knowing presence "I."

Hmm. Clearly, I was not my changing opinions or beliefs. Once I believed in demons in the closet; once I believed in a god outside myself. Same with emotions, preferences, and pleasures—they weren't *me*, they *happened* in me, in my private Imax theater.

Whatever I experience, whether it's pain or luxury, I am there. If I am hungry, I am there. Jealous, I am there. Enjoying the weather, I am there. *I am something that is always here and knows the continual flow of things and ideas.*

After I explored passages of the slim volume, I had many new questions. I really wanted to have a conversation with Spira, but he lived and worked in Oxford, England. He held retreats in Europe and both coasts of the United States, but that was way out of budget for me.

I doubt I'll ever meet him, I thought with disappointment. *It would take a miracle.*

CHAPTER 53
THE ROAD HOME

"Come help me with this," Jill said from where she stood on a ladder, pulling at a cumbersome carton.

I stared up at the box, then down at the ladder. "Are you sure? It looks heavy."

It was November, and Jill had finally gotten—and accepted—an offer on her house that we could genuinely celebrate. We were now slogging through the final clean-out—which, in this moment, meant dragging boxes and furniture out from under the house.

"Jesus, Rikki, just come over and stand here," she said, pointing to the floor under the carton. Her voice had taken on an edge that always set panic quivering in my belly.

"Well, don't get mad," I grimaced. Suddenly I felt defensive. Jill's irritation triggered physical memories of my father's dangerous rages and the wounded feelings of a confused child.

Jill gritted her teeth and squinted. "I'm not mad; it's just frustrating. You always do this."

Ouch! Jill's words could bite, especially when I was already on my back foot.

"What do I *always* do?"

"We could be done already."

After years of experience, I knew that if I got angry the conversation would escalate. Jill could outfight me every time, and I'd end up feeling shamed and defeated. Or I'd lose control and yell explosively from a deep scary place inside me.

To avoid both, my unsustainable coping strategy had long been to hide my fears and swallow pained feelings. Neither of us liked the dynamic; it was a habit that hadn't improved with age. By the time we were done packing up the house, my tolerance for confrontation was paper-thin.

Jill and I had decided on this retirement plan together, but now that we were doing it, dregs of apprehension fouled my excitement. The house I had learned to call home over the past twelve years suddenly belonged to someone else. I had few possessions of my own—some books and an old Yamaha guitar. Even my Prius was gone. I had nothing but Jill, and when we argued, I had nothing.

The day after Christmas, we pulled onto Highway 17 for the last time, descending out of the Santa Cruz Mountains in the two cars Jill still owned, a BMW crossover and a Porsche 911 Carrera. Because heavy snow blocked the mountainous northern passage to Santa Fe, we took the southern route. This meant we could stop in LA to say goodbye to my family: sisters Beth and Linda, brother-in-law, nephew, and Lauren's dad.

A couple of years after Linda's stem cell transplant, a delayed immune system attack had damaged her lungs. Now she endured a perpetual hacking cough and took a hodge-podge of blood balancers and immunosuppressants. She sounded okay on the phone, but I wanted to observe her up close.

When we arrived, seeing her stopped my heart like a finch smacking into a window. She walked slowly for only short distances using a cane. Her skin was pale and her eyes looked tired.

But she led us cheerfully to our room, and then to the kitchen, where she baked cookies and prepared noshes for everyone with her usual joie de vivre. She took breaks for breathing therapies but her buoyant laughter, though it might trigger a cough, had not diminished. Her curiosity and interest in people were as lively as ever during our overnight visit.

I could tell that she did not want pity. Rather, she deserved respect and inspired awe.

Still, I knew when Jill and I drove away that Linda's health was fragile and precarious. She had been my home base and safe haven all my life, but since she'd been sick, I'd had to stand up with courage for the whole family. Now, I understood that even a simple upper respiratory infection could take her from us.

As Jill and I said goodbye and resumed our journey, I felt a tearing near my heart, under my breastbone. *Will Linda ever be able to travel to Santa Fe? Will we ever see each other again?*

Heading east out of LA was an epic traffic nightmare. Interstate 5 was closed due to heavy snowfall, and it seemed like everyone in Southern California was with us on Interstate 10. Creeping along at twenty or thirty miles per hour in the Porsche, I followed Jill, often slipping a few cars behind. The cargo hold on top of the BMW was my target, and I strained to glimpse it through eighteen-wheelers blowing diesel smoke and SUVs constantly changing lanes.

Within minutes, I lost sight of her.

"Oh shit." My stomach lurched, and I swallowed hard. Already weakened by the grief of separation from everything I knew and loved, my insides trembled. A frisson of panic ticked up my spine. Untethered, with my limited resources in a strange place, I had not planned on navigating my journey alone. But straightening up in my seat, I bolstered myself.

"You can do this. You don't always need to lean on Jill."

With the morning glare in my eyes and my fingers clamped onto the damp, leather-wrapped sport wheel, the first throb of a headache quivered behind my right eye.

Stop freaking out! I chided myself. *You're just driving on a road! Plus, you have a cell phone and a AAA card.*

After an hour or so, Jill texted me where to exit so we could meet up for a doggie pit stop.

When I glimpsed her car, my breathing settled back to normal. *That was nothing!* I chided myself. *What's the matter with you?*

We took a short walk with the dog, then piled back into our cars. Knowing I'd probably get disconnected from the BMW, I took charge of my low-level anxiety.

"Let everything be exactly as it is," I recited, coaching myself as the miles spun out beneath me. *Yes, I have scary racing thoughts, my head's hammering, and my breath is ragged. But I am not those things.* I reminded myself that I was not my thoughts nor my feelings.

"I am something that experiences those things," I reminded myself, "but I am not the things." To help separate my stable self from my feelings, I took verbal note of each sensation.

"Here is throbbing; now there is an ominous thought. Here is a jittery sense of foreboding." I announced each thought and sensation as it arose.

"Yet I am still me."

Soon I began to smile at my descriptive captions.

By the time the sun settled into blackness the next day, I guessed we were heading east into the mountainous Apache trust land near the New Mexico border. We'd spent a restful night in Phoenix with a childhood friend of Jill's, then taken off after breakfast on the all-day drive to Santa Fe.

No highway lights or bright signs polluted the pure night. The road was deserted. Cell phone service melted as we entered the canyon.

My eyesight was poor in deep darkness. I slowed down through the curves, but Jill continued without braking. A groan rose from my tailbone to my throat as I watched her taillights vanish. Didn't she notice my disappearing headlamps? I immediately felt the deep pang of loneliness. Behind me lay my old life, safety, and community. Ahead, I glimpsed only walls of gray rock and maybe ten yards of winding two-lane road.

With my heart in my throat I swore, however alone I might feel, I would not succumb to panic or sadness. I had to find that place in myself that I could trust.

"Ok, Rikki, this is the hard part. Hang in there." I pressed on. But tears dripped down my cheeks. Abandoned, hours from a town or police station, with spotty cell service, freezing temperatures, and poor understanding of the terrain, I broke down.

I was spinning in a dark, cold, and empty landscape. My mind unleashed a flurry of grim fantasies. What if I took a wrong turn or the car broke down? I pictured myself stumbling down the freezing black road on foot. What if I got hit by an oncoming car or kidnapped by God knows whom?

Sticking to the right edge of the road, I feared overshooting my visibility. I slowed to forty-five miles per hour, then to forty, then down to thirty-five. Even with my high beams on, I peered without blinking into the gloom just to make sense of the road's shape. My stiff fingers flicked on the emergency flashers to warn cars behind me.

Head hammering, I encouraged myself out loud. "One moment at a time. Just this much. Just one breath."

Twenty or thirty miles further on, cell service returned, and Jill called.

"Where are you?" she asked, her voice flat and clipped. She sounded as exhausted as I was.

"I have no idea," I said, trying to hide the weepy rasp in my voice out of shame of being wimpy. *Hold it together!*

"I know you didn't pass me. I'm waiting for you in a deserted motel parking lot. Look for a hanging light bulb on your right. I'll watch for you." She hung up.

My heart sank. *Couldn't we have stayed on the phone until I found you?*

I took a few deep breaths and blinked hard. *You are almost there.* Another four or five minutes and I saw the dangling bulb and two red lights. But as I slid my car behind hers in the empty lot, Jill took off again.

"Damn you, Jill!" I shouted at the windshield. I'd been hoping for a moment's rest. Shifting back into drive, I accelerated past my comfort zone to keep up. More scared of isolation in a vacant, cold unknown than I was of crashing, I kept my foot off the brake and her taillights in sight.

Did I really need to race like that? *Yes*, I thought. I was scared of the dark, of the traffic in Albuquerque, and of finding the rental late at night.

But as we cruised across the desert landscape, something shifted in my chest as if I'd swallowed a big pill.

This whole damned journey, I would have been all right if Jill hadn't been here, I realized. In reality I'd made it through the worst parts by myself. I'd managed grief, panic, anger, fear, and loneliness. And I could do it again.

More importantly, I realized I was done with this victim posture. Something about my confidence and independence had to change. I had to make it happen.

That night, in bed in our rental in midtown Santa Fe, I lay quietly awake, unpacking the whole driving ordeal.

Why did I lean on Jill for things I could handle myself? Where was the gal who'd built a career among some of the most competitive people in the world? What had happened to the Mama Bear who could handle anything for Lauren?

The lesson from the harrowing road trip took shape: I was not as helpless as being broke and without possessions made me feel. Despite those circumstances, there was something in me I could count on. My deeper self encompassed much more than reactive habits; it consisted of peaceful awareness plus the rich complex of experience and wisdom that had grown in me. I was utterly capable of encountering and handling anything life threw at me, and I was beginning to know it.

That understanding marked an inflection point for the victim attitude in my psyche. If the car had broken down, I would have handled it. I had the tools and the wisdom to navigate tough situations. I never had to get swept away by panic again. I could count on myself to show up and face whatever challenge presented itself.

Jill breathed steadily next to me while our pit bull-boxer Zoey snored at the foot of the bed. A resolution affirmed itself: *I will not slip into the victim position when friction sparks between us. I will keep my footing and meet her as an equal.* I knew that shift in me would change our dynamic. It already was influencing the way I thought about our exodus.

We'd been in New Mexico for only a few hours, yet I wondered if, in some invisible way, I were being drawn toward a fresh start in an enchanted new land. The Zen Buddhists had a story about the need to empty yourself of prior knowledge and opinions in order to receive something new.

I rolled over onto my side and reached out to touch Jill's shoulder, comforted by her physical presence. I loved our partnership and camaraderie. I loved the adventures we undertook together. But now I knew if I had to rely on myself, living without family or friends in my new land, I'd be okay.

Apparently, I could handle my own shit.

CHAPTER 54
BE HERE NOW

Our new town, nicknamed the City Different, offered a plethora of things for Jill and me to explore. The wooded highlands of northern New Mexico drew people with diverse spiritual interests; I found two Zen Buddhist centers nestled in the foothills of the Sangre de Cristos, and the spirit of St. Francis appeared in much of the outdoor art and sculpture. Native pueblos often shared their ceremonies with the public, and I sensed an aesthetic of respect for the land and its creatures. Hiking trails permitting dogs curved through the city and surrounding mountains. Santa Fe Ski boasted world-class snow with great trails for Jill in winter, and the city golf course was just a few miles from downtown. We talked about getting e-bikes for zooming around the hills, or an RV for camping trips.

But it was not yet to be. In early January, huddled under the covers until midmorning in our Santa Fe rental, Jill read an article about a coronavirus outbreak in China. Week after week, we tracked its assault on the world. We were lucky to purchase a home in February and move in a few weeks before general Covid-19 panic and lockdowns ensued. Before we could furnish the house, we got cut off from family, friends, and community for the next year.

Surprisingly, however, as someone lonely and disoriented in a new place, pandemic shutdowns created opportunities for me. The ski slopes and golf courses were closed, so Jill was home a lot. Together we explored the wilderness encircling Santa Fe, took day trips to local artist havens, and hiked the trails around our house. Our new e-bikes zoomed us up and down the hills on meandering forty-mile rides. And as I acclimated to Santa Fe, the acute anxiety that assailed me during the months-long move diminished.

But I also had a lot of quiet time at home. With little to distract me, I couldn't avoid the nagging sense that something important was lacking in my life.

Am I doing what I am supposed to do? Am I fulfilling the reason I am alive?

The few times I had tried to talk with others about these questions, I heard, "There is no purpose to life. It's all random." Or, "I found my purpose in Jesus Christ, come to my church." Of course, many people find purpose in their career, service to others, accomplishments, or creativity, but those activities didn't fit the bill. I needed to know why there is something—a universe, consciousness, life—rather than nothing.

Why is there a me and a you?

Maybe that question formed in me while watching my father self-destruct. As a kid praying for him, I probably wondered why people were born just to be miserable. Later, when I was in my teens and my father asked me to procure some Nembutal to aid his suicide, I thought through everything I knew about life and death before deciding what to do.

Life is meaningless and stupid anyway, asserted my wounded, frightened teenage self.

"Okay," I'd told Dad as I stood numbly at the kitchen counter with the Frosted Flakes and strawberry jam. "I'll make some calls."

How was it possible that I had considered helping my dad end his life? Half a century later, I still wanted to know if the teenage me was right. Did I really believe my father's life was meaningless? Was mine?

At times in my life journey, I'd thought my purpose was to grow and learn by facing challenges and hard times. Many days my reason for getting up was to nurture and provide for my daughter. Sometimes creative expression like writing songs, taking photos, and producing good meals seemed enough. Who knows, maybe we were just supposed to fulfill our potential, enjoy family and friends, have exciting vacations, and create treasured memories. These were all excellent life outcomes that I'd be blessed to fulfill, but they didn't quite touch that deeper itch.

Does my life mean anything in the vast scheme of things? Does it matter what I choose?

Rupert's little gray book approached that question by suggesting I find out what I *am* before I decide what I *mean*. He then suggested that in all of existence, there is only one being, and each of us shares it with everyone else. Imagine just one gigantic being, having an infinity of experiences! No one would be a separate soul or entity with their own unique self. Even though there are billions of separate people, there would be only *one* aware entity, and it would shine in everyone's eyes.

Using ordinary language, *Being Aware of Being Aware* guided me to notice the background awareness of that being illuminating my own experience. It pointed out there were no requirements for recognizing present awareness. No religious practices, moral behaviors, or metaphysical beliefs were necessary. Because, I read, what we are seeking is already here, now, knowable as our own shared, aware being.

I pondered the idea of a singular aware being. It made surprising sense to me. Instead of one aware being per person, there would be one aware being per universe, or per *totality*. Apparently, the one single all-inclusive aware being had local "Rikki" experiences. Somehow (could science investigate this someday?) Rikki's mind had private knowledge and personal thoughts that are known by the one awareness. We name a collection of experiences "Rikki" or "Jill" but really, the exact same, unitary, awareness would fill us both.

This "one aware being" notion was a huge Einstein-level idea that immediately turned my old picture of reality upside down. I loved it. Forget the notion of individuals with individual consciousnesses that arise in individual brains. Instead, imagine one great universal self-aware creative *something* that illuminates the experiences of uncountable minds and bodies.

And yet, however much I appreciated the *concept* of one shared being, I still *felt* like a separate entity. I had my own thoughts, preferences, and memories. How would I ever be able to know for myself, with certainty, whether this one intimate connected reality thing was real? That's what I wanted to discover during the little bit of life I had left.

Actual knowing or grasping the reality of *one being* in my own experience could trigger the end of a lifelong search.

I had left everything behind—places, people, money, status, ideas, assumptions—even God—in pursuit of self-knowledge. I was almost there; I could feel it. There was nowhere else for me to go.

CHAPTER 55
WHAT THE THUNDER SAID

Sunday morning, I sat quietly in my den, on the white leather couch where I often read or practiced the guitar. A stack of books, some coffee, a notebook, and pen were all close by. Beethoven's late string quartet in A minor, which included a movement he called "Holy song of thanksgiving from a convalescent to the Deity," was gently filling my sanctuary with gratitude and joy.

The mid-March day in Santa Fe was bright and blue. I'd been reading a paper about a new philosophy called modern analytic idealism that gave an account of our experienced reality, including ordinary human consciousness. But I could not understand some of the concepts, nor reconcile others with my hard-won beliefs. In recent weeks, I'd been getting frustrated with my intellectual limitations.

Outside my east window, dreary gray light slid off ice crystals that laced the gray-green pinyon branches. Inside the den, the cellos and violins wound about each other, repeating a phrase, one descending as the other rose. I watched as red-headed house finches waited for a turn at the sunflower bar. Stymied, my head dropped into my hands.

Then a rubber band snapped in my mind, and I sat up wide-eyed. I realized I was not going to understand anything about *reality* until I understood *myself.*

How had I missed that?

I peered through the windowpane at pygmy nuthatches whacking peanut pieces with their tiny beaks. Dropping my eyelids, I silently voiced the now familiar prompt, *What am I,* then added, *Like, what the hell am I? For real?*

I began reciting my favorite mantra, "Blah, blah, blah . . . ," which I often used to block noisy thoughts. Then I coached myself: *I am the space, the quietly aware presence, in which these thoughts and sounds are happening.*

And like a dog settling into a burrow, my mind fell back into the spacious experience of simply being. Letting everything be as it is, I attended to a visceral sense of aliveness, listening as the Beethoven piece unfolded from my speakers.

Suddenly everything fell out of my mind, away from my attention. There was only the awareness of inner spaciousness, in which the quartet of strings celebrated their song. I followed thousands of notes as they danced and rolled, lifting to the heavens like leaping flames. Chord after chord, I explored the endlessly varied rhythms and registers, the beauty and harmony and colors of perhaps seven tones in the key of F Lydian.

Then me as a separate person disappeared.

Eyes closed, legs crossed, arms resting on the chair . . . my body melted into a sea of gentle vibrations. The personal interests, preferences, and story that defined Rikki evaporated the way colors do in desert sun. My personal feelings were muted; instead, a burst of freedom—like clean and pure air—soared in me with the music, lifting a weightless part of me that melted into gold and yellow streams.

I am that. I am freedom.

Beauty swelled like ripeness, warm as a rising sun, full of poignancy for everything all at once. It shone round and whole, flowing within and around everywhere.

This is me. I am beauty.

Understanding seeped into the warm animal of my body, clarifying a reality that I could not find through thinking. My personal story dissolved in the solvent of a greater reality that I sensed but could not speak, a truth beyond understanding.

Everything is made of this one truth. I am truth.

Peace undulated beneath me, as if I stood on a hidden dock on a wooded lake at sundown, mist rising. As if herons stared into glassy water and a whooshing flock of geese settled, squawking, to fish among the ripples. Everything found its place.

I am supported by peace, imbued with peace. I am peace.

Inside my heart, within the music, glowed a harmony of intricate chemical life, the fulness of an ocean, the majesty of galaxies.

I am nothing separate. I am this oneness. I am this. I am.

After perhaps fifteen minutes, I wandered into the living room and looked out the wall of windows onto the snow-capped mountains thirty miles away, miraculous and majestic. A tiny juniper titmouse landed on the woodpile and pecked lightly before springing away. April warmth emboldened tiny green spots to burst out of dry woody branches in our garden.

I saw clearly that all the thoughts, opinions, resentments, and stories that made up my egoic psychological person were not who I am. I had never been a person. I had always been beauty, truth, and goodness.

In me, as me, light, love, knowingness, harmony, fulfillment, fullness, and goodness all rested in utter quiet. I could stand there forever as emptiness knowing. I didn't have to return to my old life and pretend I was a physical person filled with thoughts and preferences.

A prayer formed out of the stillness, "Let me live in harmony with you, celebration of you, expression of you. Never let me forget you. Or what I am and what the world really is."

Jill stepped through the arched passage from the kitchen into the living room.

"Enjoying the view? There's still snow on Pyramid Peak," she said.

Smiling, I did not speak, clinging to the last wisps of my silent reverie. But when I looked at Jill, my heart jumped. I saw that she too was made of goodness and light. Everything, everything, everything was made of this beauty and harmony I'd witnessed. Within her must also be an ocean of freedom and a symphony of grace.

Do you know you are actually made of innocence and beauty? I thought, looking in her eyes.

"What do you want to have for dinner?" I said aloud. "I can do burgers, burritos . . . or a pasta? I think we have spinach and mushrooms."

We went into the kitchen to examine our ingredients. Everything—the steel two-slice toaster, the Cuisinart coffee maker, the vegetables in the fridge—was perfectly normal and the same as yesterday, except I could sense an inner quality of harmony and relaxation around me. As if we were secretly cooling our feet in a stream running through a sunlit Tuolumne Meadows in the middle of June.

"Let's have burritos," Jill said. She straightened and closed the refrigerator door.

"No problemo!" I said, clapping my hands. "I have time to take Zoey for a walk. Want to come?"

Our property ran adjacent to a fifty-acre fenced field, wild with desert grasses, trees, tiny wildflowers, and seasonal daisies. There our sixty-five-pound pit bull–boxer could run off leash, free to explore empty jackrabbit burrows and to chase traces of the coyote pack that had hunted there earlier in the day. I opened the back door, and she rushed to the rear gate. Jill moved the rock holding it shut, and we started down the trail.

I plodded along the single-lane track, my sneakers scrunching on the rocks and clay. High, scattered clouds filtered the light over the north central New Mexican highlands. Everything looked the same as always: clumps of dry grasses and crinkly daisy stalks mixed with flat-green cacti scattered among short pinyon trees and scraggly junipers. But something about my sense of self was distinctly different. I felt bigger, freer, more expansive, and inherently beautiful.

"Zoey!" Jill called, scanning the forward horizon. Our puppy popped out of the brush farther down the trail and sat to wait for us, panting. I loved that dog. I belonged to her, to this pastureland, to Jill, to Lauren. I belonged to the whole expanse of life and being, the way whirlpools belong to a river, the way stars belong to light. I was never a separate person; not really. The child who memorized the Stations of the Cross (were there ten or twelve?) and the drunk who ordered another round for her friends were me, but only in the sense that Keanu Reeves was Neo, the hero of the *Matrix* films.

I didn't want to live for an imaginary person anymore—subject to the needs, judgments, opinions and pleasures of the temporary persona named "Rikki." It was too much work! She was never content, always seeking something: a car, a house, a wife, wisdom, new clothes, status, clarity, enlightenment, God, understanding, freedom. Money. Respect. During my recent mystical vision, I had seen and felt clearly that I was literally not this person. Just like Jill, in my deepest being, I was an ocean of freedom and a symphony of grace.

Jill reached the gate at the edge of the field and opened it. Zoey followed her, running toward home. The circle of mountains beyond the trees caught my eye as I followed the path. I saw a vibrant spectacle of peaks and seasons and trees and snow and the sun all intimately entwined in a dance of exquisite symmetry.

"Wow," I said aloud. "Just wow." I'd been looking everywhere for the truth about reality, but this was completely different from what I imagined. Everything looked the same but the inside of it shone out. Somewhere in the very deep nonverbal depths of my mind I saw that the surrounding mountains and woodlands were not just mountains and woodlands, but also an endless unfolding of deep harmony into a myriad of marvelous forms.

When we got home, I put some Charles Mingus on the outdoor speakers. We settled into the cushioned easy chairs on the patio. Jill poured herself a glass of something red, and I took a hit of cannabis oil from my vape pen. Zoey was spread out on the cool tiles in the shade of the house. My thoughts were quiet and the melted-caramel feeling of deep contentment seeped into my relaxing muscles. Everything, everything, everything was OK.

Without thinking in the ordinary way, I intuitively understood that Jill, Zoey, me, and the whole world were made of a dimensionless, nameless, self-aware substance that emanated all kinds of perfect ideals like truth and goodness. In my mind's eye I saw again the swirls of colored light that were also the harmonic chords of some invisible, boundless, perfect substance. I was *that.* I didn't want to think about it; I just wanted to *be* it.

But I decided to try talking about it.

"Jill," I began, "I had a wonderful experience after meditating today. I listened to a string quartet, and . . ." I choked up and started to cry. "It was so . . ." I began to sob. "Beautiful." I could find no other words. My face fell into my palms, and my body cried while Jill stroked my shoulder.

"That's so sweet," she said, smiling at me quizzically.

How could I convey even a sliver of that magnificence? The next day I would start writing a hymn, and would be surprised and pleased when it began to focus around this whispered prayer: "Make my life nothing but singing with you."

For over half a century, within the limits of my powers, I had scrounged Western thought and Eastern religion for a kernel of genuine, no-kidding, what's-going-on truth. I'd finally given up on finding God, cosmic purpose, or supreme anything.

Wherever I looked, I only ever found myself.

Now, I'd seen a truth about myself.

Just imagine! I'd had an intuitive, wordless experience of our everyday reality that convinced me, after decades of soul-searching, that this world and our lives and thoughts, everything, the whole enchilada, all unfold as expressions of some nonphysical, exquisite, harmonious *something* that is aware of its own experiences. I am *that*.

Life had given me a fifteen-minute exposure to an aspect of what must be the *reality* of everything, including me. I now had direct, subtle "knowledge" that would, in coming months, help me answer many agonizing questions about human existence and put an end to my feeling like a separate, lonely, limited thing adrift in a sea of unknown troubles.

But I didn't want to create a belief about that reality out of memories. Rather, I wanted to embrace the astonishing truth in the present, and let all its wonderful qualities permeate my mind and body, my thoughts and actions. The gift of my unearned insight was a tiny taste, just one petal in the flowering garden of reality. I was going to need a master gardener to help me explore its inner secrets.

I googled Rupert Spira, the author of the little book I'd been reading. While sequestered at home in England due to the Covid epidemic, Rupert had been hosting online Zooms and posting segments on YouTube. There, people discussed spiritual, personal, and philosophical questions about his approach to happiness. I secretly hoped he might know a whole new way to explore the garden of reality. So, relaxing into the leather sofa in my den, I stuffed my Air Pods into my ears and hit "play" on my phone.

Rupert's face appeared in conversation with a man who wanted to find spacious awareness within himself. Much like me before my recent vision of innate beauty, the fellow was sure he was a separate "somebody" on a journey, who would change or learn enough to get enlightened someday. Rupert asked the fellow to identify very specific qualities that make him think he was merely a body with a brain that produced a mind.

The man took a moment before speaking. "When I close my eyes and attend to myself," he said, "I feel sensations and notice perceptions, like the sound of your voice. I sense my body. I don't *feel* like boundless space or awareness. My teeth are hard. My lower back hurts. I hear birds outside. My stomach is rumbling. I feel like a body," he said.

Rupert then asked the man what it is that *knows* these perceptions.

The sound or pain or sensation is experienced by *something*. What, the two explored, was the subtle *something* that knows a perception? By the time they finished, the caller reported experiencing himself less as a solid body, and more as what he called an "inner cognizance."

I was fascinated. This way of exploring private experience was utterly new to me. I observed my own experience carefully. I noticed the *presence* in each sensation, *that which* experiences various stimuli. Just like the man in the YouTube video, I could sense the inner cognizance that *knew* the sensations and perceptions recorded by my body.

Excited that I would be able to converse with Rupert about these matters, I started preparing a question to raise at his Zoom webinar the following week.

CHAPTER 56
A SURPRISE ENDING

"All you need to do is *drop the seeker*, Rikki," Rupert said to me.

The moment I heard *drop the seeker*, my eyes widened and I understood, the way you suddenly see how the threads of a movie come together at the surprise ending. *Oh! I get that.* Simultaneously, dozens of life scenes flashed through my mind.

I pictured myself as the Catholic schoolgirl singing to God at Mass with Grammy, and the teenage me on LSD melting into the starlit skies above Santa Barbara. I saw myself chanting to Buddha to find emotional peace, surrendering to a higher power to gain sobriety, and rejecting God in pursuit of a truth I could call my own. In my heart, I remembered the urgency with which I scoured the literature for the deepest truths I could grasp. My body relived fasting, repeating mantras, and hours of sitting on floor cushions. In one form or another, I had been on this quest for belonging, meaning, and truth my entire life.

During all those yearning years, I imagined myself as a persona or character, perhaps a soul, on a journey to find something I didn't already have. Or to become good enough to earn sainthood, or to know something beyond ordinary human understanding. More than any other sobriquet, *seeker* defined me.

Or did it? With Rupert's prompting, I suddenly understood that *seeker* was a role I'd played rather than what I *was*. If I dropped all my roles and personas, what would be left?

On Zoom with several hundred other people, I looked deep within and relaxed while letting my egoic persona melt. All the concerns of my crazy made-up character began to drain away. I let go of ambition, fear, envy, anger, and opinions. Struggling and seeking relaxed into stillness.

What was left?

Nothing . . . except a silent aware sense that I *am*.

Right there, in a place called *I*, pulsed the singular, great, aware being. How could I be a *seeker* of this being if it was already me? That was like a wave searching for water, a golden nugget searching for gold. I dropped the *seeker*. That wasn't me. I was beauty, truth, and love.

There was no need for better meditation or self-improvement campaigns. There was nothing my true, deep self needed to earn, achieve, or gain. In reality, I was not a seeking or incomplete soul. Any moment I chose, I could recognize myself as the goodness, light, and beauty that is the inner wholeness of everyone.

As this new understanding settled into my mind and body, my identify slowly shifted. Once I stopped imagining I was a wandering soul or a temporary arrangement of molecules, I could sense or intuit that I was an open, aware *mystery* that emanates all the qualities of love. That sounded very strange, but I could come up with no other way to think about it.

Over a period of weeks, it slowly dawned on me that the *mystery* looking out of my eyes was *identical* with that looking out of everyone else's. Not just similar, but *exactly* the same. Seeing *that* was a clear clue that the "one aware being" idea jibed with my own experience. It seemed to me as if there were one great light burning under a thick canvas that had many punctures through which the light streamed.

The emerging beams were not separate lights; they were all the same light from one source. There is one inclusive, endless, harmonious awareness, which shines here as me. And there as you.

Knowing that changed *everything*.

I started to feel myself to be that silent, aware presence. Peaceful contentment mixed with creativity energy and curiosity emerged as my basic mood. The old sense of incompleteness, of needing to *find* fulfillment in activities or achievements began to dissipate. I knew myself: not in words but in my gut. The old existential questions—what am I, what should I be doing, do I matter, will I die?—began, over time, mutating under pressure from this fresh understanding.

One evening in late June, Jill and I lounged in the back courtyard with our feet up, just back from a thirty-mile e-bike ride in the Santa Fe hills. We munched on aged Irish Cheddar and crackers, and Zoey slept nearby in the sun.

"You remember when I first spoke to Rupert on Zoom a few months ago?" I asked, breaking our silent reveries.

"I remember you were excited. You didn't tell me what he said." Jill sipped from a cold jug of ginger ale.

"He told me to drop the *seeker*."

"Hmm. What did that mean?" Setting down her drink, she watched me carefully.

My head tipped to one shoulder, and I looked at her sideways. "It meant I can stop creating the psychological illusion of being a soul on a journey seeking something. I am already that something."

"That's what I've been saying, but okay," Jill said. "Anyway, whatever you've been doing, it's working."

My brows furrowed in a question. "What do you mean?" I placed a slice of cheese on a cracker and popped it in my mouth.

"You're totally different. Confident, I don't know. Independent."

"Really?" I chewed a moment. "I guess I feel it, too."

"Maybe it's that victim thing we've talked so much about," Jill added, taking a sip of her soda.

"What, it's worse?" I asked in mock surprise, standing up to do quad stretches.

Jill laughed. "No, a lot better. You're not so reactive."

"Well, that's good to hear." I smiled to myself. The sky over the Jemez glowed purple and pink as the sun dropped. "I'm a witness and lover of life these days. Can I have a sip of that?"

Jill handed me her thermos. The sky continued its ritual evening display of color. Marigold and poppy with deep bluebell and reddish plum lit the distant mountaintops.

"I'm glad you can get to Rupert with the call-ins," she said.

"Yeah. And the philosophy behind it makes sense to me." I took a slug of ginger beer and sat down. "And it's catching on! People all over the world are discussing what it means for the world to appear in consciousness. Versus the current view that consciousness appears in the world."

Jill reached over to high-five me. "Once someone explains a new way of looking at things, smart people start to see it! That's why Elon Musk was cool when he was young," she said. "He got people to believe in things they didn't conceive of until he explained them."

"Remember years ago, you told me even though I'm not a philosopher, I am part of the revolution because of my personal research?"

"It takes people to make a movement," she answered, getting up to turn off the patio's ceiling fan.

"I'm proud of myself." I watched her long hair ruffle in the evening air. "The twentieth century is really over. We are on the verge of discovering a whole new level of our existence."

"Let's hope it's not too late for the planet," Jill said. Lengthening sunrays now painted the horizon in pure crimson and gold. "Look, you can see Jupiter near the crescent moon," she said, pointing high in the southwest. We watched in silence.

“Stunning, huh, babe?” Jill hummed.

We stood like two tiny drops of aware beauty out in the universe, under the protective gravity of Jupiter, witnessing a tiny slice of an endless miracle. Within us flowed formless harmony, displaying itself in our sacred lives. Whether writing songs, caring for relationships, or creating meals, I knew it was my responsibility to express its grace and integrity in everything I did. If my life had deep purpose, it would be found there.

CHAPTER 57

A JOURNEY OF A THOUSAND MILES

"Honestly, I actually *feel* like a peaceful energetic warmth instead of striving person," I said to my friend David in a FaceTime call. We'd known each other more than forty years, since college at Berkeley. I'd been looking for down-to-earth "spiritual" friends with whom I could discuss my recent awakenings and their influence on me. When I'd found him through a Facebook connection, I called thinking he might share a similar understanding of reality. Now we chatted every few months.

"The fear of death is gone," I said, "and the ache of loneliness—"

"Whoa, Nelly!" David cut me off. "Them's big words, Rikki. No one is free from the fear of death." David's face, innocent like that of the young man I once knew, glowed in my video rectangle. He was a gentle, well-read, inquisitive soul. The kind of guy you'd want at your bedside if you were dying.

After a moment, I said "You're right. That wasn't honest, it was BS."

"It sounds like bypassing. I don't mean to dismiss the importance of insight, but . . ." David went quiet.

"Of course, I'm afraid of death," I admitted. "But I think it's possible that *I*, as aware being plus some remnant 'Rikki' vibrations, won't get obliterated. I will persist in some form or state."

"Yes, I share that intuition. I think most people do."

I enjoyed having someone to talk to. Since my troubles began, I'd been avoiding people. Unworthy feelings kept me from reaching out to old friends. But that pain belonged to the imaginary individual who feared she did not measure up. I now knew I was not that phantom; I was beauty and love unfolding.

"It's true I still get depressed and lonely. And angry," I went on, "but also . . . none of these emotions really disturbs the expansive pool of peace deep inside." *Even when I am alone in the dark. Even during an anxiety attack.*

"Until they do," David joked.

I laughed. David had been a Nam-myoho-renge-kyo chanter with me back in the '70s. He had much happier memories of those days than I did, but we shared a cynical sense of humor.

"I don't mean to squelch your enthusiasm," he said. "I'm sorry. Go on."

"Well, the basic nondual philosophy is idealistic rather than materialistic, asserting that mind—awareness, consciousness, whatever-you-want-to-call-it—is fundamental and prior to matter. The physically experienced world arises within that consciousness. I've found a few scientists online talking seriously about it. There's a neuroscientist in Wisconsin, a physicist cum philosopher in the Netherlands, and a cognitive scientist in Southern California. They all start their research with the assumption that consciousness exists independently of brains."

"That's interesting," David said and paused. "But I guess I've always thought that."

"It excites me that people are considering alternatives to seeing ourselves as mere things made of molecules, despite the resistance of the scientific community. It opens the way for people to find happiness within themselves instead of trying to get it from the world."

"I agree, Richarda, we need to stop seeing people as consumers and instead as facets of the jewel of being. And it's our inner, conscious lives that make us interesting and real."

"Well said, my friend!" I gestured a thumbs up and smiled at his image on my iPad screen.

"I find it uplifting to know I am not confined to this existence, that there is endless experience available to my unending being," David went on.

"Yes," I said. We let a moment pass silently. "There's no reason to assume that in death the deeper layers of the mind fully unravel back into the One."

"Just admit it—the soul persists after death."

We both laughed. David was an ardent student of the afterlife and the potential transmigration of souls. We playfully disagreed on some of the details.

"But as living people here on earth," I said, "the possibilities give me a shard of hope for the survival of humanity. Perhaps with a firmer foundation in actual reality, we might learn to live in balance with our world. To respect the many forms of the one life we all share."

"From your lips to God's ears," David said.

Astonishingly, like the lilies of the field in the Gospel of Matthew's Sermon on the Mount, I found that when I let myself blossom as the One in this body-mind, all of my needs were met. I had a beautiful home, an intimate relationship, and a very loving family. Creativity took the place of anxiety and struggle. My health was still terrific, and I had enough money for my lifestyle. My family was thriving. And I had learned from life. It had brought me here, to a kind of self-knowledge I had not anticipated.

I had come home to myself, a journey of a thousand miles that required not a single step.

EPILOGUE
WHERE DID SHE GO?

The following year, in late August 2021, my family and a few friends stood talking softly under scattered clouds outside a small mausoleum in Santa Monica, California. Next to us on a metal stand waited a pinewood box. Inside it, my sister Linda's body lay naked, wrapped in linen, still cool from refrigeration. Six of us planned to carry her a short distance to Woodlawn Cemetery's Eternal Meadow, where she would organically decompose to become part of the cemetery's natural wildlife.

I wrapped my left hand tightly around the pallbearer's pole on my side. The sanded surface of the smooth but unvarnished wood scraped my fingers and warmed my palm. The pole felt solid and true, no-nonsense. I smiled at my nephew, who took the bar on the opposite side as others lined up behind us. I hefted my end.

Linda had been two when I was born. She was my first friend, shelter from the storm, and reading teacher. I had begun this life's journey holding her hand. Now she was gone from her body. I had kissed her cold forehead gently through my tears not thirty minutes earlier. But where had she gone? Did she go out like a light when her brain stopped? Or had her awareness withdrawn shyly, only to hide now among wafting late-summer grasses?

Gripping the handle with all my heart, I stepped firmly on the path among inlaid headstones toward the small living meadow reserved for green burials. The six of us set Linda's plank casket on the bier that someone had placed over a freshly dug hole in the earth. My eyes flicked to a vivid orange and black monarch butterfly flexing its wings on a spray of summer-blue salvia. The tiny brightness looked up and stared right at me before bobbing gaily around the burial site and settling on a bit of nearby yarrow. I glanced away to lock eyes with my younger sister, Elizabeth. We both raised our brows: Linda?

Why did we look for her in a butterfly? Many of our group believed Linda ceased when her body stopped. Some of us suspected that her awareness continued, free of that body's limitations and constrictions. Nonetheless, we all felt her presence that day as a loving, warm, embrace; a sense of appreciation that permeated the whole gathering. In death, her life brushed against ours like a gentle exhalation.

A few years after her stem cell transplant, a rogue immune reaction had left Linda's lungs scarred and her immune system suppressed. Since that day she had known an infection from something as simple as a cold would eventually take her life. Two weeks ago, a rhinovirus had penetrated her compromised immune system.

When the hospital sent her home to die, family and friends had arrived to tell stories, laugh, share memories, and sing favorite songs. Linda's last moments, as she drifted in and out of consciousness, had been filled with the warm patter of her children, sisters, husband, grandchild, in-laws, nieces, and friends moving around the house, eating food, and comforting each other. She had wanted her death to be at home like this, among the happily living.

Now her body lay warming in the pine box that we would soon lower into the grave. We would cover her with earth, and she would become food for new life. That part was clear and straightforward. What opened a world of questions was the equally clear intuition that something about her had not gone anywhere. The same angel-like substance that permeated the space around her bedside was with us at her gravesite.

We shoveled earth onto her casket of wood; all the dirt in the pile set out for us. We scattered flowers on top of the mound while the little monarch fluttered among us. Then we sat in a circle to say our goodbyes.

Gently we read poems, sang, and wept as we told her how we would miss her. I could feel her right there, though she could no longer add her wit, insight, or laughter. I wondered if she could hear our voices. Was she saying goodbye, even as she found a new home among other resting, rejuvenating friends?

Clarity grew in me as Jill and I walked away from the Eternal Meadow. Linda—and Mom, Nick, Terri, Dad, and all the others—had not gone out like broken lights. Bodies had been buried or burned but the beautiful ever-present awareness that once animated them had only hidden itself from the limited perceptions of our human minds.

It was still here, somewhere, invisible to our senses, always shining as the ever-present beauty that gives rise to us all.

READER INQUIRY QUESTIONS

Part I: The Problem

1. What are young Rikki's strategies for coping with family turbulence during her childhood in Northbrook, Illinois? What strategies worked for you during your own childhood?
2. What do you think Rikki's fierce loyalty to her family is based in? Fear and anxiety? Love and belonging? Or something else?
3. Rikki begins to question her family's religion at a young age. Did you go through a similar process? At what age? How did you bring your questions to resolution?
4. Every family has conflicts and core issues. For Rikki, those center on her father's alcoholism and temper. Were there core issues in your family that absorbed everyone's time and attention?
5. Who created all this? is a big question for young Rikki. Have such questions puzzled you? Which ones still make you scratch your head?
6. Rikki grows up in a mostly white world; she awakens slowly to realities of life for Black and Brown people. When did your exposure to another class, color, or ethnicity start to shape your understanding of the world?
7. It takes Rikki nearly fifteen years to understand and accept herself

as a lesbian. Nowadays, society challenges us to accept and understand a variety of gender and sexual choices. How comfortable are you with this societal shift, and in what ways has it impacted your life and family?

8. Rape compromises Rikki's sense of worth, but she denies its subtle effect, compartmentalizing it for years. What are your experiences with handling unwanted sexual advances? Attitudes toward sexual violence have changed a great deal over the last fifty years, particularly in the last decade. Have you reevaluated any prior experiences since this shift took place? Have you shared your thoughts with anyone?

9. Rikki's disappointment about medical school initiates a descent into dangerous addictive drinking. Years pass before she learns coping strategies for triggered emotions. What tools have you discovered that empower you to stabilize, understand, or recover from disappointments?

10. Rikki sometimes relinquishes her power to other people (like Diane and Daniel and the chanting Buddhists) and even to ideas (like the existentialist ideal of sexual liberation). Over the course of her life, she slowly reclaims herself, her power, and her dignity. The process demands that she confront painful truths. Have you ever had to face something about yourself that you could no longer hide from? What was the outcome?

11. Rikki undergoes a period of dark despair that makes her think she wants to die. Experts say that most of us have felt suicidal at some point in our lives. Have you experienced anything like this in yourself or a loved one?

Part II: The Partial Fix

12. As Rikki gains longevity with Alcoholic Anonymous, she becomes willing to face weaknesses of character such as playing the victim or acting out rage. What are some landmark moments you've experienced in your own character development?

13. Rikki relies on the AA community to help her learn to live life as it comes. In what ways have communities in your life helped shape you?

14. Rikki accepts a "higher power" into her life without having to profess any beliefs. Relying on that inexplicable and unexplained presence, her life improves. Have you witnessed such beneficial effects from relying on an intangible presence? How do you explain that to yourself?

15. Rikki learns to meditate, to visualize forgiveness, and to empower herself through Buddhist practices like meditation. These help her stay present with her dying father. When he passes, she struggles to understand where he went or if he went anywhere at all. Have you lost someone who made you deeply wonder about an afterlife? Do you have prayers or rituals to help ease your grief over your loved ones' passages?

16. As a trained scientist, Rikki seeks an explanation for life that is consistent with science. But science has no explanation for how the awareness in our minds is able to hear the vibrations of a guitar string as a melodious tone, or know the love of our favorite people. Clearly, we are aware of our experiences; where do you think that awareness comes from?

17. Following her friend's example, Rikki creates a family with two fathers. What are your thoughts about creating a unique family shape?

18. Rikki falls in love and desperately tries to create belonging with

the wrong person. Her grief over that relationship leads her to search for her true self; what initially seems like a tragedy ultimately leads her to many beneficial outcomes. Have you experienced similar twists of fate? What do you think is going on, if anything?

19. Rikki struggles to stay financially afloat after age fifty. To maintain her spirits, she tries to find some truth or power she can really rely on. Ultimately, she finds answers within. When the going gets tough, to whom or where do you turn?

20. During her life, Rikki extracts herself from two cult-like organizations. Have you ever realized you were under someone's sway and broken away to learn to think for yourself? How did you handle it?

21. When Rikki tosses overboard all the concepts, ideals, images, and expectations about an external higher power that she has carried with her through life, a fresh energy blossoms from within. Have you had similar moments of self-discovery? How did they come about?

Part III: Getting Real

22. During a moment of grief and despair, Rikki hears a booming proclamation: "I have always been here for you." The voice is her own, not a stranger's. What do you think that voice means, and where does it come from?

23. After her friend Terri dies, Rikki experiences what seems like Terri's presence, saying goodbye. What do you make of such experiences, common and familiar to many people?

24. Late in life, Rikki senses that her inner life is more real than the external social character she portrays. What do you think she means by that? Have you had similar intuitions?

25. Quantum mechanics reveals that tiny entities, like atoms, do not always obey the laws of physics; they can "dissolve" into possibilities that are not determined by any known laws. If you are not truly a thing made of atoms, what are you?

26. For the briefest of moments, Rikki experiences herself and the world as ultimate goodness flowing forth from something beautiful, harmonious, and truthful—something we could call "God." Many people have professed similar mini-revelations of beauty and love at the heart of all that is. In what ways have you encountered a similar mystery?

ACKNOWLEDGMENTS

My deepest gratitude to Jill, Robert, Julie, and Rupert—without you, there would be no Empty Bowl.

Heartfelt thanks to Illana, Krissa, Kim, and Evelyn for all your help and insights.

ABOUT THE AUTHOR

photo credit: Reenie Raschke

Rikki West, a former spiritual seeker and UC Berkeley–trained scientist, spent decades trying to reconcile scientific explanations of existence with her ordinary, real-life awareness. One adventure at a time, she found her way to a peace and beauty that changed all the questions. Her book *Rootlines*, a memoir of family healing, was published by She Writes Press in 2020. Mother of Noli and Godmother of Morgan, Rikki loves being outside in the alpine desert of northern New Mexico, where she lives with her wife Jill and her dog, Zoey.

Looking for your next great read?

We can help!

Visit www.shewritespress.com/next-read or scan the QR code below for a list of our recommended titles.

She Writes Press is an award-winning independent publishing company founded to serve women writers everywhere.

THE EMPTY BOWL